EARLY ACCLAIM

Shakespeare and the Moral Curriculum

From **Northrop Frye's** letter to the author:

"Thank you for *Shakespeare and the Moral Curriculum*. I enjoyed it, and would find it hard to disagree with its central premise that literature can be an ideal source of moral instruction, certainly better than simplistic discussions of current issues, because, as you put it, it moralizes without being moralistic. I also find it quite believable that students of the current generation, despite the widespread view of them as numbed and demoralized relativists, can be readily fired up, given competent teaching, over questions about values.... The book is lively and engaging, and should generate worthwhile discussion.... I wish you the best of luck with it!

> — NORTHROP FRYE is the author of such works as *Fearful Symmetry: A Study of William Blake; Anatomy of Criticism: Four Essays*, etc. Until his death in January of 1991 he was University Professor at Victoria College of the University of Toronto.

"In the last ten years I have taught over a dozen graduate courses in the teaching of English for secondary school teachers.... This text would be particularly helpful for these courses, and for English teachers and department chairs. I would certainly use it for the arguments it could raise, and for all the ideas and suggestions it provides."

> — DAVID WATERS, English chair,
> Isidore Newman School, New Orleans

SHAKESPEARE AND THE MORAL CURRICULUM

Rethinking the Secondary School Shakespeare Syllabus

by Peter Roberts

Includes the Results of a Survey of over 200 English Department Chairpersons Nationwide

Pripet Press
New York

Library of Congress Catalog Card Number: 91-66911

ISBN Number: 0-9631311-0-9

The cover photo is of a scene (II, v) from a December 1990 production of *As You Like It* at the Princeton Day School in Princeton, New Jersey. (The photo was taken from a video shot by a PDS parent, Charles Hardy.)

Here Jacques (David Wise) forces one of Duke Senior's co-mates in exile (Mrinalini Kamath) to cover her ears, as he launches into an off-key rendition of "If it do come to pass/That any man turn ass...." Managing to listen with open ears is Amiens, played by Lemington Ridley. (That is another of the Duke's companions, played by Bryan Taylor, just visible to Ridley's left.)

Scenic design was by Ross Hindley, costume design by Karin Sconzert and Lemington Ridley. The production was produced and directed by the head of the PDS Performing Arts Program, Paul Bernstein.

B.T. 17.10(1860)
6/30/93

This book is dedicated to **Barbara Chesley Roberts** and **Donald Austin Roberts**, great independent school teachers for over thirty years, without whose support it could never have been completed.

Emerson remarks in his journal that "appreciators" are almost invariably the offspring of appreciators, and such certainly seems to be true in my case. Had I not grown up in a household where Laurence Olivier's recorded extracts from *Hamlet* and *Henry V* were always near the turntable ("...upon Saint Crispian's dAYYYY..."!), and where the children all but demanded that their father christen a female cat and dog with the names of Shakespearean heroines (Ophelia and Desdemona were chosen!), the joy I have experienced these past two years, in immersing myself in the genius of William Shakespeare, might never have come my way. Thank you, folks!

The conduct of our lives is the true reflection
of our thoughts.

— MONTAIGNE

If man is sick, is unable, is mean-spirited and odious,
it is because there is so much of his own nature
which is unlawfully withholden from him.

— EMERSON

. . . when too, I remember how much character is formed
by what we read, I cannot look upon it as a light question,
to be passed over as a mere amusement, like a game of
cards or chess. I have never been able to tame down
my mind to think poetry a sport, or an occupation for
idle hours.

— COLERIDGE

CONTENTS

To the Public or Parochial School Teacher

O ne of the many rewards of being a teacher, appreciated most keenly by those of us who worked in other fields before becoming such, is that one can address a fellow teacher as "colleague" without feeling the term to be a grandiloquent one. For while I suppose even investment bankers have their secret handshake, and warm to a splendid conviviality at board meetings, we teachers are more firmly bonded by the knowledge that our calling is both a noble and a difficult one.

Thus it gives me the greatest pleasure, as someone who has done most of his teaching in independent schools, to extend a warm welcome to my public or parochial school colleague, and to offer a few frank words about the book he or she now has in hand.

First of all, let it be stated right up front that my working subtitle for this book was "Improving the Shakespeare Syllabus in the *Independent* School," and noted as well that its focus is still very much on the independent school. As my colleague will discover as he or she reads on, this whole project began with a survey on the teaching of Shakespeare that I sent out to independent school English chairpersons in October of 1989. At that time I had no real idea that a full-fledged book would soon be born from the survey (and from my own thoughts and experiences as a new teacher), and therefore I would have dismissed as outlandish the idea that I should broaden my database by also sending it out to public and parochial schools. The relatively self-contained world of the independent school seemed to me then — and still seems to me now — an ideally delimited one for a survey such as mine, and about all a one-man polling outfit could handle.

Thus I can assure my public and parochial school colleagues that there is no more of the exclusionary and the snobbish in this book than there is in its author — which is to say, very little indeed — and that I certainly never made any conscious decision to "include them out" (to employ one of my favorite Samuel Goldwyn-isms). That said, it does remain true that the Shakespeare syllabus I attempt to ameliorate in this book is the independent school syllabus (as brought to light by the survey), and true as well that in envisioning my own "ideal" syllabus I have had in mind the independent school as I have come to know it. (Hence the references throughout this book, albeit rather few and far between, to the specific effect this or that play will have on the "privileged" independent school student.)

Yet while my public and parochial school colleagues are hereby advised that they may have to do some mental transmuting to bring my observations and suggestions into line with whatever situations obtain in their own classrooms, I would never have been so bold as to give my book its present subtitle if I thought that there was some impassible chasm dividing the realms of public and private education. I suspect I resemble most writers on education in being simply a social critic in not very effective disguise, and therefore no one would rejoice more heartily than I if a project that had set out to reshape only the tiniest segment of our society — English departments at independent schools — managed to remold an even more imposing piece of clay.

Now for two final messages, one to the public and one to the parochial school teacher. First, the public one.

I think it is worth noting, given the fact that I do make a few explicit references throughout this book to the "privileged" independent school student, that my depiction of the adolescent as a hardheaded pragmatist (in Chapter 1) may be an even better likeness of the public school student than the private. Therefore, given the fact that virtually every conclusion I come to in this book derives in one way or another from my conception of the adolescent, it is entirely possible that this book will have even *more* to say to you, the public school teacher, than it does to the private one.

To my parochial school colleague, a more personal note. While you may be put off by the position I adopt in Chapters 2 and 3, to the effect that moral education should have nothing to do with religious instruction, I hope other passages throughout this book that reveal me rather clearly as being a "believer" will lure you at least part of the way back to my camp. For while it is indeed my personal belief that formal education should confine itself to arousing in young people a sense of the ethical, even when this or that teacher fervently hopes that someday the ethical sense will blossom into the religious sense, it is my even more passionate belief that the adult in whom the religious sense has never flowered will never understand the true glory or the full import of ethics.

Thus I'm sure you, my parochial school reader, and indeed you, my general reader, will recognize as you read that religious values in the broadest sense have indeed informed many of my judgments on the various plays in the canon, and have also (to cite one of many possible examples) led me to argue in a number of ensuing contexts for an anti-tragic view of life. My drawing the reader's attention to this fact in no way constitutes a "confession," nor does it prove that I'm any less serious than I have said I am about steering well clear of all religious proselytizing in the classroom. It is one thing to proselytize, quite another to hope that the student who has been trained to think seriously about moral issues will at some later date ask himself the most vital question in ethics: Is the ethical sense self-supporting, or can it only grow, vine-like, by clinging to a support that points to heaven?

At this point the parochial school educator might well raise the objection that such an approach leaves the student far too alone in his quest for God, and that adults have an obligation to do more than just *hope* that young people will someday find the theological pot of gold at the end of the ethical rainbow. To a certain extent, I agree with him. For although I do believe that hard thinking about ethical issues should be at the center of secondary education, and believe as well that the topic of God must be handled with the greatest possible delicacy and detachment, I am sure that our culture is impoverished whenever public and private school teachers, fearful of even being *thought* by some observer to be proselytizing, squelch all talk of God in the classroom. Surely it must be admitted, even by he who holds the position that we humans created God rather than the other way around, that God is humankind's most interesting and philosophically important creation. We can hardly overlook "Him," even if we would prefer to lowercase that "Him" or change the "him" to "it" — or "she"!

A WORD ABOUT
THIS BOOK

To an extent characteristic of no other institution, save that of the state itself, the school has the power to modify the social order. And under our political system, it is the right of each individual to have a voice in the making of social policies as, indeed, he has a vote in the determination of political affairs. If this be true, education is primarily a public business, and only secondarily a specialized vocation. The layman [and the new teacher] will always have his right to some utterance on the operation of the public [and private!] schools.[1]

— JOHN DEWEY (BRACKETED INSERTS MINE)

No single factor has been so important in helping me to understand what sort of book it is that I have written, and to explain that book to my reader, than a suggestion about changing it that was made by a few of the teachers who read it in manuscript form. While all of those teachers spoke highly of the book, and cited numerous examples of passages that they felt had been of real benefit to them as teachers, they still wondered aloud whether many of their colleagues might not be put off by the prospect of taking tutelage from a rookie teacher with far fewer years of teaching experience than they. (I have been teaching for four years, much of that time as a substitute teacher, and have taught only five Shakespeare plays: *Macbeth*, *Caesar*, *Shrew*, *Midsummer*, and *R & J*.) Why is there a need, these teachers asked, to make mention of your relative pedagogic inexperience at all? Why not just play it so far down that the veteran teacher reading your book will have no opportunity to be troubled by it?

While there was much sense in that suggestion, and while clearly it was made in a spirit of kindness and helpfulness, I'm

[1]From *Moral Principles in Education*, as quoted by Charles Silberman in *Crisis in the Classroom* (New York: Vintage Books, 1970), pp. 523-524.

sure that even in the process of making it my early readers were asking themselves the very same questions I was. Wouldn't it be sheer duplicity on my part to pretend that my recommendations on the teaching of a number of plays were based on many years' experience teaching them (for doubtless that's what my reader would assume, unless I told him or her otherwise), when in fact I have never taught them at all? And however much respect one might have for the speculative approach to curricular thinking taken in a book such as mine, wouldn't it be absolutely necessary to remind the reader of not only the strengths but also the patent weaknesses of such an approach?

The answer to both questions, of course, is "Of course it would." I can hardly expect my infinitely more experienced colleagues to read this book or to take it seriously until they have heard me confess a) that my speculations are doomed to remain forever only that unless and until they put them to the test in their classrooms, and b) that many of those speculations are likely to fail that test. Trapped as in many ways I am within the magic circle of theory, I can only, Prospero-like, implore the veteran teacher to draw upon all of her wisdom and pedagogic lore and

> release me from my bands
> With the help of your good hands.
> Gentle breath of yours my sails
> Must fill, or else my project fails,
> Which was to please.

Yet even as I admit that speculation must always be followed up by on-the-scene observation, and that every theory is only as good as the facts it seems actually to have accounted for, I would also remind my reader that we moderns never so clearly evince that impatience with intellect that is our besetting sin as when we blithely offer "guesswork" as an adequate synonym for *speculation*. In its most proper sense *speculation* means simply *vision*, and therefore we should always be wary of dismissing out of hand as "mere speculation" what may perhaps be a vision of things somewhat more penetrating than the average.

If I give evidence in this book of possessing even a bit of that more penetrating vision, I think I know how I came by it. It was given to me as a gift when I became a teacher. Unaccustomed as I was to daily contact with adolescents, every day on the job granted me some new revelation as to their intellectual, moral, and personal characteristics. When I had at last managed to yoke together a few of those lightning flashes to illumine a more rounded vision of the adolescent, I then resolved to see whether I could reshape the current Shakespeare syllabus so as to bring it into closer conformity with that vision. This of course required both a complete rereading of the canon as it might be seen through the eyes of a young person, and also the gathering of data from independent schools all across the country. (I have explained in the foreword to the public or parochial school teacher what factors led me to "poll" independent schools only.)

If then the virtue of the approach to curricular reform taken in this book is that it gives evidence of some clear vision of young people, of the Shakespeare plays themselves, and of the standard Shakespeare syllabus as it exists in most independent schools across the country, and if its defect is that it tends at times toward the strictly speculative, are there any defects or deficiencies in the kind of curricular thinking being done by veteran teachers that this book might help to remedy?

While I'm not about to attempt a definitive answer to that question before my investigation into it — this book itself — has even begun, I would go so far as to suggest that if there is blurriness or distortion in the veteran teacher's curricular vision it arises from his or her being too close to the object of vision to see it clearly, or dispassionately.

Let us take as a hypothetical example a teacher of fifteen years' experience who for most of those years has been teaching *Othello* to 11th-graders, and doing so with extraordinary aplomb. I would suggest that if we wish to subject to the most searching scrutiny the notions that *Othello* is a) the proper food on which young minds should be nourished, b) the right work for 11th-graders, or even c) a popular work with students, we would do well to balance the comments of the person who has something of a vested interest in teaching *Othello* with those of a relative newcomer to the teaching scene. For while I, as the son of teachers, know full well that teachers are always rethinking what they do, and are by no means the most dogmatic or hidebound of mortals, I do think we err if we assume that because of this the teaching trade is powered less than any other by that most silent and cost-efficient of energy sources, Inertia. There is, after all, an understandable tendency in every profession to go with what "works," and too often it is the very highest possible Working of that profession which suffers from this.

Thus, to return to the points listed above, the teacher who has fallen in love with teaching *Othello* may be more resistant than anyone to the idea that it is an entirely inappropriate work for study in the secondary school. She may also, by mere force of habit, be unable to visualize teaching it or any other work at a grade level different from the one she has grown accustomed to. Most surprising of all, her ability to judge just how deeply this or any other work is affecting young people may be not quite so transcendent as we have assumed it to be.

To begin with, students have an obvious incentive — their desire for a good grade — to appear excited about a work even when it in fact leaves them cold. Then too, the teacher's own love for a work, and/or his love of teaching that work, may lead him to give too high an estimate of the number of "I loved it"'s he has heard from students over the years, and too low an estimate of the number of bored and/or confused gazes that have stared back at him in that time.

The most important fact for us to note here, however, is that if the gauging of a play's popularity with students is hard, then the gauging of just how much it has benefited them morally and spiritually is far harder. I use the word "spiritually" here in its widest and loosest sense of exalting or thrilling the spirit, and I use it, rather than "intellectually," advisedly. Good students will always be able to write good papers and have good discussions about almost any work, but only a few such works will genuinely move or change them.

If then it is at least plausible that many a veteran teacher is too close to a curriculum to reform it as it should be reformed (perhaps not unlike a spouse whose love for a partner prevents him or her from saying things that should be said), the person who can see things in perspective is, perhaps, the relative outsider. Indeed, the very etymology of *speculate* confirms us in this suspicion, for the word derives from *specula*, or *watchtower*. The person with the best view of the battlefield is not the valiant warrior himself, but the observer gazing down from above.

As someone who has been a substitute teacher for two of his four years in the profession, and who therefore has seen many schools and taught students of all ages, I am, I believe, the outsider who can see no, not the whole truth, but perhaps a few of the truths that the insiders cannot see, or can no longer see. Then too, if Will Durant is right when he says that the God who created substitute teaching found he then had no need to create a Hell, no one could be better suited than I to play Virgil to my reader's Dante, leading both of us up the path to some pedagogic Paradise — or at least Purgatory.

A Word About
the Survey

The speculations that make up the body of this book would have been idle ones indeed, had I not been able to compare my thinking with the thinking of those who are framing today's Shakespeare syllabuses, and then do more thinking based on their thinking. This was made possible by the survey of English department chairpersons, the results of which appear in Appendix V.

My purpose here is not to describe the survey — I do that at the beginning of said appendix — but to explain why findings so crucial to this study appear at its end rather than its beginning. There are two reasons for this, one having to do with the essential nature of this project, the other with more pragmatic considerations.

First, it has seemed appropriate that in this book speculations should come first, confirming data second. For while in some cases I have worked from a fact to a theory — for instance, it was by musing on the fact that *R & J* is now *the* 9th-grade Shakespeare play that I came to challenge the logic of its placement there — my more usual modus operandi has been to start with a conviction based on my view of young people and of a particular play and then to gently chide my colleagues for their failure to make use of that play as I feel it should be used.

Second, the comments I make about the survey's various findings can properly be appreciated only by the reader who has become well acquainted with my positions on the various plays.

Yet while it has seemed best to place the survey at the end

rather than the beginning of this book, the reader probably will want to run his or her eyes over the data in the "most widely taught plays" category (question number one, on pages 226–227) before beginning the play-by-play commentaries that begin on page 27. References to those findings are made fairly routinely throughout the play commentaries, but doubtless the reader will wish to a) acquaint himself or herself with them early on and b) flip back and forth to them as he or she reads.

Two final points. First, let it be noted that the survey has been made the last of the appendixes not because it is the least important of these — it is the most important — but so that the reader can locate it quickly at the back of the book whenever he or she wishes to consult it.

Second, while most references throughout this book to the various comments my colleagues jotted down on their survey forms are general ones, there are a few direct quotations here and there. Seeing as I had stated on the survey form itself that I had no interest in prying into the affairs of particular schools or particular teachers, but was simply trying to get an overview of current teaching practices, I have thought it best to respect the anonymity of my sources and leave these quotations unattributed.

ACKNOWLEDGMENTS

I t is a truism that writing is a lonely trade, but only the first-time author is in a position to appreciate just how true the truism is. For months ideas about his book have been popping into his head day and night, but only after the long, long slog of thinking and writing has resulted in a completed manuscript can he share those ideas with others.

How lucky I am, then, to have been rewarded for my labors by being given such astute critics and such friendly and helpful people as the first readers of my manuscript!

Three teachers and/or administrators in particular have been good enough to sustain me with their enthusiasm for this project, to make innumerable truly invaluable suggestions, and to endure what must have seemed an unending barrage of letters from me: Craig Kerrick of the Saint Mark's School in Massachusetts, David Waters of the Isidore Newman School in New Orleans, and Judith Michaels of the Princeton (New Jersey) Day School. My thanks also to my friend Cyrus Veeser, both for his own very helpful comments on the opening sections of the manuscript and for referring me to Nancy Brandwein, who made many truly superb editorial suggestions, and my friends David and Vicki Newman, for the loan of a valuable computer — and even more valuable computer knowhow — at more than one crucial juncture in the writing of this book.

Lastly, I must take a moment to salute the memory of Northrop Frye, who found time in the last months of his life to read and comment favorably on my manuscript. When I consider that over the years no single book has lifted my spirit higher than *Fearful Symmetry*, his transcendently great study of Blake, the fact that Professor Frye actually had read some words of *mine* before he died seems as wonderful as it is improbable. My thanks to him for all that he gave to me, and to others.

PETER ROBERTS
NEW YORK CITY

INTRODUCTION

The most recent incitement to curricular reform has come from those who inveigh against a course of study that they see as too rigidly masculine and too unswervingly Western. Whether one stands with this particular group of reformers or against them, surely one can see much merit in one of their movement's central tenets: Curricula do not exist in a vacuum. Even in the case of those rare works about whose greatness virtually all parties are agreed, any failure on the part of educators to take into account the needs and nature of those to whom such works must speak will usually undermine their ability to do so. Yet even as we adopt this sensible doctrine we should demand that it be tested for a far wider applicability than its rather narrow partisans heretofore have dreamed of. We should insist that no agenda for curricular reform can be worth its salt if it brings to our attention new or overlooked voices yet fails to provide us with a fuller understanding of, and better uses for, what has come to be thought of as the traditional curriculum.

Of all of those "dead white males" whom academics soon will have to detain for questioning in a kind of purgatorial customs area, Shakespeare almost certainly will be one of the few to be waived right through without so much as a glance at his passport to Immortality. Matthew Arnold could have told us as much: "Others abide our question; thou art free." And yet for those of us proud of being as democratic in our intellectual as in our political judgments, there is something repugnant in such exception-making. While there may be no pressing need to subject Mr.

1

Shakespeare to a body-search (i.e., to question the fact that greatness of one kind or another is indeed his), we are determined to
linger over his papers (the plays upon which his reputation is
based) and to betray no trace of obsequiousness in our dealings
with him.

The reward for our thoroughness and self-possession may be,
not a cry from Mr. Shakespeare that he has been ill-used, but
our own discovery that we as teachers have made ill use of the
Shakespeare canon. That discovery in turn may prompt English
chairpersons to do that which it is the whole purpose of this
book to convince them to do: reshape the Shakespeare syllabus
in the image of its young, ardent, morally eager[1] user, rather
than, as it seems it is being shaped today, that of its middle-
aged, rather melancholy, aesthetically-minded maker.

[1]When I refer here to the adolescent as being "morally eager," or
speak of him/her as being a "moralist" a few pages from here, I certainly do not mean to imply that he or she possesses a greater degree
of moral perfection than the adult, or even that he or she is much of a
hand at moralizing. I simply wish to suggest that at this age most (but
certainly not all) young people are eager (if only subconsciously) to
"walk in the paths of righteousness," if only some adult will consent
to lead the way down them.

1.

THE ADOLESCENT AS
STUDENT — AND TEACHER

> Children are all foreigners. We treat them as such.
> We cannot understand their speech or mode of life,
> and so our Education is remote and accidental and
> not closely applied to the facts.
>
> — EMERSON

For two reasons, this book could only begin with the
following sketchy but I hope telling portrait of the
adolescent. First, as the genesis of this whole project was
a new teacher's vision of the adolescent, it seems only fitting that
that genesis, like its more famous capitalized counterpart, should
come first. Second, if it is indeed the case that educators who are
unwilling to let their gaze linger long on the adolescent are all
too likely to sin by shaping a curriculum in their own image
instead, we can show our own determination to eschew that sin
by gazing long and hard. Let it be noted, however, that the portrait painted below is by no means of the full-length variety —
rather it is a silhouette of sorts, sketched by the light of one
adolescent intellectual strength and one weakness.

Certainly the most salient characteristic of the adolescent as
student is that he is "a severely practical person."[1] The honors
student, Harvard-obsessed, and the borderline dropout are equally
likely to demand of their teacher, "What's all of this *for?*", even
if the former is purportedly trying to ascertain the relation of the
work in question to doing well on the SAT and the latter its
relation to being the life of every party. Ultimately, of course,

[1]Samuel McChord Crothers, *The Dame School of Experience* (Boston and
New York: Houghton Mifflin Company, 1920), p. 33.

3

such a merciless pragmatism is utterly destructive of the values of a liberal education: One must, after all, examine life before one can assert that the examination has yielded tangible benefit. Nonetheless, the wise teacher will make a virtue of a necessity and learn to respect or even reverence this student passion for (excuse the sixties term, hoary with age) relevance.

For while at first glance he may have mistaken the adolescent's angry-visaged skepticism for genuine cynicism, or mislabeled as mere shiftlessness what is in fact the student's ardent desire to discover *value*, or *values*, in the work under discussion, the enlightened teacher has learned over the years to disregard the crusty surface without and train his gaze on the molten idealism ready to burst forth from within. He knows that, while there are genuine cynics among the adolescent as among the adult population, the far more common type has been immortalized in the figure of Holden Caulfield: the passionate seeker after truth, prompted by compassion (where do the ducks in Central Park go in the winter?), and the poet keenly alive to the combined pathos and humor of life (the prostitute who says "like fun"), both bravely putting up a united front as one hard-drinking, foul-speaking realist, the only genuine article in a world where phonies are a dime a dozen and Phoebes a pearl beyond price.

Thus I would suggest that the good teacher is he who takes with the utmost seriousness that eternal student cry of "What for?", and who hears in it not merely the whining petulance of the homework-avoider (although there's always a large admixture of that) but also a clarion call summoning him to the most rigorous examination of his own motivations and practices.

For English teachers in particular it is of the utmost importance that that jab — "What for?" — be received not merely as the wild, flailing punch of the academic lightweight trying to bring down the heavyweight, but as a highly tonic slap in the face, to which the only sage response can be, "Thanks, I needed that!" For the delights of literature are so varied and sweet, its siren call so seductive and alluring, that it is the besetting sin of the academic decadent (so to speak) to think that art and literature need never submit to the great pragmatic and moral tests. One need not be a mere censorious prig, a Jerry Falwell or Jesse Helms, or conceive of the word "moral" in their own debased fashion, to consider the decadent entirely in the wrong on this issue, or to feel that too many curricular choices are made (generally, one assumes, on a subconscious level) so as to conform with his faulty first principle. Indeed, it will be the business of many of the coming pages to suggest that too often students throw down their books in disgust only because the moralist and the pragmatist in them — or if you will, the phoniness-spotter and the truth-teller — see all too clearly that what is the matter with many of today's curricula is that they contain far too little moral "matter."

Without making any pretense to comprehensiveness in this analysis, we might before leaving the subject point out a preeminent weakness in the adolescent mind, just as we have singled out its "idealistic pragmatism" as a characteristic strength. Simply put, the adolescent, caricatured as being far too group-conscious, is on a deeper level dangerously ignorant of the social dimension to both life and truth. If the Judaic tradition in religion has emphasized man's connectedness with the cosmos (i.e., his relation to God), and the Catholic tradition man's interrelatedness with his fellow humans, then the typical adolescent is a pure Protestant of the "Inner Light" variety. Because her ego is undeveloped and therefore feels to her vulnerable and exposed, the whole tendency of her being is to glorify that ego and to vilify (in the manner of all adolescent poetry and song lyrics) all those around her, even those who wish to help, as "insensitive," "backstabbers," and so on.

So too, while it may have been tailored to his specifications by adult psychologists, no concept is so quintessentially adolescent as that of "peer pressure," with its rather comical vision (like that of some poorly executed medieval woodcut) of a young person's classmates holding out to him, serpent-like, a golden apple, in whose reflection the bright lights of Sunday night's rock concert can be seen to glow mightily, luring him away from his homework. While of course such a vision *is* true to the very real temptations besetting the adolescent (drug and alcohol abuse, etc.) temptations that often lead to tragic consequences and that the young person has every right to take as seriously as he does, from an adult perspective it remains a rather crude caricature of a generally salutary process. Namely, the process by which society reminds each of its members that her pretentions to absolute uniqueness and autonomy are only that, and invites her to forsake solipsism in favor of full integration in the human community.

For although the years may have robbed the adult of much, they have also instilled in her the essential truth that mere self, far from being the only heroic thing in a trivial world, as the adolescent conceives of it as being, is too often either silly and ineffectual or downright unregenerate: conceited, lazy, foolish. She has learned that she is never more truly "herself" than when she is working for or with family and community members, rising above her mundane self via art or scholarship, and virtually losing her self altogether in the contemplation of the surpassing greatness of the Universe, or God. In all of this she is as different as can be from the adolescent, who feels deep in his heart — even as he whoops it up with his pals, chugs a beer, and seems to be having a riotously good time — that there is something unclean or unholy about all group activities. (Hence his extraordinary readiness to accept *Lord of the Flies* not as powerful myth-making but as uncannily accurate sociology.)

The pedagogic implications of the adolescent's inevitable self-centeredness seem relatively plain to me, although I'm not sure most secondary school educators are as cognizant of them as they should be. I would suggest, for instance, that while conformism is as much or more of a danger in American life now as it ever was, and while educators do have a solemn obligation to include in their syllabuses works such as *Babbitt, The Catcher in the Rye,* and *One Flew Over the Cuckoo's Nest* — with their insistence on the supreme value and importance of the individual, and on the fact that, as Emerson warns us, society is perpetually in conspiracy against each of its members — at least two considerations should keep us from giving all such works the key to the syllabus while we lock out others that perhaps have an even more important lesson to teach young people.

First, most works of literature by their very nature feature a protagonist "fighting against the world," so works that deal overtly with the theme of nonconformity perhaps only give adolescents more of what they would get enough of anyway in four years of study. Second, and more importantly, works preaching a defiant individualism are likely in a certain sense to be preaching to the converted, in that most adolescents are already convinced "the world's against me" and are therefore perhaps immune to the deeper intellectual implications of such works.

Thus while every English teacher and his brother have long been in the habit of consciously choosing works that feature non-conformist heroes, on the theory that this is what the young both want and need, I would suggest that we should begin to give the young something that they may not want but that they desperately need: works that stress the essential interrelatedness of person with person, and of each person with the cosmos. (Such works will be referred to throughout these pages as being those offering "social vision.")

As I see it, a balanced curriculum should guard against including too many works that allow an unrestricted view of a character's inner world but seem to crop right out of the picture that bounteous social and cosmic landscape from which he draws his sustenance. (For example, all of those innumerable coming-of-age novels that the junior high student now seems to read back-to-back and day after day.) An exemplary exception to this rule would be a work such as *Hamlet*, which helps us to extirpate the adolescent faults of brooding and solipsism by giving them superb voice.

My final word on the adolescent may strike some as being unbearably coy or ingenuous, but judging by some curricula it is too often forgotten: The adolescent is youth-full. This means that any text submitted for her approval should be as full of the spirit of youth as she, although it should be well noted that this does *not* necessarily mean these works must deal with young people, or be marked by a spirit of fancy or whimsy (both of which fallacies will be examined soon by the light of the Shakespeare syllabus). It does mean that we should be suspicious of works that seem to be marked less by the mercurial energy of Mercutio than by the droning ponderousness of Polonius, or in which a precious artiness has been allowed to preempt that moral seriousness which — all appearances and misconceptions notwithstanding — is native to Youth.

Above all, perhaps, it means that English teachers should be far more alive than they seem to be to the keen irony involved in our offering young people — overflowing as they really are (despite all of Youth's fears and uncertainties) with hope and high spirits — one *tragedy* after another!

2.

THE MORAL IN LITERATURE

Even if Youth does in fact want to sink its teeth into works conspicuous for their high moral-fiber content, the questions remain: What do we mean by "moral content"? Is it of the essence in the study of literature, an irrelevance, or downright pernicious? How can we spot it and, having spotted it, should we nurture or uproot it?

To many, the very mention of the word *morality* in connection with imaginative literature (I mean by that term all those works that we routinely refer to or think of as "fiction") summons up thoughts of all that they find offensive in certain works: a fudging of life's bitter moments in favor of a treacly, death-of-Little-Nell sentimentality; a tendency toward the clumsily allegoric rather than the holding of the mirror up to Nature; and a style in which the author is all too omniscient, perpetually preaching homilies rather than letting his characters and situations tell their own stories.

While no one sensitive to imaginative literature can ever be in favor of any of the above tendencies, the first duty of the critic who confesses — nay, proudly proclaims — that he views literature's chief function as being the promotion of genuine morality in the reader, is to deny that the moral need appear in any of the above-mentioned guises. Yet before I can do so in any effective fashion, I must first provide my reader with at least a working definition of that "moral content" (or "moral wisdom") to which I shall routinely be referring.

What I do *not* mean by the term is any delimited or limiting code of conduct, as best exemplified by the Decalogue.[1] Rather, to me moral wisdom is the expression of any general truth[2] about human beings and their cosmos (whether stated explicitly, or implicit in the work as a whole) and/or (and again, implicitly or explicitly) advice about how best they may acquit themselves in that cosmos. I also feel that there are in essence two modes of moral discourse in imaginative literature, the first genuine and fully contextual, the second sham and always seeming to have been imported into the work to do labor the author should have delegated to her or his characters and situations themselves. The first I herewith denote the moral*izing* faculty, the second the moral*istic*.

Shakespeare is in fact the perfect author to turn to if one wishes to prove that there is in fact a profound difference between these two modes, in that he was without a doubt one of the most moral*izing* authors who ever lived while at the same time being perhaps the least moral*istic*. We can all readily recognize and appreciate the moralizing aspect of Shakespeare's art. Throughout every scene in Shakespeare, and out of the mouths of virtually all of his characters — be they Gertrudes or Isabellas, Henry V's or Richard III's, Lears or Fools — there flows a steady stream of commentary about the nature of human life and the quality of human action within it. Examples come as readily to hand as fruit in harvest time, but here one will suffice.[3]

[1]Of course I intend here no derogation of the Commandmants, which are themselves brilliant pieces of moralizing that time has robbed of little of their luster. I refer only to the habit unreflective people have of imagining that these ten, or even these ten plus some additional hundred and one, could ever in some comprehensive way account for all of man's moral moods.

[2]I am well aware that it is presently the vogue among many academics (particularly those calling themselves "deconstructionists") to disparage the usefulness, or even to deny the existence, of general truths. What more can I say here, given my limitations of space, but that I think them utterly — and tragically — wrong?

[3]Readers who are naturally suspicious of those who speak of "moral education," assuming that almost all of those who do so actually have some religious bill of goods to sell, will pounce on the fact that the passage offered here concerns itself with God. I can only assure them that I am as opposed to any form of religious proselytizing in the classroom as they are, and that I have chosen this passage only because a) by touching on the cosmic, it is as adventurous a piece of moralizing as any writer

Hamlet has just recounted to Horatio his providential escape from pirates, and caps his tale with the profound thought, "There's a divinity that shapes our ends, rough-hew them how we will."[4] As A. C. Bradley points out, to Horatio — a thoughtful man, but of conventional intellect — such a thought is a commonplace, "a thing of course" (his response is "That is most certain"), but for Hamlet it is clearly "a discovery hardly won."[5]

Conveniently for our purposes here, each of these attitudes can be seen to correspond nicely to our two different modes, the moralistic and the moralizing. Because such a truth could never be more than a dead truth to Horatio, any story he might construct using it as its moral tag doubtless would strike us as being trite and moralistic. Yet as employed by Hamlet it not only crowns his story as gracefully and organically as a flower crowns its stalk, but seems indeed to crown his whole earthly existence up to that point. Thus while it is likely that the atheistic reader would have bridled at the moral tag had it come at the end of Horatio's tale, he may find himself, despite himself, as moved and consoled by this tale and its tag as Hamlet obviously is.

If we seem almost to stumble on the genuine moral truth, finding it suddenly at our feet as lovely, pliant, and unassuming as a wildflower, the merely moralistic might be compared to a scarecrow, one that an author plants in the middle of his artistic landscape to frighten off those ugly crows known as critics, who otherwise might descend upon it with their own false theories and interpretations. A better example of moralistic utterance could scarcely be afforded than the following lines from the Epilogue to *Pericles*. Given the fact that their moralistic — as opposed to moralizing — tone is in general conspicuously absent from Shakespeare's work, and seems in fact to have been anathematic

might assay, and b) because it allows me to make some of the points I wish to, in the discussion that follows, as to the "moralizing" versus the "moralistic." Needless to say, there *are* countless non-religious pieces of moralizing in Shakespeare: "All the world's a stage," "Lord, what fools these mortals be!" etc. and ad infinitum.

[4] Profound, yes; nonetheless a modern thinker, determined to account for the fact of evolution in any world-view he might formulate, would doubtless decide that the statement makes better sense when its terms have been reversed: "There's a divinity that rough-hews our ends, shape them how we will."

[5] A. C. Bradley, *Shakespearean Tragedy*, as excerpted in the Signet Classic *Hamlet* (New York: New American Library, 1963), p. 205.

to him, one can only assume that (if Shakespeare did pen these lines at all) they have been tailored by the Bard to fit Gower and the morality play over which he presides:

> In Antiochus and his daughter you have heard
> Of monstrous lust the due and just reward:
> In Pericles, his Queen and daughter, seen,
> Although assailed with fortune fierce and keen,
> Virtue preserved from fell destruction's blast,
> Led on by Heaven, and crowned with joy at last.

Perhaps one final thought on the moral in imaginative literature will not only help to disarm those who find the very word offensive in connection with such literature, but also throw some light on Shakespeare's greatness from a new and unusual angle. Too often in speaking or thinking of morality we narrow our minds to too paltry a conception of goodness: We are good if we pay our taxes, love our children, and refrain from murder. Yet surely we should more often think of goodness and morality as simply synonyms for human richness and maturity. When we use the term "good" we should apply it to men and women, or to moments in our lives, exactly as we would use it to refer to a piece of fruit that has reached a perfection of ripeness and has no sourness of taste or blemish of surface to offend us. Shakespeare — the poet, after all, who tells us that Ripeness Is All — is in this additional and somewhat unorthodox sense the most moral of poets. The unrivaled richness of his poetry is a perpetual admonishment to us to *linger* over each of the important moments of our lives, and to ponder (literally, *weigh*) them with the same grave deliberation we give to each line of his poetry — or even, for that matter, the perfect pear that we revolve in our hand for a moment before (very slowly) consuming it.

3.

THE MORAL IN EDUCATION

Is the name of virtue to be a barrier to that which is virtue?

— EMERSON

T hus far it has been suggested that two propositions are true: Students have a genuine appetite for value, or meaning, and works of literature are perfectly capable of containing such meaning without degenerating into mere moral tracts. The next order of business is to determine whether this student appetite is being sated — knowing as we now do that there is no dearth of intellectual provender — and, if it is not, to demand on precisely what grounds this moral nutriment is being withheld.

While the problematic nature of "ethical instruction" in the schools has always made it and always should make it a cause for concern among both parents and educators, and while we will directly address that concern in a moment, let us begin by trying to determine whether the troublesome word *moral*, when it is used in connection with education, should frighten educators as much as I would guess it does. To do so we will have to look first at the word itself, and then at the emotions it arouses in many of its hearers.

Etymologically, the word *moral* is derived from the Latin *mos*, or *custom*. This would seem to provide ammunition for the anti-nomian, in his argument that *morality* is only a more sanctimonious version of *mores* (also derived from *mos*), those group customs which the unthinking are perpetually exalting into

13

God-given and inalterable codes of conduct, graven in stone. And indeed, no thinking person can do other than concede that throughout the ages *morality* has in fact been a by no means adequate synonym for that simple word *goodness*. More commonly, it has been the word the herd invokes whenever it wishes to trample underfoot its shepherds, or to nudge its weakest or most unusual members off the edge of the nearest cliff.

Yet while none can deny that *moral* is an historically tainted word and *ethical* a relatively pure one, unless I am mistaken *moral* has a brighter future than *ethical* in much the same way as a regenerated "sinner" has a better chance of becoming a good person than the goody-goody who has never strayed. For if we ever see the day when *morality* has come to mean not the custom or "way" of a particular nation or people but that almost Taoistic "Way" which is the path not to blind conformity but to genuine righteousness and human fulfillment, on that day too educators may have come to look on the term "moral education" as being not an oxymoron but a redundancy.

Before that day does come, however, a much larger group of men and women than those who had assumed *moral* could mean only *priggish* or *self-righteous* will have to have rethought their basic conception of morality. For those who stand in the way of a new definition of morality are not so much the relatively few cynics and skeptics, but all those countless thousands of human beings who assume unhesitatingly that they are walking embodiments of morality, and this because (to recycle the examples cited a page or two earlier) they refrain from murder, love their children, and pay their taxes. One could hardly expect those of today's educators who share this limited conception of goodness to get very worked up about a new "moral" curriculum, because by their definition virtually everyone they know is already "moral," which is to say at least relatively kindly and decent.

Thus if there is one thing the modern moralist must insist upon it is that there is both negative and positive morality. While negative morality has done magnificent work down all those long ages in which humankind has been struggling to put beastliness behind it, now more than ever, at this point in human evolution, we must demand of ourselves full *positive* morality, which is to say conduct that not merely eschews evil but that actively seeks out and promotes the good.[1] The woman or man

---

[1]That negative morality's day of apocalypse really is at hand is attested to by the Woodstock festival and all of its clones — those orgies of self-

who votes but votes foolishly, who pays for her children's education but has no interest in it, who pays homage to heroes whose credentials for greatness he has not the least interest in examining, who positively glories in his "populist" contempt for the highbrow and wears his ignorance like a badge of honor, and so on and so forth, is by no means deserving of the high honor of being called "moral" or "good."

Now if I have thus far suggested that a person of intellectual honor cannot run away from the word *moral* merely by pretending that either *self-righteous* or *humanly decent* is an adequate synonym for it, I have still by no means made the case that, simply because there is such a thing as positive goodness, as well as an inadequate but indispensable word called *morality* to describe it, it is therefore the business of educators to somehow ensure that the moral be made an intrinsic component of their thoughts and their curricula. Many English teachers in particular will object that they have their hands quite full enough already, thank you, with trying to make their students literate and to arouse in them a love for literature that (it is hoped) will last a lifetime. Allow me to address my first comments to educators in general, and then add a word or two to English teachers in particular.

When educators argue vociferously that their job is to impart information (something, we should note in passing, that an encyclopedia or a computer could do almost as well as they), not to "inculcate a moral sense," one can be entirely sympathetic to what they *think* they are saying and still believe that their thinking has been hopelessly hampered by their assumption that *morality* can only mean today what it has in the past, the rigidly prescribed (and proscribing) code of conduct of a particular nation or social grouping. It is hardly surprising that the educator who thinks "teaching morality" means loudly proclaiming "Don't push in the hallways!" or "No sex until you're married!" becomes more elated than one might have expected at the prospect of being a mere knowledge-peddler.

Those who balk at the idea of "teaching morality" have of course good reason for doing so, in that some religious schools, for instance, do attempt to lay down the law of right conduct for their students. (Whenever the term "right conduct" is used in these pages it is used in the quasi-Buddhist sense of "appropriate"

congratulating grooviness. To sit in a muddy field, heavily sedated by drugs, and yet still manage to refrain from murder and riot — here, surely, is the ne plus ultra of human virtue!

rather than prescribed conduct.) All one can do is to assure such educators that *true* morality, in its "regenerated" modern sense of goodness in all its infinite facets, *cannot* be "inculcated" in the same fashion a teacher might din the periodic table into students' heads, for the simple reason that it is not a set of rules or guidelines, however subtle or carefully worked out, but a spirit, an orientation toward life.

At any rate, let it be noted that the teacher who feels no need to blush or stammer when the word *moral* arises in connection with education derives his equanimity from his understanding that there is no such thing as "teaching morality," only the *raising of moral issues.* He knows as well — or if he doesn't know now, I hope he will by the time he's finished this book! — that it is a relatively easy matter to tell morally weighty from morally negligible literature (*As You Like It* from *Much Ado About Nothing*, for instance — but more on that anon), and that the morally weighty should always have the greater claim on a syllabus-shaper's attention, but that whether the moral content of an *As You Like It* is worthy of being referred to as "moral *wisdom*" must be left entirely up to the reader (or student) to decide.

Unfortunately of course, and despite my best efforts to give the word *morality* a new lease on life, its unfortunate connotations will continue to make many teachers so uncomfortable with the idea of "moral education" that all analyses of whether our curricula are value-rich or value-poor will have difficulty gaining an impartial hearing. Many English teachers will return with a sigh of relief to their two functions as they see them, that of drilling students in the basics of grammar and of seeking to arouse in them a love for literature.

Yet as I see it, to precisely the same extent as English teachers shirk their responsibility — a responsibility only they are in a position to assume — of making students aware of moral complexity, will they fail to arouse in them a genuine love of literature or convince them that the communication of meaning and value — which is all that "good writing" can ever be — is something not only worth doing but worth doing stylishly.

For as we have seen, students have a ravenous appetite for value, and whenever we attempt to make a "good writer" and a "good appreciator" of a student who is all but starving for value we make fools of ourselves by offering a man whose ribs are showing a tuxedo and a ticket to the theater rather than a juicy steak. Just as we must feed a man before we can hope to develop in him a taste for moral and intellectual nicety, so too, in education, unless we can manage to convince our students that picking up a pen or opening a book *matters* even the A students will go through all four years of high school with a sardonic, weary grin on their faces, convinced that watching *Batman* on video is the funny, sexy person's preferred mode of entertainment, and that *Hamlet* is strictly for the humorless and the paunchy.

Clearly, the anti-intellectualism those students' grins betoken is not confined to young people but runs rampant through all segments of the American population. While none of us can gauge precisely how much of the blame for it should be laid at the doorstep of educational institutions, one thing at least seems clear: Whenever those institutions evade their responsibility to bring a sense of value into the lives of our young people (almost certainly on the mistaken supposition that neither students nor teachers are value-ready, so to speak), they sell both themselves and this nation very short.

In my opinion much of the blame for this must be assigned to that whole school of English teaching that undoubtedly would lend its endorsement to the notion I once saw expressed in the Introduction to a writing manual, that the best way to teach writing is to treat it as a "craft" and disregard content entirely — i.e., conveniently to forget that human language, when value and meaning have been drained out of it, is the most vain and pathetic of gibberish.[2]

We will know that a new educational era is upon us when the subject we now call "English" takes — no, not a step *backward*, as in that writing manual, to become that hideous thing "language arts" — but a step forward to become (not necessarily in name, but certainly in spirit) Philosophy, the love and pursuit of wisdom.

As we wait for that to happen, we English teachers can take a giant step toward *making* it happen by becoming not less but more content-conscious when we are drawing up our curricula. This does not mean we must suddenly begin to emulate Mrs. Grundy, and demand of every work submitted for our approval

---

[2]I realize that, given the current voguishness of the study of linguistics and semantics, many academics will reject this statement as patently false. My own belief is that these scholarly people go wrong when they assume that the law they have unearthed — that many of humanity's languages are sustained by the same principles and exhibit similar structures — is of necessity the highest law. The letter may indeed have quite a bit of "residual spirit" in it, so to speak, but it is still only the spirit itself that can make the letter come vibrantly and *morally* to life.

that it say only the "right" things, but it does mean that we should begin to emulate Socrates, and insist of our texts (as he seems to have done of his companions) that they *do have something to say.*

For while it may seem the height of perversity or effrontery for a new teacher to remind his more experienced colleagues that virtually every work in a secondary curriculum should be *about something,* I am driven to do so by my belief that the Groves of Academe too often are enchanted ones, where the books in the running brooks and the sermons in stones speak volumes to academics but insist on remaining stonily mute when students assemble dutifully before them, stifling a yawn. The supreme irony here is that the grove's spell can be broken if the teacher can simply summon up the courage to utter the word "moral," but this is the very word an evil and deceiving wizard (looking something like a cross between Oscar Wilde and Gustave Flaubert) has assured him it is death to utter: for him, for the grove, and for all of its young visitors.

4.

CAVEATS AND DISCLAIMERS

Before I can offer my colleagues my judgments as to the pedagogic suitability, or lack of it, of each of the plays in the canon, I must first throw out a few caveats and disclaimers.

1. One criticism I would like to forestall, if at all possible, is that which accuses me of being a moral monomaniac, intent on banishing from the Shakespeare syllabus a work of pure beauty such as *Midsummer*, or of pure fun such as *Shrew*, or of pure sensuality such as *Antony and Cleopatra*.[1] Let it be known, then, that I disclaim any such intention. By now my position with regard to the moral in literature and in education is, I would hope, clear:

A) *Virtually* all of the world's greatest literature is, by definition, literature that trains our attention on the moral difficulties with which life is fraught, and perhaps also trains us (in that word's other sense), to comport ourselves honorably when we are confronted by such difficulties. The word "virtually" is crucial here, because there is of course a whole world of literature — from *Midsummer* to S. J. Perelman — whose avowed purpose is

[1] Of course I don't mean to imply here that any of these plays, or for that matter any play by Shakespeare, is entirely without moral content. However, it does seem to me undeniable that, *as far as the effect these plays will have on secondary students goes*, it will be those other qualities of fun, sensuality, etc., rather than the moral subtext, that make the greatest impression.

to delight rather than instruct.

B) *In general,* "moral" literature is better suited to the secondary classrooom than "amoral," in that it a) satisfies the young person's appetite for value and b) lends itself to the kind of discussion and analysis that are the bread and butter of humanistic studies. This does *not* mean that the *Shrew*'s and the *Antony and Cleopatra*'s have no place in a well-balanced syllabus, and it *certainly* does not mean that any work should be excluded simply because it is "too frivolous" or "too sexy," i.e., because some syllabus-shaper has crossed the line and decided that works which are more or less *a*moral are, for pedagogic purposes, *im*moral.

What it does mean is that if we are to teach the *Shrew*'s etc. to add balance to the syllabus, they must be balancing *something,* and here "something" can only mean more morally rigorous works. What it also means is that, cognizant as we now are that it is the "moral" works that are most likely to generate the best class discussions etc., we must show *more* rather than less care in assigning the "amoral" works to their proper grade level in order to ensure that they will a) yield the maximum amount of fun possible, and b) provide "amoral relief" (so to speak!) at just the right moment, when the rest of the "moral syllabus" has perhaps begun to weigh down unduly both student and teacher.

2. It seems likely that many veteran teachers, when they hear some of my comments as to the virtually insurmountable barriers students at various grade levels are likely to come up against in their study of certain plays ("barriers" here meaning language that is too tough for them, or themes that are too foreign to them), will feel that I err too much on the side of caution when I proceed either to "banish" those plays from the syllabus or to reposition them at a different grade level. Then too, they may feel that some of the plays I am recommending be taught more often are just as difficult, or perhaps even more so, as those I have "banished." How am I to answer these charges?

As for seeming to err on the side of caution in many of my judgments, I can only say that I feel I have indeed done so, and for a reason. It is my conviction that a culture stands or falls not so much on whether its intellectual elite has a passion for books and learning — it always does — but on whether the average nonintellecual person goes through life having at least a modest liking for literature and ideas, and a certain grudging respect for the men and women who produce them. We are unlikely to engender such liking and respect in the average student if we ask him to study a work that he simply doesn't have the verbal skills to handle, or whose theme is one that means a great deal to his teacher but next to nothing to him.

With regard to the latter issue of thematic inappropriateness, I would take this opportunity to remind my reader that the very thesis of this book is that too often secondary school curricula are shaped in the image of their adult intellectual makers rather than, as they should be, that of their young unintellectual users. Given that fact, it certainly seems fitting that I have cried foul whenever it has seemed to me that a widely taught play is distinctly unsuited to the nature of adolescents and/or fails to address their needs.

As for the second charge that could with reason be leveled against me, that a few of my play choices, particularly those for Shakespeare electives and/or Advanced Placement courses, may be just as difficult in terms of "reading level" as some of the plays I have banished, I would simply say that if it does prove to be true it will be true *only* of those elective/AP choices. My hope here is that students who have *elected* to study some new and different Shakespeare plays, or whose high ability has earned them the right to be part of an AP course, will be ready and willing to rise to the challenge their stylistic complexity may indeed pose.

Now I am well aware that my reader's most golden opportunity to throw all of the above words back in my face will come when (or if) he disagrees with my judgment later in these pages that *Troilus and Cressida* is a play seniors should be able to read quite easily, and to comprehend (after much hard thought) quite fully. It may well seem to him that in recommending that play I am, par excellence, the adult forcing his extremely intellectual tastes on the unintellectual youth.

My answer to that prospective critic, which I give in passing in the commentary itself but think it helpful to stress here, is that there is a whole world of difference between demanding that our students study incredibly cryptic and opaque passages of the kind one finds in *Lear* (think, for instance, of the ravings of "poor Tom," where the profoundest sense and the wildest nonsense are inextricably intertwined), and passages of the kind one finds in *T & C*, passages that are remarkably easy to *read* but by no means easy to *understand*. For the simple fact is that the student who manages to decipher poor Tom's ravings in *Lear* proves himself merely *clever* (or an adept reader of footnotes!), whereas the student who, after much prior thought and study, is at last ready to give the class a coherent account of what Ulysses is saying (and how he is saying it) in his great "Take but degree away" speech in *T & C* proves herself a *thinker*.

The deeper point I'm trying to make here is that if there really is a certain flabbiness to a good deal of modern schooling on the liberal arts side, what has allowed that flab to grow is our subconscious conviction that there is something almost dangerous about demanding that students *think*, and think hard. We would never dream of rebuking the math teacher who has told a slow student that unless she can master a particular theorem she simply won't pass the course, period, but our sympathies would be entirely with the student, not the teacher, if an English teacher were to take the same stance vis-à-vis some "theorem" (i.e., difficult but philosophically profound passage) of Shakespeare's.

3. I would guess that among the most severe critics of a book such as mine — one that looks closely at each play's intellectual and moral content and, as often as not, decides that a particular play is not suited to a particular grade level, or perhaps not suitable for study by secondary students at any grade level — will be the drama teachers, and also the "theater people" who often visit schools to conduct workshops, stage performances, etc. It seems likely that many of these men and women, they who have spent a good bit of time in our classrooms and auditoriums "turning kids on to Shakespeare," will find ludicrous the idea that there is such a thing as "*the* 7th-grade [or 12th-grade, etc.] Shakespeare play," and downright blasphemous the notion that there are some plays not right for secondary school students at all. Should these folks indeed decide to make me the object of their scorn, how will I react?

I hope, with understanding and with tolerance. For while my reader might expect that I would return such scorn with scorn, and insist that my more theoretical approach to Shakespeare studies is the only one, I am glad to confound that reader's expectation. Clearly, the men and women who come into our schools (or who are already on the staff of our schools) and get kids up and on their feet to perform scenes from Shakespeare's plays are themselves performing an invaluable service. And if in the rendering of that service they use scenes from plays that in the course of this book I suggest are the wrong ones for book-study in general, or for study by students at a certain grade level in particular, there's little or no harm in that.

That said, I must go on to say that I think teachers deceive themselves enormously if they think that the initial thrill a student may well feel at seeing or being part of a Shakespeare production will necessarily linger on for years in the form of intellectual excitement, and deceive themselves far more dangerously if they assume that that thrill — however intense, and however important in breaking through a student's "block" about Shakespeare — can ever be a substitute for the kind of moral and intellectual growth that only the *study* of Shakespeare's plays can bring one.

Granted, Shakespeare *was* a consummate man of the theater, but the fact is that we revere him today not so much because he once trod the boards in body as because he still walks abroad in spirit. In other words, it has been the consensus of cultivated men and women for many generations now that Shakespeare is not only a genius but a particularly rare sort of genius (more on this in Appendix II), and that his works all but *demand* to be studied, not simply performed. Thus, in my view, one of the most dangerous pedagogic delusions the English teacher can fall victim to is this: to imagine that the student with a cloak of felt on his back and a foil of lath in his hand has been fully equipped to thrust right to the heart of Shakespeare's genius.

One final and I think very important word on this subject. In referring to my approach to Shakespeare studies as being "theoretical," and thereby leaving all those more attractive adjectives such as "spontaneous," "fun-loving," "kid-oriented" to the theater folks, I have perhaps left an impression in my reader's mind that I am the old and gray fuddy-duddy, the taskmaster with the birch rod in his hand, and that the drama teachers etc. are of necessity the innovators and the true friends of youth. Given the fact that this whole book has no reason for being whatsoever unless it can be thought of as a true friend of youth, I'm sure my reader will understand that I don't intend to let that impression harden and dry.

Let it be said then, that if I seem to be merely cruel when I say that the majority of our students' time simply must be spent with their heads in the texts of Shakespeare's plays, not with their arms outstretched in the performance of those plays, I am cruel only to be kind. For while the theater person will of course win most of the kudos in the short run, and students will flock to her standard as their deliverer from the bondage of book-study, in the long run, I truly believe, those same students will come to see that it was that taskmaster with the birch rod in his hand who was the best friend they ever had.

4. The teacher who has been teaching only *R & J* and *Macbeth* for twenty years, and feels herself quite content to go on doing so for another ten, may think it rather absurd that I've taken the trouble to examine *every* play in the canon, on the assumption that even *Timon of Athens* has the right to a fair trial before it is sentenced to banishment. I think two responses may be made to her objection.

First, as it will be one of the primary contentions of this book that much good and even great Shakespeare is indeed going unmined by today's syllabus-shapers, thoroughness demands that we sift even the slag lest a bit of the precious ore should escape our notice.

Second, even if my reader finds he cannot endorse my lists of favored and proscribed plays in Chapter 6, this book may still succeed as a morale-booster of sorts. It will do so if it reminds the teacher of the glories of the whole canon, and suggests that, while many a play is far from being a teacher's dream, there are indeed a few very "dreamy" but lonely plays out there, shyly waiting for those teachers bold enough (and bored enough?) to stride up and ask them if they might have the pleasure of this dance.

5. While the focus of this book is almost entirely on the pedagogic value, or lack of it, of each of the Shakespeare plays, at times in order to get a good shot of my subject I have had to remove a large object positioned between it and the camera. By that "large object" I mean the preconceptions about certain plays a good number of my readers almost certainly hold. Thus I have taken the time to analyze at relatively great length the "intrinsic" *Merchant of Venice, Hamlet*, and *Troilus and Cressida* (and to a lesser extent a number of others), simply because I have recognized that only by first getting my reader to share my view of the "intrinsic" play can I hope to convince her to put it to the pedagogic uses I have envisioned for it.

While I do feel that even in the midst of the longest of these commentaries I am never unmindful of, and never finally fail to articulate, some pedagogic objective, I hope my reader will agree that I also perform a valuable service if I simply stimulate new thinking among teachers about certain of the plays. Some of these (*Hamlet*, for one) they perhaps have been too close to for many years to take a fresh glance at from a further remove, and others (*Troilus and Cressida* being a likely candidate here) so far away from since leaving university that the out of sight has been put quite out of mind.

In particular I am thinking here of my commentary on *Hamlet*, which I admit sticks out a bit by reading for much of its length more like a critical essay than a pedagogic piece. While of course I make no claim to complete originality in my comments there (although I do pride myself on having made a few original observations), I think I have been able to synthesize much of the "new" thinking on *Hamlet*, thinking that I hope will energize my colleagues as they return to the teaching of this the most central (both intrinsically and pedagogically) play in the canon.

6. The final warning I have to offer is in a way two warnings, one directed primarily at myself and the other at my reader.

The warning I have often had to give myself, and which my reader is invited to listen in on now as well, is to consider well the possibility that just as the imponderable is at the heart of life so it may be at the heart of education. However convincing a theoretical case I may at times make in favor of teaching one play and forsaking another, it would be folly for me to forget that theories are only tools, and that tools alone may not be sufficient to pry open the door behind which Truth is barricaded. Thus there is always a very real possibility that the play that looks like a classroom winner on paper may still, even when it has been given a chance to enter the race, come in a distant second to the present front-runner.

The warning to my reader is this. While she has a right to be comforted by my confession of fallibility above, whenever she is feeling the urge to cry out that I am inveighing too strongly against the teaching of a much-loved play, that comfort should not lull her into thinking that a return to a complete curricular relativism and sujectivism is thereby justified. This book will have served no purpose whatever if it has not impressed upon my reader the simple fact that each Shakespeare play differs significantly from all of the others, and that these differences inevitably have important pedagogic implications.

This book *will* have served its purpose if, after weathering the "attacks" I make on the teaching of various plays, teachers are in the future better prepared to defend their decision to teach them. It will have failed if teachers continue to think that either a play's popularity (with their students or, even more to the point, with them) or its inherent greatness is in and of itself grounds for continuing to teach it. As a number of the play commentaries in the next chapter will show, a play may be popular precisely *because* of its relative lack of moral weight, and an inherently great play may either be too tough for secondary students or teach lessons that are not the ones young people have the greatest need to learn.

5.

PLAY-BY-PLAY
COMMENTARIES

For lack of any better mode of presentation, the plays have been ordered thus. Plays that either I or current practice deem best taught at a particular grade level are first discussed, beginning at grade 7 and moving on to grade 12. For instance, the first play analyzed is *Midsummer*, because the survey reveals that it is at present the most widely taught play in the seventh grade, the second play *As You Like It*, not because it is now being taught much in junior high but because I believe it should be.

This does not mean, however, that the reader will note any neat coupling of "bad play, good play" as he reads, merely that I am working my way in rough fashion from grade 7 to 12. The most important thing for my reader to note is that she is not being asked to intuit, merely from this mode of presentation, my final decisions as to the best grade level for each play. She will find those judgments in the chapter following this one.

After the 7–12 "standards" come the plays now being taught in electives or AP courses, or thought by me to be good elective/AP choices, and after these those plays which are, to some extent or other, the pedagogic "losers." In arranging both the elective/AP choices and the "losers" I have been more concerned with varying topic and tone for my reader's pleasure than with ranking the plays from good to not-so-good, or bad to worse. For those rankings as well, the reader is referred to the next chapter. Now for two final points.

1. While references will be made, as part of the commentary on virtually every play, to at least one and generally all three of the pedagogic attributes we have said a work ideally should possess if it is to be adopted for study at the secondary level — moral weight, social vision, and youthfulness — I have spared both my reader and myself the pedantry of labeling each section of my commentary with one of the above rubrics, and indeed have not made explicit mention of them in every case. I'm sure both my reader and I are quite capable of debating the relative moral weight of this play, or the degree of youthfulness of that, without repeating the terms themselves ad nauseam.

2. While in most of the commentaries I refer somewhere to the play's "most taught" ranking in the tabular data that follows the first question of the survey (pp. 226–227), the reader is reminded that he or she may wish to look over that data (and perhaps other data as well) in Appendix V before reading each commentary. It is likely that a play's ranking will make a greater impression when it is seen in tabular form, with other plays above and below it, than when it is mentioned briefly by me in the course of a commentary.

A MIDSUMMER NIGHT'S DREAM

One of the first and most difficult adjustments anyone new to the teaching profession must make (and it is particularly difficult for anyone with a keen sense of humor), is to banish from one's banter even the slightest hint of the sardonic. A new teacher quickly apprehends the fact that the crystal cabinet housing the adolescent ego is brittle beyond belief, and shatters at the slightest imputation of incapacity. Yet as time passes and he learns to scour daily from his countenance any trace of mocking wit at student expense, at last he is brought up short by a sudden and deeper revelation: Irony in any form, however impersonal its target, is utterly alien to the adolescent mind.[1]

[1]Many a veteran teacher, with a career's worth of raucous student laughter echoing in her ears, may wonder if she heard that assertion aright, so improbable did it sound on first hearing. Yet if she will simply summon up any single memory of a young person attempting to be sarcastic — the stagy delivery, the oh-so-pregnant pause, and all of it climaxed with that quintessentially adolescent "yuck yuck yuck" — I'm sure she will quickly

The reason for this is not far to seek. Irony is above all a vision of the incongruous, of the lamentable discrepancy between the ideal and the real, the intended and the unintended, the blissful dream and the grumpy awakening. Striving mightily as they are to find and make fast both mental and social connections, young people have had no chance to develop any of the adult's ability to wryly accept missed connections as an inevitable part of both mental life and life as a whole.

Now whimsy, it might be said, is simply the spiritualized form of irony. It strives not to close but to widen the gap between the mundane and the ethereal, generally in order to suggest that the mundane is all too earthy-gross. Surely the fact that the butt of all the rather cruel tricks played by leprechauns and fairies is the country clodhopper, or an occasional "rude mechanical" who has strayed beyond city gates, suggests that such sprites are the agents through whom the human imagination chides the most unimaginative humans for their benightedness. And when we also recall that those to whom such leprechauns and fairies appear are proverbially not children but old folk[2] — the family retainer trudging down a country road in the gloaming, on his way home from the pub; the crone out just before dawn to inspect her garden plot — we have in fact gathered all the data we need to dispute the pedestrian notion that any play containing fairies and a man with a donkey's head must perforce be ideal for the young reader.

For given the fact that *Midsummer* is essentially four acts of whimsy and a final act — the play within a play — of potent and undiluted irony, any bits of evidence we may have been able to glean suggesting that adolescents are indeed insensible to one or both of these qualities should be taken under strict advisement. I myself first stumbled on such evidence when I committed the blunder (for so it still seems to me) of having some 7th-graders get to their feet and (book in hand) perform the play within the play. As I tried to impart some modest direction to

join me in the conviction that adult irony and adolescent goofball humor are the twin poles of the comic sphere.

[2]There is a passage in *Merry Wives* that illustrates this for us nicely. In Act IV, scene iv, as the plot to place some very real horns on Falstaff's head is being hatched, there is talk of the ghost known as Herne the Hunter. Mrs. Page then says: "... and well you know/The superstitious idle-headed eld [old folk]/Received, and did deliver to our age/This tale of Herne the Hunter for a truth."

the very halting proceedings, I marveled at how *completely* impervious these young people were to the humor of the scene they were trying to enact, and felt ashamed at myself for having cast these awkward, shy creatures in the role of dupes.

The fact that to an adult Bottom and company are *lovable* dupes, and that the adult likes to think at least that he is laughing with them and not at them, availed not a whit these poor student players who had "never laboured in their minds till now." As I observed their struggles I felt I could only exclaim with Hippolyta, "I love not to see wretchedness o'ercharged/And duty in his service perishing," or advise any other spectators to avert their eyes "unless you can find sport in their intents,/Extremely stretched, and conned with cruel pain...."

The difficulty for early adolescents[3] of the play within a play is compounded by the fact that the sardonic asides of Theseus et al, as they pass amused judgment on their social inferiors, are fraught with puns, archaisms, and double entendres, all of them utterly beyond the ken even of the gifted 7th- or 8th-grader. Indeed, it should here be noted, of the poetry of *Midsummer* in general, that it is Shakespeare at his most opulent and rococo, and by no means ideal for the first-time reader of Shakespeare. For instance, a speech such as that by Theseus (IV, i) in praise of his "hounds... bred out of the Spartan kind" is about as gorgeous a piece of word-music and word-painting as the language affords, but it is certain to stump the young reader in two ways.

First, he will have immense difficulties with the language ("So flewed, so sanded... dew-lapped like Thessalian bulls"), difficulties even the footnotes are unlikely to conjure away (should he deign to read them at all, which is always unlikely). Second, the pragmatist in him continually will be wondering, "What does all this *mean*, both in and of itself and in relation to the story?" How to tell him that it means essentially nothing, being simply a piece of artistry as exquisite and as superbly constructed as the hounds it describes?

Even if some or all of these speculations about *Midsummer* in the classroom are on the mark, it seems likely that it is a popular

---

[3] Just so my reader and I can be sure we're talking the same language, let me briefly note what I will mean in this book by early, middle, and late adolescence. Early adolescence I take to be roughly ages 12–15, and from grade 6 through the middle of grade 10. Middle adolescence is roughly ages 16–19, and from the latter half of grade 10 through the freshman year in college. Late adolescence is the last three years of college, up to age 21 or 22.

play with many students. (Although more so with girls than with boys, according to a few survey respondents, and although its showing in the survey's "most popular with students" category — p. 231 — looks a bit lackluster, given the fact that this is the sixth most widely taught play nationwide.) I'm not especially concerned to deny this, but I would note that the student who has been mesmerized by the play (particularly if study of the text has been supplemented with viewings of a video, or of a live performance) may also be he or she who is then too sleepy-headed to wish to grapple closely with its difficult poetry.

So too I find no fault with the notion that the study of Shakespeare should begin with a play of assured popularity, but I do insist that that notion will hold weight only if it is ballasted by others of at least equal weight. Chief among these must be the notion that educators have a duty to provide their students with works that challenge them as much as they delight them, that instruct even as they amuse.

Thus, while he who utters a single stern word about this lovely play feels that he is breaking its fairy spell, and playing the killjoy to boot, nonetheless it must be noted that *Midsummer* is a work of almost no moral content whatever. Can any of us think of a single *lesson* it has to teach, beyond perhaps "fools are lovable, and we are all fools," or "love is blind"? There are of course a few nice instances of moralizing in the work, such as the one that opens Act V: Theseus the philosopher-king reminding us that "The lunatic, the lover, and the poet/Are of imagination all compact." Yet not only are these bits of moralizing in every way aloof from the rest of the work, but their very aloofness — that urbane and condescending tone of Jovian wisdom which is Theseus's — is certain to leave the thirteen-year-old cold.

If, then, even such minimal moral content as *Midsummer* does possess is of entirely the wrong sort to offer to young people, and if the "irony issue" I raised a moment ago is in fact a valid and important one, one can only conclude that this is not the Shakespeare play junior high students should first encounter. For surely the young person who is at last making the acquaintance of a genius of whom she has heard so much deserves to part from him not only happier, but wiser. If we have any doubts as to that, perhaps these words, spoken by one very great man about another, will help to dispel them:

His wisdom draws men to him. We do not go to
him to have our ear tickled with the tune of his verse

nor our fancy amused with flowers and rainbows. But we
go to him because, whilst he yields us these gratifications,
this wondrous Sage takes possession of our heart and
mind, and instructs and elevates us.[4]

AS YOU LIKE IT

The accusation has been made that the potent enchantment of
Midsummer has beguiled the teacher into hearing as the lyric
voice of youth what are in fact the stately euphonies of a mature
singer highly adept in the arts of whimsy and irony, and has so
enthralled the student that she can scarcely keep her eyes focused
on the words spread out on the page before her. Yet of all the
ill curricular effects this bewitchment has wreaked perhaps none is
sorrier than this: Like some Puck-struck lover, some new
Demetrius, we have plighted our troth to the wrong play.
Smitten as we have been by *Midsummer's* ravishing beauty of
body (the fable itself) and mellifluousness of voice (its ornate
poetry), we have pretended to see in her those more perdurable
inner qualities that we know, in our heart of hearts, her somewhat homelier cousin is infinitely richer in. Need it be added that
that cousin's name is *As You Like It?*

Indeed, while we are invoking the spirit of wonder and astonishment, I must confess that no aspect of the survey results so
genuinely astonished me as the discovery that *AYLI* is not only
hugely under-taught,[5] but that when it is taught it is generally as
part of an 11-12 elective. This, in my view, amounts almost to a
scandal. For while of course nothing could be more absurd than

---

[4]R.W. Emerson, *The Early Lectures of Ralph Waldo Emerson*, ed. Whicher
and Spiller (Cambridge: Harvard University Press, 1959), p. 303.

[5]As corroboration of sorts of the survey's finding in this regard, I might
note that I had a good bit of trouble tracking down a cover photo for
this book that showed young people performing a scene from *AYLI*.
Other plays are far more commonly used for such student renditions —
Midsummer, R & J, The Tempest, etc.

My own hunch is that, far from proving that *AYLI* is intrinsically
unsuited to young people, what this really "proves" is something quite
different and more interesting. To wit, that those choosing relatively
"doable" scenes for kids to perform from Shakespeare recognize, if only
subconsciously, *AYLI*'s true moral weightiness, and decide that it would

to think that any of Shakespeare's plays originally was intended to be taught at a particular grade level (or even taught at all), the fact remains that this play has PERFECT FOR YOUNG PEOPLE written under its title in invisible ink. Its virtues in this respect are almost numberless, but perhaps we can work our way through some of them.

First and foremost, *AYLI* is without doubt the *greenest* of Shakespeare's plays — the Forest of Arden being a more genuine Arcadia than the fairyland of *Midsummer* — and surely today's young people, trapped as they are in a grimy urban world and beset by acid rain and ozone depletion, richly deserve the opportunity to cavort across a bucolic landscape in those more innocent days "when the world was young."

On a deeper level, *AYLI* has what *Midsummer* only feigns to have, a genuinely youth's-eye view of love. Consider Silvius's rebuke to Corin, when Corin says that he can sympathize with that youth's lovesickness, because he too has "loved ere now": "No, Corin, being old, thou canst not guess,/Though in thy youth thou wast as true a lover/As ever sighed upon a midnight pillow." Or hear the very voice of youthful impatience and joy in Rosalind, when she has discovered from Celia that it is Orlando who has been defacing tree trunks with his doggerel: "What said he? How looked he? Wherein went he? What makes he here? Did he ask for me? Where remains he? How parted he with thee? and when shalt thou see him again? Answer me in one word." By contrast, the view of love in *Midsummer* is like that seen through the veiled lids of a mocking giant (i.e., an ironic adult) as he tosses the lovers back and forth in his hand and laughs uproariously at their agitations.

Note too that the source of contention between Helena, Hermia, and Demetrius is physical beauty, or the lack thereof, whereas clearly what first endears Orlando to Rosalind is the fact that he, like she, is "one out of suits with Fortune." In general the obsession with physical appearance only gets into full swing in middle adolescence, whereas one of the genuine charms of the twelve- or thirteen-year-old is that she still retains much of the divine inwardness of childhood, and is still capable of "those obstinate questionings/Of sense and outward things" of which

be wiser to try a bit of fluff from *Midsummer*, farce from *The Tempest* (Trinculo sharing Caliban's gaberdine in II, ii) or passionate athleticism from *R & J*. If this is true, I think it in fact helps me to make the case that *AYLI* is the play junior high students should be *studying*, regardless of which scenes from which plays they are acting out.

Wordsworth has spoken.

If the vision of young love in *AYLI* is truer and more compelling than that of *Midsummer*, so too the images it offers us of love and friendship can genuinely move and teach us, whereas the ceaseless bickering of Hermia et al can at best amuse and at worst annoy us. Helena and Hermia may in happier days have been "two lovely berries molded on one stem," but Puck, with his harshly sardonic (and therefore adult) sense of humor, has joyed to blight them both. The young person who has, or is, a best friend, will see little to admire in Helena and Hermia, but may well be deeply touched by the constant companionship of Celia and Rosalind, those two being "like Juno's swans...coupled and inseparable."

So too nothing in *AYLI* is more moving than the mutual devotion of Orlando and Adam. The early adolescent, often just awakening to the realization that his elders are not mere stock figures from an MTV video but genuinely human beings who suffer and joy as he does, may well feel filial piety stirring within him as he observes Orlando's solicitousness for a sick old man who has done his family good service.

Even with all its many excellences, *AYLI* might not merit a place in an already crowded curriculum if, like *Midsummer*, it were devoid of moral content, or without a theme. Yet *AYLI* does have moral content, and most of it has been placed at the service of its theme, one of the mightiest: that of the striking spiritual contrast between gratitude and ingratitude. Each of us, this play suggests, owes a twofold debt: one to existence itself, another to our fellow humans for whatever love and support they have rendered us throughout our life. The unfailing mark of the bad person is that he or she is in arrears on both of these payments.

Needless to say, the idea of the ingratitude of man to man is at the core of this play's plot, in that the usurping Duke and the usurping Oliver have both failed in their obligation of fraternal love. It should be noted in this regard that any play which is set in motion by sibling rivalry and flagrant injustice should have an immediate double appeal for the early adolescent. No student who has a brother or sister has escaped the contentions that are an inevitable feature of family membership, and it seems likely that it is from her perpetual recourse to parental adjudication that that sense so powerful in the adolescent — of the necessity of fair play, and the egregiousness of injustice — is born.

Later in the play the note of ingratitude, lest it fade away altogether as the evil-brothers plot element wanes in importance, gathers other notes to itself and breaks into song:

> Blow, blow, thou winter wind,
> Thou art not so unkind as man's ingratitude;
>   . . .
> Freeze, freeze, thou bitter sky,
> That dost not bite so nigh as benefits forgot.

Of course the countervailing theme of gratitude is first broached, in immortal fashion, in the great speech by the banished Duke that opens Act II, a speech whose merits alone would make *AYLI* an indispensable text for all secondary students. A great spirit, it suggests, can find good not merely in almost everything — many people can do that — but even in adversity, even in the "churlish chiding of the winter wind."

This theme of gratitude is so potent that it manages to insinuate itself into even the unlikeliest of places, such as the mouth of the melancholy Jacques. In giving Amiens his reason for having avoided the Duke, he says: "He is too disputable for my company. I think of as many matters as he, but *I give heaven thanks* and make no boast of them." Then too in a later scene, Rosalind, as if to cajole Jacques back into the wisdom we just had a taste of, uses irony in order to chide him out of his sullen peevishness: "Look you... be out of love with your nativity, and almost chide God for making you that countenance you are...."

Yet perhaps most miraculous of all are those moments when Shakespeare seems to suggest that ultimately there is only one gratitude, not two, and that those who most cherish existence are also those most likely to serve their fellow human beings best, and vice versa. As might be expected from so great an artist as Shakespeare, these revelations crop up in the most unexpected places, as in these words of old Corin's when he first meets Rosalind and company: "My master is of churlish disposition,/And little recks to find the way to heaven/By doing deeds of hospitality." Or these of Orlando: "I chide no breather in the world but myself, against whom I know most faults." Or these of Rosalind to Phoebe: "But mistress, know yourself, down on your knees,/And thank heaven, fasting, for a good man's love."

Can there be the slightest doubt that a text such as this, full of fun and passion as it is, yet with so much to teach the young about the firm connection between a certain natural piety and an honorable and happy life, should be one of the firmest fixtures of our syllabus? It may be objected that junior high students are incapable of analyzing fully this theme of gratitude versus ingratitude. So they undoubtedly are — but what of it? If our contention from the opening pages is correct, that the moral in imaginative literature, when it is genuine, is an organic outgrowth of the whole rather than a graft imposed from without, and if our faith in Shakespeare's artistry is unshakable, we need not doubt that this great theme will do its work silently, in the subconscious of each reader, without a word of analysis needing to be spoken.

The only other conceivable objection to teaching *AYLI* to junior high students is that Touchstone's jesting is a) not very funny, and b) recondite in the extreme. True again. Yet provided there is some fairly active teacher intervention, explicating the passages quickly and moving students through them quickly, these need not bring the otherwise lively and rewarding proceedings to too screeching a halt.

JULIUS CAESAR

It seems likely that, throughout all the years teachers have been offering *Julius Caesar* to their younger students, they have done so with a slight twinge of regret and with a profound sense of irony. Regret, in that *JC*, for all its greatness, does tend a bit toward the stolid, and knowing as the sensitive critic does that the more stolidity there is about a work the less it is characteristically Shakespearean, it has always seemed a shame to introduce students to the Bard on one of those rarest of occasions when he is wholly sober and mirthless. Irony, in that the sight of thirteen- to fifteen-year-olds, creasing their smooth and carefree brows as they ponder portentous political happenings and linger over exquisitely drawn psychological portraits, can only evoke in the mature mind faint (and perhaps not entirely reliable?) memories of a Little Rascals episode, one in which a togaed Spanky cries out "Et tu, Brutè?" as Alfalfa plucks his cursed steel away.

Yet despite the fact that there is much in *JC* certain to elude the young reader, and while it is certain that we dishonor this great play whenever we conceive of it as being strictly "student Shakespeare," its pedagogic merits — strong plot (in both senses), fascinating characterizations, and above all immense readability — will continue to find it a place in most curricula. For the plain fact is that the number of Shakespeare plays suited to the 7-9 syllabus is very limited, and doubtless teachers will continue to turn to *JC* as they have always done: with some ambivalence, but with more than a little relief that so trusty and well-tried a pedagogic tool is ready to hand.

Yet while *JC* almost certainly should be read by all students before they've left the 9th grade, my own view is that it should *not* be the first Shakespeare play a student reads in junior high. Given the fact that the perfect junior high play, *AYLI*, is a work as characteristically Shakespearean as *JC* in many respects is not, surely it makes more sense to introduce students to the Bard when he is attired in his usual doublet and hose than when his distinctive form has been obscured by a toga.

ROMEO AND JULIET

To no one's surprise, the survey reveals that (as far as teachers can tell) *Romeo and Juliet* is the Shakespeare play most popular with students. Yet this play's very popularity presents the teacher with a dual challenge. First, he must do everything in his power to ensure that students actually *learn* from *R & J* rather than merely absorb it, that they come to grips with Shakespeare's demanding verse rather than simply abandon themselves to Zeffirelli's images. Second, he must see to it that the play's most striking themes and effects have a chance to resonate as deeply within the student's being as possible, so that she will still be able to hear their muffled echo even a generation hence.

I would assert that both of these challenges can be met successfully only if *R & J* is taught at the proper grade level. I feel that while 9th-graders (at the moment the play's single largest group of readers) may be marginally equipped to deal with its complexities of language, they are simply too immature sexually and emotionally to have a full appreciation of this passion-filled work. In the "ideal" syllabus I present in Chapter 6, I have placed *R & J* not merely in the tenth grade but in the second semester of the tenth grade. As all veteran teachers know (it was a veteran teacher, my father, who first made me aware of the phenomenon), the division between the fall and the spring terms of the tenth grade is also the boundary between early and middle adolescence (for most if not for all students). The second-semester sophomore possesses a sexual and emotional maturity worlds removed from that of his freshman counterpart. As an added dividend, positioning *R & J* in the second semester means that students will be reading it in the spring, or as spring approaches — should it ever be otherwise?

Before we take a longer look at some of those factors that have contributed to my assessment of *R & J* as a far more adult work than it is generally recognized as being, let it herewith be noted that numerous survey respondents have indicated that *R & J* does pose serious language problems for many of today's non-reading, vocabulary-impoverished students. One department chairman had this to say: "In terms of language, we found it one of the most sophisticated plays we were teaching, and while the kids loved it, we found far too much evidence that they couldn't really read it." If there is as much truth to that statement as I would surmise there is,[6] one could state unequivocally that, on the basis of language difficulty alone, those who teach *R & J* in grade 7 or 8 err in so doing. When one also pauses to consider how many highly adult features there are to *R & J*, the wisdom of teaching it to twelve- to fourteen-year-olds comes to seem all the more dubious. Let us examine some of them.

In many ways the atmosphere of the whole play is established in its first scene, that in which the servingmen of the houses of Montague and Capulet quarrel and then fight. This is an atmosphere not of sex alone ("maidenheads") or of violence alone ("choler") but of the two combined — of rape ("women... thrust to the wall," "cut off [the maids'] heads"). Romeo, when we first meet him brooding darkly over the fair Rosaline, is suffering not from a case of unrequited puppy love such as any 7th-grader might recognize and empathize with, but from ungratified desire. This Romeo is no Petrarchan lover, content to cherish for untold years one glimpse from afar of some golden Laura, but a passionate young man sulking over the fact that Rosaline is "in strong proof of chastity well armed" and refuses to "ope her lap to saint-seducing gold."

---

[6]Some corroborating evidence of my own: In my first year of teaching, I taught *R & J* to a very slow group of seniors (the play was chosen because, surprisingly, no one in the class had encountered it before). While all seemed more or less well as the class read through and discussed the play, the dismal performance by virtually everyone on the exam convinced me that very few of these students actually had been making much sense of Shakespeare's English.

Or consider Mercutio. Often mistaken for nothing but a mad-cap youth, the quintessence of high spirits, in fact Mercutio is quite likely a genuine manic-depressive. His famous Queen Mab speech, which the careless reader revels in as nothing but a marvelous bit of *Midsummer*-ish fluff, is in fact one of those supreme moments in Shakespeare where the poet and dramatist join forces to create a stunning emotional effect. As the imagery in the speech subtly shifts from "moonshine's watery beams" to "dreams... of cutting foreign throats" and "maids [that] lie on their backs" (note again the link between sex and violence), so too we see Mercutio being transformed before our eyes from a mere fantastic into a man perilously close to insanity. The moment when Romeo brings his friend back to earth with a few soft words in his ear — "Peace, peace, Mercutio, peace! Thou talk'st of nothing." — is to my way of thinking the most genuinely heartrending in the whole play.[7]

Let it also be noted that the Mercutio whom we meet in the sweltering piazza in Act II, scene iv, spoiling for a fight with Tybalt and growing bawdy with the Nurse (sex and violence, yet again), is no mere adolescent cutup or class clown, but a man whose swaggering bravado certainly would have gained him admittance to the Sharks or the Jets if only he had lived a few hundred years later.

Yet of all the aspects of this work that so plainly suit it to the middle rather than the early adolescent, none is so plain as its very theme, which is intergenerational conflict. Just as we have seen how a superficial assessment of *Midsummer* finds in it only childishness rather than highly adult whimsy and irony, so too it is an all too common error to think of *R & J* as merely "a story of young lovers" rather than as what its prologue proclaims it to be, a cautionary tale depicting how the sins of one generation are visited upon the next. It is doubtful whether any book, play, or film about the 1960s has ever shown a young person so utterly alienated from her elders and driven back on her own resources as Juliet is, in that terrifying scene where she is confronted with a violently angry, utterly loutish father ("Out, you greensickness carrion! Out, you baggage! You tallowface!"), a useless mother ("Talk not to me, for I'll speak not a word"), and a nurse who, in knowingly counseling her to bigamy, forfeits, in the space of

---

[7]All of these insights into this scene, if insights they be, never would have come into my head had it not been for John McEnery's magnificent and moving performance as Mercutio in the Zeffirelli film.

thirteen lines, all of Juliet's love (and ours) forever.

Now the point here is that the middle adolescent is in a position to genuinely feel this intergenerational conflict in a way the early adolescent cannot possibly do. The twelve- to fifteen-year-old is of course at odds with her parents over curfews, allowance, overnights, and so on, but only in middle and late adolescence do the real arguments over alcohol and drug use, sex, college and career choice, and so on really get under way.[8] This is of course a time fraught with peril and anxiety for both parent and child, and few works of literature could do a better job than *R & J* does of providing the middle adolescent with a genuine catharsis for the emotions threatening to consume him at this period of his development.

One might also note that the middle adolescent generally feels a greater need than does his younger counterpart to go beyond the confines of the family group in search of adult role models and counselors. He may well be moved, as a thirteen-year-old never could be, by the figure of the good Friar Laurence, that eternal symbol of adulthood willing to lend an unbiased ear and a charitable hand to youth in distress.

If any or all of our conclusions thus far have been valid, a question suggests itself: Who or what is it that keeps ordering *R & J* up to the front lines of the curriculum, when there is so much evidence to suggest that it would do far better service if it were allowed to stand just a file or two back in the ranks? Three answers seem plausible.

1. Perhaps the one fact about *R & J* the average reader finds most engaging is that the lovers are not only teenagers but early teenagers. She is both startled and charmed by this potent reminder that the life cycle of the short-lived Renaissance person moved at a far faster clip than its modern counterpart. One is probably justified in assuming from this that many a teacher, having fallen under the spell of this singular fact, goes on to decide that a play *about* early teens must therefore be the right play *for* early teens. This decision almost certainly is an ill-considered one, and for two reasons.

First and foremost, while *R & J* may concern itself with early teens, its author was himself no early teen. This is the work of a

---

[8]The reader might argue that this is a vision of the early adolescent as she existed in a more innocent era, but no longer. The objection is sustained, but nonetheless I will stand by my statement as one that is still true *enough* for purposes of the distinction being made here.

mature artist, writing poetry that is as difficult as it is evocative. Second, most attempts to find equivalences between the lives of modern men and women and those of earlier ages are certain to miscarry. For while we moderns doubtless are exceedingly similar to our ancestors in terms of biology, the fact of early death must certainly have given each stage of human development in eras prior to our own a very different flavor and significance.

2. Knowing as teachers do that students love *R & J*, and having an understandable desire to gratify their students (and perhaps bask a bit in the reflected glow of their gratitude), they simply can't resist offering it to young people who are in fact emotionally and intellectually unfit for it.

3. By overlooking *AYLI* as an ideal junior high text, perhaps by being too bored with *JC* to remind themselves that their students are sure to enjoy and profit from it, and by conveniently ignoring the adult aspects of *R & J*, teachers manage to convince themselves that "there really is no substitute" (which is how one or two survey respondents put it) for *R & J* in the junior high Shakespeare syllabus.

A final thought. While the thinking that has made *R & J* the third most commonly taught play nationwide — presumably, that it would be almost a crime to deprive students of a work so quintessentially youthful, and so grippingly dramatic — seems in most respects compelling enough, perhaps I would be doing all of us teachers a service if I challenged it for a moment.

Mightn't one formulate a theory that certain works — in the canon, *Midsummer* and *R & J* immediately come to mind — not only grab a student's attention but shake it violently, and that these works are as little likely to develop a student's power of reasoning as they are very likely to excite him emotionally?

For while doubtless we are right in perceiving as a dour and blinkered pedant the educator who insists that education can only be about mental, never about emotional growth, and right in thinking that if schools *are* about emotional growth as well as mental growth then *R & J* is every bit as indispensable as we have come to think it, nonetheless one can't help but wonder whether this play (particularly when it is taught in conjunction with the Zeffirelli video, which in my opinion it unavoidably *must* be) gives students the *learning* experience we teachers are pledged to provide them with. We have a right to demand that students struggle to comprehend the actual text of a difficult poetic drama, and students have a right to sit back and emote as that drama unfolds before them on the video screen, but almost certainly those two rights can and do conflict, and conflict violently.

At any rate, one thing does seem clear: The teacher who decides *not* to teach R & J has no real reason to upbraid himself for having thus chosen. The Zeffirelli video is widely known, and at some later point in life the student could easily become acquainted with it and/or the text of the play. More importantly, there are if anything *too many* Shakespeare plays perfectly suited to the tenth grade (see Chapter 6), so the teacher who decides to move R & J from there to an 11-12 elective (probably quite a good place for it, in fact, given its maturity and the difficulty of its language) is also simplifying her life by making the choice of a 10th-grade play an easier one.

RICHARD II, AND THE HISTORIES

It pleases me to consider that, while my colleagues may have disagreed with this or that assertion thus far, they are bound to agree with at least one: Most students who turn away from Shakespeare in disappointment or disgust do so because of the difficulties of language they have encountered therein. The new teacher, in particular, notes well the look of disgruntled bafflement on the faces of students who are struggling to comprehend Shakespeare's complex verse, and seems to see graven there the question, "Why does this guy have to write this way?" (For some thoughts on how best to erase that look, the reader is referred to Appendix III.)

If there is in fact a collegial consensus as to the difficulty of Shakespeare's language for almost all students, one might assume that English teachers spend a good bit of their time searching for their own version of the Holy Grail, the perfectly readable Shakespeare play. Yet if they've ever held a copy of *Richard II* in their hand, their quest at that moment had already come to an end. For with respect to this issue of readability, *Richard II*'s position within the canon is wholly anomalous: Of no other play by Shakespeare can it be said so truly that the average reader can make his way from the first to the last act without once having to stop to consult a footnote. Yet if this play does possess this extraordinary pedagogic virtue, how are we to account for the fact that it is so little taught?

Two answers suggest themselves. First, *Richard II* obviously has been eclipsed by *Richard III* in many curricula. This is regrettable in and of itself, in that most mature minds feel no hesitation in proclaiming *Richard II* the far superior work, *Richard III* — despite its many show-stopping attributes — being little more than a rather tiresome harping on one note, the note of absolute evil. It seems certain that teachers turn more often to *Richard III* simply because they imagine that such a "good villain" must surely be a crowd-pleaser with students. While on the surface there might seem to be a certain wisdom in such a judgment, I would suggest that in fact there is implicit in it a condescension that should be rejected by any teacher with an exalted view of his calling and an unshakable belief in the intellectual capabilities of his students. One might in good conscience recommend a movie or other light entertainment simply because "the villain is too good to miss," but to choose on such a basis the great literature on which young minds must be nourished can only be an error.

The second likely reason to help us account for the fact that *Richard II* is so underutilized in the classroom is simply that it is a history play, for clearly there is a widespread feeling among teachers that, as one survey respondent simply puts it, "the histories are hard for kids." That the history plays do indeed pose special pedagogic problems is a proposition every teacher readily would assent to, and few of us would be so intrepid as to assert that they will inevitably "go over" with every group of young people. Thus I will confine myself here to pointing out four of the histories' indisputable pedagogic strengths and to suggesting that, if properly presented, there is no reason why they shouldn't succeed in the classroom. (Let it be noted that throughout this discussion by "the histories" I will mean *Richard II* and *Henry IV*, the only two history plays that, in my opinion, can have a serious claim on the attention of secondary teachers. See the individual commentaries on the other histories for my opinion as to their varying levels of pedagogic suitability.)

1.   We have noted of the adolescent that he is a stern pragmatist, and that he feels most at ease educationally when he is confident that what he is studying has some rock-solid relationship to the real world. Given that fact, his knowledge as he reads one of the histories that "all this really happened" (more or less, at least) probably will steady him and cause him to persevere even when he begins to be buffeted by difficulties of comprehension.

By contrast, the student puzzled by the language or the strange goings-on of *Midsummer* may be tempted, when it occurs to him that "all of this never happened, anyway" to write the whole thing off as a bad job.

2.   By virtue of their broad tableaux of characters, the histories provide students with one of our curricular desiderata articulated earlier: a vivid sense of that all-encompassing social order in which, like it or not, each of us must find his place. For while *Richard II* is every bit as much a personal tragedy as, for instance, *Hamlet* or *Macbeth*, one feels that its secondary characters — Bolingbroke, John of Gaunt, the Duke of York, and so on — are secondary in a literary sense only. Unlike characters such as Horatio and Polonius, whose chief function seems to be to reveal to us different aspects of Hamlet's character through their interactions with him, or Duncan and Banquo, who are essentially nine-pins fated to fall when Macbeth's ambition bowls them over, the supporting cast in *Richard II* is like that supporting cast that surrounds each of us in the drama of our daily life: one composed of all-too-real people, people whose passions and opinions often conflict with our own, but without whose stern counsels and unbending inclinations (think, for instance, of John of Gaunt's blunt and manly speech to Richard before his death) we would be even more foolish and self-centered than we already are.

3.   If *Richard II* and *Henry IV* are studied in that order and in the same year (the reader will find a discussion of the pros and cons of this approach in Chapter 6), the student can gain an immensely valuable sense both of the transience of individual glory and of the enduring effects — for good or ill — of a political legacy. In the education of Americans in particular — a people more prone than most to impatiently dismiss history as "bunk," and to fondly imagine that an untrammeled individualism will of itself cure all social ills — any work of literature is to be valued that instills a sense of that larger corporate identity that redeems each of us from our all-too-personal pettiness and vanity.

4.   As has been said, chief among the pedagogic virtues of the histories — *Richard II* in this respect preeminent among them — is their straightforwardness of language. In general it might be asserted that Shakespeare's verse is most difficult for the average reader to follow a) when the Bard is consciously exulting in his

poetic powers, and writing poetry that is complex, highly "conceited," and elliptical (*Measure for Measure* comes to mind), and b) when characters are indulging in that "arid badinage" (Durant's perfect phrase[9]) — rich in puns, allusions, and archaisms — so excessively dear to Elizabethans and often so tiresome to us. In the history plays Shakespeare is devoting too much of his attention to sticking to the historical facts (or rather, to Holinshed's often erroneous version of the facts) to indulge greatly his taste for the former, and the lack of Fools (at least of the professional variety) provides a welcome respite from the latter. Thus, while in reading a history play the student may well be brought up short, and quite often, by the problem of titles and allegiances, I would hazard the guess that, in reading the tragedies and "comedies,"[10] he is confounded far more often by their complex verse and labored wit.

Although there is of course some variability in this clarity of language from one history to the next — with *Richard II* at one end of the spectrum and *King John*, perhaps, at the other — all that need concern most English teachers is that the whole of *Richard II* and most of *Henry IV* are genuinely "easy reading." Granted, scenes in *Henry IV* involving Falstaff are often thick with archaisms, but at least the humor which they subserve is quite straightforward, with little of that double- or triple-pronged punning that occurs whenever a Fool is on the job, and the student's chances of actually being rewarded for his struggles with a *laugh* are higher here than elsewhere in the canon. The more "historical" scenes — all those *not* featuring Falstaff — boast an almost *Richard II* degree of clarity.

Now the question that every English teacher should ask herself is this: "Given this extraordinary pedagogic boon [the clarity of language we have been speaking of], what should it mean to me, and how can I make the best use of it?"

The answer to the first part of the question is clear. While many English teachers doubtless feel it to be almost a professional obligation to assert that Shakespeare is always and everywhere perfectly understandable, by both academic and lay person, when

[9]Will Durant, *The Age of Reason Begins* (New York: Simon and Schuster, 1961), p. 92.

[10]For a full explanation of why I insist on always placing this term in quotes, whenever it is being used in its Shakespearean sense, the reader is referred to Appendix I.

and if they are candid with themselves they can only admit that various factors — among them Shakespeare's not-so-occasional preciousness, and the changes the language has gone through in four hundred years — militate at all times against complete comprehension. (For a more extended discussion of this matter, see Appendix III.) Therefore any tool that comes to hand — and none could be handier than *Richard II* — that the teacher can use to pry open the steel door that students slam shut as soon as they decide about Shakespeare's characters that "people don't really talk that way" is entirely invaluable.

The second part of the teacher's question, as we have noted, is "How do I put this wonderful tool to its best use?" After much considered thought on this subject, I have come to the conclusion that the student should see — or rather, *hear* — *Richard II* on video before she ever sets eyes on the text. For if we ever wish to convince our students that Shakespeare really can speak to them directly, without the need for translation by footnote or by teacher, *this* is our most golden opportunity. Needless to say such an approach hinges on whether one's school has taped or purchased the BBC video (see Appendix IV), but the teacher can be assured that the video, if she can gain access to it, is an absolute stunner (again, see appendix).

In addition to proving to students that Shakespeare really *can* still speak to us directly, after four hundred years (and also, it should be noted, giving them a chance to revel in *Richard II*'s exquisitely lovely verse), having students see the video *before* reading should in and of itself help to loosen (if not completely untie) two of the knottiest problems the histories pose for students and teachers.

The first of these problems has to do with the fact that characters in the histories often have more than one title or nickname, and are related to other characters by potentially confusing ties of blood and shifting political kinship. The student who has *seen* Jon Finch in his magnificent portrayal of Bolingbroke will find it far easier than the mere reader to comprehend the fact that Harry of Hereford and Darby, the Duke of Lancaster (after John of Gaunt's death), and Henry IV, are indeed one and the same person: "Oh yeah, he's the cute one with the brown beard that was banished but then came back."

Second, the viewing of the video not only will serve to release from its dreary confines within the covers of a book all the color and pageantry of medieval life, but in so doing give the student an almost instinctive understanding of a concept central to medieval life but utterly alien to her own: that of the divine right of kings. Merely by observing how Richard comports himself, before and after losing the crown, and how others behave when in the presence of their sovereign, the student viewer will have an infinitely better chance than the student reader of understanding, for instance, the wrenching emotional changes York goes through as he is forced to transfer his fealty from a bad king — who is nonetheless God's annointed vicar on earth — to a better king — who is also a traitor and a usurper.

Yet while there can be little doubt that video will help teachers to deal with the very real pedagogic problems the histories do pose, in and of itself it will not make them disappear. Thus it certainly would be wise for the teacher to, for instance, prepare a mimeo or xerox giving all the names and titles of the major characters, and depicting in a simple format those ties of blood or political allegiance referred to above. Above all, however, the teacher should stress, either orally or on the mimeo, two things. First, that what the class is studying is a work of literature, not a "history" in any genuine sense, and that therefore they need achieve only such mastery of the historical facts as will allow them to comprehend and appreciate the work of literature. Second, that if the student keeps his eye firmly fixed on the five or six major characters he need not let the references to the innumerable minor characters distract him unduly.

It should be noted here, also, that (in marked contrast to *Richard III*) the student needs relatively little background information in order to understand and enjoy *Richard II*. Only Act I, scene ii, in which the Duchess of Gloucester remonstrates with John of Gaunt for not having taken action to avenge Woodstock's death (a scene rare in Shakespeare, by the way, in that it seems to lead absolutely nowhere nor to contribute to dramatic unity), will require a good bit of teacher explication if it is not to derail students only moments after their journey into *Richard II* has gotten under way.

Having said this much about a few of the more obvious pedagogic pluses and minuses of the history plays in general, the time has come to take note of the chief factor that makes *Richard II* itself a work ideally suited to the secondary classroom. While there is no point in pretending that there is anything *overtly* youthful about *Richard II*, or that it will ever be as popular with students as *R & J*, the fact remains that Richard's tragic flaws — his callowness and his egotism — are the adolescent weaknesses par excellence. Our students couldn't help but benefit from witnessing the spectacle of a man who is made both sadder and wiser by his realization that the claims of the ego are not always admissible in the open court of public life, and that those who laugh at others' cares are likely to end their days as care-full men indeed.

HENRY IV

We have suggested — tentatively, and with a full awareness of the pedagogic problems attendant upon the teaching of the history plays — that *Richard II*, particularly when it is taught in conjunction with *Henry IV*, simply has too much going for it pedagogically to exclude it from the curriculum. Yet while it has moral weight and social vision we have admitted that there is little overt youthfulness about it. Thus it certainly seems a good thing that the student who has been sobered by *Richard II* can laugh again on meeting Hal and Falstaff. The objection some undoubtedly would raise to teaching both *Richard II* and *Henry IV* — that it is too much of the same thing, and deprives student and teacher of that variety which is the spice of life — is in most respects invalid. For while *Henry IV* does follow *Richard II* in historical sequence, the plays themselves are as utterly unalike as their protagonists.

Before we can begin to list some of *Henry IV*'s pedagogic assets, we must of course take note of its chief debit, which is, as with *Richard II*, its large and potentially confusing cast of characters. As was suggested in our discussion of *Richard II*, some sort of mimeoed handout detailing political allegiances would go at least some of the way toward alleviating student confusion, as would a directive from the teacher to students counseling them to keep their eyes on Hal, Falstaff, and a few others and not let the rest overly concern them. Unless I'm mistaken, this whole issue of character recognition and identification is likely to be a good bit less troubling in *Henry IV* than in *Richard II*, in that many of the names referred to in *Henry IV* are only that, names of various lords amassing their powers offstage somewhere, rather than, as in *Richard II*, characters quite consistently in the thick of the action.

In compiling our list of *Henry IV, Part One*'s pedagogic pluses, pride of place certainly must be given, as with *Richard II*, to the relative straightforwardness of it language, at least in the "his-

torical" speeches that make up the bulk of Part One. (The scenes
in Part One in which Falstaff appears send the reader far oftener
to the footnotes, but that seems a small price to pay for the
pleasure of his company.) Note also that many of these speeches
are not merely straightforward, but memorable; perhaps no other
play in the canon — well, aside from *JC* and *Hamlet* — offers so
many wonderful pieces for student memorization as this one.

Of course the first such to leap to all of our minds is
Hal's great "Yet herein will I imitate the sun" soliloquy, but
others are every bit as worthy and perhaps even more fun,
among them Hotspur's marvelous recounting for the king of
the fop "perfumed like a milliner" who pestered him like a
popinjay and "demanded my prisoners in your Majesty's
behalf." Speaking of Hotspur, let it be noted that the mere fact
that this character appears in *Henry IV* would be enough, in
and of itself, to make this work an indispensable part of any
curriculum. For not only is he a delightful and consistently fascinating creation, one certain to engage and hold young people's attention, he is also a man from whom the young have
much to learn. Like them, Hotspur is infinitely charming and
yet far too rash and self-centered. The young probably have
more to learn about the dangers of pure egotism from observing Richard II, but when it comes to learning how to moderate
their passionate outbursts of both joy and anger the study of
Hotspur is certain to prove highly rewarding.

Yet of course it is Hal and Falstaff who are at the center of
Part One, and the depiction there of their relationship has not
one but two pedagogic merits to recommend it. Its first merit is
simply that it is fun; there is far less pure fun in Shakespeare
than there is that labored "wit" so dear to Elizabethans, and the
former is as likely to play well in the classroom as the latter is
to close in previews, so to speak. Its second merit is that it provides the privileged independent school student (and for that
matter, the "non-privileged" public or parochial school student as
well) with an important sense of the moral ambiguity that
inevitably shadows all relations between the classes. For while we
admire Hal hugely for having the common touch and having it
in such abundance, we are always suspicious (and for good reason, as it turns out) that he is only slumming in keeping the
company he keeps. We see in his attitude toward Falstaff et al
much genuine affection, and it pleases us immensely to think that
the future king of England can see real worth in even the lowli-
est of his subjects; yet we also see in Hal the less savory side of

class privilege, in that he never hesitates, when the mood seizes him, to speak of Falstaff in the most brutal (albeit accurate) terms: "thou bolting hutch of beastliness," etc.

Yet all of the other factors that go to make *Henry IV* an absolutely indispensable work for young people pale almost to insignificance when one considers how perfectly suited to secondary education is its central theme, "the Reclamation of a Profligate Prince."[11] *Henry IV*, in both of its parts, is perhaps the greatest depiction in all of literature of the sowing of wild oats. For young people intent on sowing plenty of their own, yet always conscious that the time is not so distant when they will be harnessed to the yoke of adult responsibility, the study of this work should offer the opportunity not only for profound emotional catharsis but for a great leap forward in self-knowledge.

Unfortunately, as *Henry IV* presently is being studied this great central theme hardly has a chance to be noted by students, much less analyzed by them, simply because only a handful of schools are taking the plunge and doing both parts of the play back-to-back. While one can appreciate this reluctance to teach Part Two (more on this presently), the fact remains that only the student who has read Part Two can go back to Part One and suddenly recognize the immense significance of those four most important words in the play(s) as a whole, Hal's "I do, I will." Those words, in which Hal asserts that he does at that moment begin to banish Falstaff from his affections, and will so banish the entire world that Falstaff represents when he becomes king, can only be well nigh meaningless to the student who has been denied the opportunity to read on into Part Two and discover their literal, prophetic truthfulness.

Now before I make the case for having students read at least selected portions of Part Two whenever they read Part One, let us first take note of one powerful objection to studying Part Two in its entirety. While Part Two is at least as great a play as its predecessor, in it the former play's ratio of history to comedy essentially has been reversed. Whereas in Part One the student benefits from the fact that most of the speeches are "historical" and therefore remarkably straightforward in language, in Part Two the history tends to serve as little more than "serious relief" to the many more scenes involving Falstaff, scenes

---

[11]Oscar James Campbell, Introduction to *Henry IV, Part II* (New York: Bantam Books, 1964), p. 1.

that perpetually send even the adult reader scurrying to the foot-notes in an effort to partake of Elizabethan drollery. Thus we note again the recurring paradox, that Shakespeare at his most serious is often easiest for the student to follow, Shakespeare at his wittiest the most difficult.

If then Part Two is a work that, when studied in full, may not pay a high enough pedagogic dividend to merit the invest-ment of time and effort, how can we still ensure that every high school student will see that which, in my view, he simply *must* see, Hal at his father's deathbed and his subsequent spurning of Falstaff? I would suggest that teachers should simply xerox and hand out to students the final third of Part Two, beginning at Act IV, scene IV, the scene in which the King expresses to Hal's brothers his grief over Hal's profligacy. The only difficulty here — a minor one, to my way of thinking — is that the stu-dent will have to be introduced by the teacher to Justices Shallow and Silence (and a few other characters of lesser conse-quence), whom he has not met before by dint of not having read the first three acts of the play.

The merits of such an approach are many. In passing over the first three and a half acts the student is spared much difficult wordplay, two intensely amusing sketches of senility that will almost certainly mean nothing to him anyway, and a revolt against the king that, despite the dramatic interest of Lancaster's going back on his word to the Archbishop of York et al, seems but a faint reprise of that earlier insurrection which brought Hotspur low. Far more importantly, such an approach ensures that the student will not have left high school behind her without first having encountered two of the most powerfully affecting scenes in all of literature.

Of the first of these — that in which a heartbroken Hal, thinking his father dead, wanders away from his deathbed wearing his crown, only to break that father's heart when the latter awak-ens to behold a seemingly callous and power-hungry son — all I can think to say is that the man or woman who can read or view it without a lump in the throat shall never be friend of mine. Literature doubtless contains many scenes equal to it in emotional power, but few could surpass it. It seems likely that the adoles-cent who is moved by this scene will also experience a powerful catharsis of all his deep but ambivalent emotions toward his par-ents. The second scene, that of the rejection of Falstaff by Hal, is every bit as emotionally wrenching as the first; more to the point, it is sure to provoke heated and valuable debate in the classroom, as students argue both sides of the eternally contested question: Is Hal simply doing what he has to do, or is he at last revealing his essentially cold and calculating nature?

The chief objection to thus making the best possible use of all of *Henry IV* will come from those who protest against this flagrant tampering with Part Two's artistic unity. While no one with an eye for form could fail to feel genuine qualms at thus dismembering an artistic whole, the decision to do so still can be defended in three ways.

1. While scholars always will debate the question of whether *Henry IV* is one play in two parts or two plays that happen to cohere rather nicely, if the former happens to be true then it could be said that we are not so much truncating one play as we are skipping over some relatively inconsequential scenes in the middle of another, greater play.

2. While we may not know much about the life and character of Shakespeare (although it should be noted that we do know a good deal, more than is generally assumed), his one personal quality that shines forth from every account is that absolute unassumingness that earned him the universal sobriquet "sweet Will." Can there be the slightest doubt that sweet Will, if he could join us around the conference table, would roar with laughter at our modern critical fastidiousness, dismissing us with a wave of his hand and his blessing to teach the plays in whatever way might maximize their impact on young minds? We can be all the more sure of this when we recollect that the King's Men themselves often had to cut and tailor Shakespeare's plays to fit the great variety of venues in which they were offered.

3. If there is any one feature of modern intellectualism that is unwholesome, it is the way in which aesthetes of the Flaubertian and Henry Jamesian schools bow down before the golden calf of artistic form rather than pay homage to the true God, philosophic content, or Truth. When we balk at enriching our students' lives with such great scenes as those under discussion here, merely out of a simpering fear that we will be throwing out of kilter an artistic balance that may indeed be a feature of *Henry IV, Part Two*, we reveal ourselves infinitely lesser and more cowardly people than Shakespeare himself — a man so unpedantic, we always should remember, that in the

course of his life he never lifted a single finger to oversee the uniform publication of his own works.

In our effort to present *Henry IV* to students as an artistic unity, video certainly can help us to do so effectively. The teacher who resolves to do as I have suggested and have students read all of Part One but only the final third of Part Two, yet who feels uneasy about leaving out altogether that big chunk in the middle, might simply show the video of the first three and a half acts of Part Two, take a few days to allow the students to read and discuss the last one and a half acts, then show the rest of the video. This is in many respects an ideal arrangement, in that those first three and a half acts are about as well larded with footnotes as any in the canon, and therefore a real chore for the student to get through, yet in performance one scarcely takes note of the various obscure Elizabethan references, these being obscured by the riotously funny physical comedy involving Falstaff, Mistress Quickly, Pistol, Bardolph, and those divine old dotards, Justices Simple and Shallow.[12]

As to the best use to be made of video when studying Part One, my instinct is that the student not only will be able to visualize this play far better than she can visualize *Richard II* but will in fact have *fun* visualizing it. Therefore I think I would, in this case, show the video in installments only after the students had read at least a couple of acts. I might even wait until they had read the whole play before showing it, although it is more likely I would want them to *see* the Gad's Hill robbery and its crucial aftermath at the Boar's Head Tavern (scenes ii and iv of Act II) as soon as they had finished reading them.

MACBETH

I have only two points to make about the teaching of *Macbeth*. The first of these relates to the teaching of the play and is very

[12]What a revelation it has been for this new teacher, as to the nature of human communication, to see just how easily students get the point (or at least seem to!) when they are watching a performance of a play rather than reading the text! Clearly, a vast amount of human communication is effected by gesture, whether of the face or the rest of the body. Needless to say this fact, while it must be noted and given due consideration, is not offered here as part of any attempt to wean students away from the written word.

simple and concrete, the other relates to the play's place in the syllabus and is a bit more complex and abstract.

As for the teaching pointer, it is simply my strong recommendation that teachers make use of the Polanski film in conjunction with the reading of the text. (For the whys and wherefores of that decision, see Appendix IV.) *Macbeth* is a play that simply *must* come alive for the student, and the Polanski film is as certain to succeed here as many a stage production is likely to fail.

As for *Macbeth*'s place in the syllabus, I would say this. First, let it be noted that I have no quarrel with the fact that *Macbeth* is the second most commonly taught play nationwide. It is, after all, not only a riveting tale and a great work of art, but a work whose high artistry is attested to by the fact that its consistent moralizing is *felt* by the viewer as drama more than it is pondered by her as moralizing. Then too, the relative simplicity of the central theme as to the dangers of ambition makes it well suited to study by those sophomores who are by far its most numerous readers at the moment, and somewhat compensates pedagogically for the fact that *Macbeth*'s poetic "density" makes it one of the Bard's more difficult works to read. All of which means that the student who reads *Macbeth* finds herself thrilled by its plot, interested in moral issues almost without being aware that they are such, and challenged but not utterly overwhelmed by the language — surely, a potent pedagogic mix.

What I would suggest, however, is that when it comes to pedagogically ideal Shakespearean tragedy — full of complex poetry and simple moral meaning, high passion and low blows — *Macbeth* represents the top of the line. While the reader will have to consult my commentaries on the other tragedies to discover precisely what strictures I pass on the pedagogic *Othello* and *Lear*, and to a much lesser extent the pedagogic *Hamlet* and *R & J*, my point here is simply that it is doubtful whether any of the other tragedies is so perfect a "textbook tragedy" as is *Macbeth*. The significance of that, as I see it, is that whoever wishes to construct a Shakespeare syllabus that will reflect as many aspects of the Bard's genius as possible, teach students as many different lessons as possible, and diversify students' intellectual interests as much as possible, will do well not to overrepresent the tragedies in that syllabus if *Macbeth* is already a part of it. My reader has just heard my recommendations as to the judicious use of certain of the history plays toward this end of diversifying the syllabus, and my similar endorsement of some of the "comedies" begins with the next commentary.

THE MERCHANT OF VENICE

Perhaps there is no more stirring sight, whether in life or in art, than that of a great work of art, only very imperfectly comprehended or appreciated over the centuries, at last finding itself an audience — yea, a world — that has evolved to the point where it can truly *see* it for the first time. In my opinion this process is just now beginning for *The Merchant of Venice* — Dustin Hoffman's genuinely epochal performance on Broadway as Shylock perhaps marking its genesis — but is a long way from being over with — witness the unthinking and critically hidebound reviews the Hoffman/Peter Hall production received from so many of the critics. Nonetheless I'm convinced that the tide has indeed turned, and that the scholar who seventy-five years from now dares to repeat yesterday's already stale cant about *Merchant* will be hooted off the stage as if he were another Launcelot Gobbo, rushing off, stage left, with that bogeyman — the Devil Jew — hard on his heels.

It seems clear, from comments made by a surprisingly large number of survey respondents, that it is indeed — *still*, and even at this late date in the history of Jewish–Gentile interrelations — the bogey of anti-Semitism that is scaring away many teachers, otherwise fully cognizant of this play's high intrinsic and even higher pedagogic merit, from teaching *Merchant*. From a pedagogic point of view this is almost tragic, in that *Merchant* not only is about as well-rounded a play as one could hope to present in the classroom, but its moral complexity and potency — the very qualities, by a bitter irony, driving teachers away from it at the moment — are precisely what our curricula stand in eternal need of. While it is true that *Merchant* is the tenth most commonly taught play nationwide, it is also true that it is taught only half as much as *Macbeth* — surely, a wholly disproportionate state of affairs.

Therefore let us see if we can rescue this great and oh-so-teachable play from ourselves, as it were — from our own misconceptions and baseless fears — and bring it back to the syllabus, its rightful home. Let us begin to make the case for a definitely non-anti-Semitic *Merchant*, and do so by blasting away at the muddy, tradition-crusted thinking that for too long has been allowed to obscure the real *Merchant* from critical view,

on the subconscious assumption that there is something there that
is best left hidden.

Our first target will be the following words by John Russell
Brown, taken from his Introduction to perhaps the most esteemed
scholarly edition of Shakespeare, the Arden:

> Whether his [Shylock's] suffering forces him to be a
> villain, or whether his villainy causes him to suffer,
> Shakespeare is not concerned to say.[13]

Now if my reader's reaction to those words is at all the same
as mine, he will wish to demand of the speaker how on earth he
has managed to hear, and yet not to hear — particularly when
their cumulative effect is like the ominous rumble of distant thunder — Shylock's impassioned defenses of himself and of his great
and beloved nation against the hideous calumnies heaped upon
them by religious persecutors:

> *He hates our sacred nation*, and he rails,
> Even there where merchants most do congregate,
> On me, my bargains, and my well-won thrift,
> Which he calls interest. *Cursed be my tribe*
> *If I forgive him!*

> Signior Antonio, many a time and oft
> In the Rialto you have rated me
> About my moneys and my usances:
> Still I have borne it with a patient shrug,
> (For suff'rance is the badge of all our tribe).
> You call me misbeliever, cut-throat dog,
> And spit upon my Jewish gaberdine,
> And all for use of that which is mine own.

For if Brown had heard those words (and of course, if every
performance he had seen featured a Shylock closer to Warren
Mitchell's in the BBC video than to Dustin Hoffman's, he may *not*
have heard them, but heard only a thick, Yiddish-like accent
instead) and heard many more that we shall soon listen to ourselves, could he have doubted for an instant that, whatever else
Shakespeare might conceivably have been feeling about Jews, or

---

[13]John Russell Brown, Introduction to the Arden edition of *The Merchant
of Venice* (Cambridge: Harvard University Press, 1959), p. 21.

about "Hebraic legalism," one thing is dramatically certain: Shylock is driven to become a villain because the sufferance which is the badge of all his tribe has come to seem to him — as a later badge, worn by a later generation of Jews, would appear to those who lived to look back on it — a badge of dishonor and of vile submission. This Shakespeare emphatically *is* concerned to say, and this could be questioned only by someone willing to overlook all of those passages (two of them quoted above) which — when delivered by an actor of Hoffman's ilk — bring a tear to the eye, a lump to the throat, and the very same words to one's lips as those Heine overheard a fellow playgoer exclaiming through his tears: "The poor man is wronged!"

Yet while it may seem as plain as day to many of us that Shylock is driven to the exaction of the pound of flesh simply because he, a patient member of a long-suffering tribe, has at last lost all patience, and if we are equally confident that it is Jessica's elopement — nay, apostasy — that has at last made firm the link in Shylock's mind between things Christian and things spiritually unclean (pork at the dinner table), civically frivolous (the "shallow fopp'ry" of masqued reveling), and fiscally imprudent, we would certainly be remiss in our duty of examining all of the evidence if we failed to look closely at the crucial scene (I, iii) in which the bond is arrived at — the scene, one assumes, that Brown had in mind when he penned this comment:

> Shakespeare has created in Shylock an outcast who suffers and is driven to extremity in his suffering, but no matter how harshly the Christians treat him, he remains the Jew who intends to kill his enemy, a harsh, cynical, and ruthless villain.[14]

Far from it being true that Shylock is so black a devil as Brown paints him here, it is clear that it is Bassanio and Antonio who, in their self-righteousness, are decidedly unlovely, whereas it is Shylock — by turns citing Scripture to good if rather sly effect (Jacob's ewes), sharing an excellent jest ("I make it breed as fast"), and using irony to make a serious moral point ("Hath a dog money? Is it possible/A cur can lend three thousand ducats?") — who strikes us as being both humanly winning and genuinely desirous of reconciliation. Above all —

[14] Ibid.

and this is a moment one can scarcely linger over too long — the evidence is clear that it is the blatantly anti-Semitic Antonio who *goads* Shylock into posting exactly the kind of morally dangerous bond he does:

> If thou wilt lend this money, lend it not
> As to thy friends, for when did friendship take
> A breed for barren metal of his friend?
> *But lend it rather to thine enemy,*
> *Who if he break, thou mayst with better face*
> *Exact the penalty.*

Yet even when thus goaded, Shylock either seeks or seems to seek (the former, in my opinion, but clearly a director could opt for the latter interpretation) interdenominational friendship:

> Why look you how you storm!
> I would be friends with you, and have your love,
> Forget the shames that you have stained me with,
> Supply your present wants, and take no doit
> Of usance for my moneys, and you'll not hear me.
> This is kind I offer.
>
> O father Abram, what these Christians are,
> Whose own hard dealing teaches them suspect
> The thoughts of others! ... I say
> To buy his favour, I extend this friendship.
> If he will take it, so; if not adieu,
> And for my love I pray you wrong me not.

Of course even someone as decidedly pro-Shylock as myself must confess that the lines above could be delivered (and doubtless were, in productions of the play staged during the Elizabethan and later eras) in a tone positively dripping with false sincerity and genuine malevolence, and that, stung by Antonio's previous taunts, Shylock may already be in deadly earnest about getting his pound of flesh (despite his avowal that his proposed bond is merely a "merry sport"). In support of this view one might cite Jessica's later statement to the Belmont company (III, ii) that she had heard Shylock lust after his pound of flesh to Tubal and Chus. If the testimony of this disgruntled daughter can be given much weight in the court of criticism — which is doubtful — such a fact might indeed seem to indicate that

Shylock had begun to feed his grudge even before Jessica's elopement. If so, one must still note that this one fact, however salient, seems out of keeping with the dramatic and emotional logic of events, all of which hinges on the elopement.

Yet while some critics will always point to the above speeches and accuse those of us of the pro-Shylock party of being deaf to the malevolent irony they might contain, we can retort that when the reader refuses to take Shylock at his word he proves himself every bit the engrainedly suspicious bigot we know Antonio and Bassanio to be. Shylock may indeed be posting this bond only as a kind of absurd gentleman's wager, in an attempt to prove himself as much or more a gentleman as these stuck-up Venetians, and when we readers insist on hearing only irony in the crie de coeur of a lonely social outcast — "And for my love I beg you wrong me not" — we almost certainly prove ourselves as hardhearted and intolerant as they.

Of course, those who take a position akin to Brown's on these matters have, if they are wise, waited until this moment in the proceedings to play their trump card: the fact that Shylock is on record from the very beginning as wanting to "catch [Antonio] upon the hip" and "feed fat the ancient grudge I bear him." They will also remind this writer with a sly smile that Shylock (savvy fellow that he is) is well aware that all of Antonio's "means are in supposition," (i.e., rolling about on the high seas) and that "ships are but boards, sailors but men."

If we were not the good sports and the fair-minded people I know we are, we of the pro-Shylock party might at this point, driven to exasperation by those smug smiles facing us across the card table, kick the dratted thing over and storm from the room. Yet the mature way of rebutting the points made above is not to deny that there is real moral complexity in *Merchant*, or to insist that Shylock is something other than human — which is to say, at least half rogue — but to suggest that, in the long run and the big picture, they are not the points that matter. The first point that matters is that Shylock's grudge only picks up a full head of steam, so to speak, after Jessica's elopement. And surely we are right in deducing from this that in Act I Shylock really did wish, in one part of his soul at least, to be friends with Antonio and have his love. The second point, however, matters much more, and it is this: Even if Shylock *is* pushing Antonio up against the wall in Act I, scene iii, push has come to shove *only because Antonio (and the whole Christian community) pushed first.*

There can be not the slightest doubt that, however Shylock was portrayed on the Elizabethan stage, Shakespeare — in his infinite genius and, in this case, propheticalness — has taken great care to portray Shylock and his people as not only the butts of the Christian world but as their unwilling pupils in sin:

> If a Christian wrong a Jew, what should his his sufferance be by Christian example? Why, revenge. *The villainy you teach me I will execute*, and it shall go hard but I will better the instruction.   [III, i]

Unfortunately, even the reader who has come to agree with me that Shylock is a man infinitely more sinned against than sinning still will be troubled by one other aspect of his character that seems a blatantly obvious bit of racial stereotyping: his conspicuously high regard for money, particularly as it is manifested in his cry (as related by the highly anti-Semitic and therefore unreliable Solanio) of "My ducats, and my daughter!". Three things may be said here in Shylock's defense.

1. Shylock's constant references to his "thrift" need not be interpreted in anti-Semitic fashion as an absurdly transparent euphemism for "greed." After all, if Bassanio had been more thrifty with the money Antonio had first lent him, all concerned would have been spared much heartache. Then too, we debt-ridden Americans, of all peoples, are in no position to cackle cynically at the word "thrift"!

2. Shylock's love of money is entirely human, and refreshingly honest. His final comment on fiscal affairs — "You take my house, when you do take the prop/That doth sustain my house. You take my life/When you do take the means whereby I live." — is a thoroughly sensible one.

3. It is entirely likely — and somehow Hoffman, in his performance, managed to convey this — that Shylock's deepest pain has come a) from the loss of his daughter, and b) from her defection to the Christian "side" — not from the disappearance of the ducats she has taken with her. In support of a) one can simply point to the fact that before Solanio has had a chance to get rhetorically overheated and report Shylock's words as having been "My ducats, and my daughter!", he has given them in their more likely order and proportion: "My daughter! O my ducats! O my

daughter!" In support of b) one can go on to cite the very next words Shylock, according to Solanio, uttered: "Fled with a Christian! O my Christian ducats!"

After all, Shylock himself provides us with better proof than any we could have hoped to dig up on our own, that human values are indeed dearer to him than fiscal ones, when he laments the fact that Jessica has sold a turquoise ring that had been given him by his wife Leah: "I would not have given it for a wilderness of monkeys." (This was an enormously moving moment as played by Hoffman.) Then too, we get a real feeling for the dignity of both Shylock and his "sacred nation" when we consider that he would never even consider bandying a wedding ring about in the cavalier and frivolous fashion Portia and Nerissa later do.

Having at last, it is hoped, sent packing the bogeyman of anti-Semitism that has continued to frighten numbers of teachers away from teaching *Merchant*, we have now before us not the duty but rather the vast pleasure of enumerating a few of *Merchant*'s almost innumerable pedagogic attractions. Let us begin, simply for continuity's sake, with that very moral complexity we have been analyzing thus far.

Can anyone doubt, even for a moment, that every young person will take delighted part, at least in their own thoughts if not loudly and insistently in classroom discussions, in the good Shylock/bad Shylock, anti-Semitic/not anti-Semitic debate? Or that young people — those champions of the underdog par excellence — will be deeply moved by Shylock's great speeches in defense of himself and his people, and sniff out like bloodhounds even the tiniest scraps of evidence that can be used to convict the "Christians" of duplicity and cant?

Of course many a teacher who really does have no doubt as to any of that, and who no longer fears that in having his students study *Merchant* he may be turning them into anti-Semites, will still be reluctant to have them study a work of such true moral complexity, a work in which no character whatever is without some taint of sin. I understand and appreciate that reluctance, and would grow concerned myself if every play in the syllabus were as morally problematic as *Merchant* is. Yet when I recall, for example, the extraordinarily acute psychological analyses a group of 9th-graders once came up with, in a discussion we were having of the argument between Brutus and Cassius in Act IV, scene iii of *JC*, I grow more certain that young people will not sink into the morass of relativism and nihilism if we lead them carefully through the potentially treacherous terrain that is *Merchant*.

Next on our list of *Merchant*'s pedagogic pluses is the simple fact that this play has, in Portia, what far too few of the commonly taught Shakespeare plays have, an attractive and intelligent female protagonist to inspire and fascinate female students. It must be left to each syllabus-shaper to decide how large this factor will loom in his or her decision-making, but I would suggest that it should loom very large indeed.

Then there are two of *Merchant*'s seemingly most superficial but actually marvelously compelling attractions, its exquisite verse and its infinite variety. As for the verse, it boasts almost a *Richard II* degree of clarity, and it has just enough of the "metaphysical" complexity of a *Measure for Measure* to fascinate but not enough to daunt. As for its variety, does any other play by Shakespeare offer so dazzling an array of intellectual treasures? Excellent fooling with the Gobbos, junior and senior; gorgeous tableaux and rich fantasy (with a pedagogically ideal moral underpinning) with the choosing among the three caskets; the moral complexity and potency of Shylock etc.; the adventure of eloping lovers; for the female student, Portia and Nerissa making a mock of men and men's institutions; for the male student, the solid comradeship of Bassanio, Antonio, et al. If we have indeed chased away the bogeyman of anti-Semitism, what cause we teachers have to exult in the treasures he has stood jealous guard over all these years!

To conclude: While discretion may indeed have been the better part of valor, as teachers steered clear of *Merchant* during all those years when it was enshrouded in those very clouds of suspicion and misunderstanding it can do so much to dispel (if given a good chance and a good performance from Shylock), we will prove ourselves both wise and courageous if we decide that it is no longer. For while there is indeed some moral ambiguity in *Merchant*, and much moral ugliness as well, if we refuse to guide our students through this harsh terrain and seek instead to spend all of our time strolling with them through the flowers of *Midsummer* or along the strand of *The Tempest*, we are certain to lose most of them along the way — many of them perishing of boredom, and others sinking into a stupor brought on by sheer moral inanition.

If we do take the road less traveled by, we can be assured of seeing many a sight — Old Gobbo feeling his son's "beard,"

Bassanio rejecting outer in favor of inner worth, Portia illumined by a good deed in a naughty world — every bit as amusing or heartening as that of Shylock is sobering and thought-provoking.

OTHELLO

In all of Shakespeare criticism there is perhaps no single pronouncement so wildly farfetched as one of Harley Granville-Barker's. Nothing could more perfectly capture all that is unintentionally comical in the bardolatrous spirit — that spirit which, in attempting to defend some indefensible weakness or defect in the Bard's work, only commits itself to a position all the more indefensible — than Granville-Barker's assertion that "we shall find neither trickery nor anomaly in the battle for Othello's soul."[15] Neither trickery nor anomaly! To any sensible critic it must be clear that there is nothing *but* trickery (as supplied by Iago) and anomaly (as supplied by Dame Fortune) in the battle for Othello's soul, and that while these go to make *Othello* an exceedingly potent melodrama they also debar it from consideration as a great work of the moral imagination.

That *Othello* is indeed a melodrama, and not a tragedy, seems certain. For although there will always be disagreement as to the proper definition of tragedy, surely true tragedy can be distinguished from false by the fact that in it the protagonist is brought to grief less by external forces than by his own failings, "some vicious mole of nature ... the stamp of one defect." While most would assert unhesitatingly that Othello has such weaknesses of character — a destabilizing sense of racial insecurity, a mind less well trained than his will, and of course consuming sexual jealousy — one doubts greatly whether it is fair to think of these as intrinsic defects of character at all. Which of us *wouldn't* feel racially insecure if he were one of Venice's most respected commanders and yet had to hear himself spoken of by Brabantio as "such a *thing* as thou," or hear honest Iago impugn Desdemona's honesty on the grounds that she had chosen a mate not "of her own clime, complexion, and degree"?

So too, even such a term-paper thesis as "Othello, while thoroughly noble of character, is brought low by his tragic flaw, which is sexual jealousy," is undoubtedly specious. For with a demon such

[15]Harley Granville-Barker, *Prefaces to Shakespeare* (London: B.T. Batsford Ltd., 1982), p. 34.

as Iago whispering in our ear — and remember that the fact that Othello trusts in him cannot be construed as a failing, in that Iago's honesty is the subject of widespread panegyric — which of us *wouldn't* become sexually jealous?

Yet even were we to accept for the sake of argument the idea that Othello's failings are indeed his own, one would hope there are few among us so rash as to assert that it is above all these failings that are responsible for the overthrow of Othello's better nature, rather than a whole battery of external agencies brought to bear against it by two supreme tacticians — Iago and Dame Fortune. For if one were to judge by this pair's extraordinary adeptness at ego destabilization and relationship subversion, one might well conclude that they had trained together in some covert operations unit. Let's briefly review a few of their accomplishments in the field.

Iago urges Cassio to "importune" Desdemona and thus seem to be consorting with her; places the handkerchief in Cassio's chamber; arranges for Othello to see and misinterpret his conversation with Cassio; and of course tortures Othello with a thousand lies and insinuations. All very commendable work, but when one has had a chance to peruse Dame Fortune's curriculum belli one immediately realizes that it is she who has been in command all along, the evil woman behind this greatly evil man. She gives Cassio a weak head for wine; provides Iago with the perfect henchman and stooge in the person of Roderigo; causes a certain handkerchief to fall at a certain moment; strikes Othello with an epileptic fit so that he has no chance to confront Cassio and perhaps learn the truth; and above all, makes an otherwise chatty, sensible, worldly-wise and all-seeing Emilia blind and dumb in precisely the right areas and at precisely the right moments.[16]

As I have watched this endlessly vulgar parade of trickeries

---

[16]That Granville-Barker himself sensed the fatuity of his boosterism for *Othello* (as quoted in the opening lines of this commentary), and sensed subconsciously that its inhererent improbability has less to do with the renowned "double time" dilemma than with Emilia's inexplicable failures of insight and action, is evidenced by his remarks on her character. In essence he tells us that Emilia is mere "coarse clay," a carbon copy of the Nurse in *R & J*. The falseness of that judgment must be clear to all those who agree with Hazlitt in his argument against Dr. Johnson, to the effect that Shakespeare creates not universal "types" but true individuals. While Emilia is to a great extent the same lower-middle-class social type as the Nurse, and shares much of her garrulity and a bit of her bawdiness, she is otherwise entirely her superior in intelligence, good-heartedness, and probity. The intelligence is attested to by the way in which she diagnoses

and anomalies pass before me in review, I have been driven to the conclusion that just as it is these that go to make *Othello* such jolly "good theater" so too it is these that make its vision of human life and destiny such an utterly false and degrading one. For while none can say whether Shakespeare was led to such a vision by that pessimism he seems to have had to fight against in his later life and work, or only stumbled upon it inadvertently in his pursuit of powerful drama, the fact remains that the ultimate "moral" of *Othello* is a blasphemous one. As in the works of Thomas Hardy, which offer us an utterly outlandish and impossibly bleak romanticism that we are asked to accept as a genuine vision of human life, so too there is that in *Othello* which seems to suggest that in this life goodness is inevitably overpowered by evil men working in collusion with some malignant cosmic Will. For those of us who hold, with Chesterton, that the depression of the people is a crime even more culpable than the oppression of the people, all such works are poison, and should above all else be kept out of the reach of young people.

Now knowing as I do that *Othello* is one of the firmest fixtures in the independent school syllabus (the fourth most commonly taught play nationwide), and acknowledging as well that many of its intrinsic — and, to a more limited extent, pedagogic — merits are as real as many teachers claim them to be, my work clearly is cut out for me. If I am to convince my reader that this play's "one defect" — its construction of a false universe in which the "demi-devil" gets all the breaks and the good man none — is so deeply defective that all the rest of this work's virtues "in the general censure take corruption from that particular fault," I must convince her that its pedagogic virtues are limited both in number and nature, and that the majority of its intrinsic virtues are not also pedagogic ones.

The three simplest and most basic of *Othello*'s pedagogic virtues are its strong plot (in both senses), its relative readability, and its richly baronial verse. Chief among these, surely, is its

Othello's malady even before Desdemona does ("Is not this man jealous?"), by her ability to moralize ("[Jealousy] 'tis a monster/Begot upon itself, born on itself"), and, above all, by the fact that she and only she deduces the fact that Othello has been "abused by some most villainous knave." The good-heartedness is attested to by her unfailing solicitude for the lady she serves, the probity by the way in which, even as she considers committing what one might call the sin of her class — adultery — she shows remarkable moral tact in evaluating the circumstances under which she would or would not commit it.

plottiness — the single most important factor in keeping students'
eyes open.

Yet even as I concede that *Othello*'s story line represents at
least a modest pedagogic strength, I can't refrain from wondering
whether a work that is Shakespeare not only at his most operatic
but his most Verdian is actually well keyed to the emotional
tenor of youth. I would have thought that the Rossinian *As You
Like It* or the Tchaikovskian *R & J* would strike a deeper chord
with adolescents than the Verdian *Othello*. After all, if one wished
to introduce young people to opera (perhaps the musical world's
equivalent of Shakespeare from one point of view, in that both at
first strike the lay person as being utterly alien), one would be
better advised to start them off on an *opera buffa* such as *The
Abduction from the Seraglio* than an *opera seria* such as *Il Trovatore*.
While if we can believe the survey's "most popular with students"
category (page 231), *Othello* does hold its own with students (it
comes in fifth in that horse race, although a fifth that is *well* out
of the money), my hunch is that this means only that students
find it remarkably tolerable for a book they have to read in
school, not that they have fallen in love with it.

As for *Othello*'s intrinsic thematic strengths, I would rank
them from greatest to least thus: its depiction of jealousy (the
romantic jealousy that Othello feels vis-à-vis Desdemona, but far
more importantly the spiritual jealousy that prompts Iago to do
Othello such vile wrong); its depiction of a black man suffering
mistreatment in the white man's world; its depiction of the struggle between romantic idealism (Othello) and Machiavellian pragmatism (Iago). Let us now assess just how much pedagogic hay a
teacher can expect to make of this relatively rich harvest of
intrinsic strengths.

There can be no doubt that in Iago Shakespeare has given us
one of his most telling portraits of the complete scoundrel. To
my mind Iago is both a more believable and a more symbolically
significant figure than Richard III, precisely because (far from
being driven, as Coleridge rather oddly insists, by "motiveless
malignity") he has an even deeper motivation for evil-doing than
Richard with his deformity and his ambition. For while purportedly at least Iago has been goaded to malefaction by his resentment of the fact that Cassio has been promoted over his head,
and by his fear of having been cuckolded, in truth his ambition,
unlike Richard's, is preeminently spiritual rather than material.
His deepest desire is not so much to rise in the world as to
dethrone from its higher rank a nature that he himself realizes is

essentially more noble and magnanimous than his own ("The Moor is of a free and open nature"). While there can be no doubt that the naked greed and lust for power made manifest in Richard wreak immeasurable havoc in our world, it seems likely that the kind of deeply engrained petty-spiritedness we see so much evidence of in Iago — the all-too-human refusal to honor the truth in Blake's maxim, "The most sublime act is to set another before you" — wreaks as much havoc or more.

The question before us, then, is not whether, as representations of "absolute evil" go, that of Iago is an uncommonly good one, but whether teachers have been right in assuming that teenagers are in a position to appreciate the deep-seated jealousy a less happily constituted nature can feel for one that is more so. While doubtless many teachers will cry out, "But adolescents are *constantly* catfighting and jockeying for social position!", my own retort to that would be that it is one thing to suffer from a disease, quite another to be able to recognize its symptoms. Quite clearly, the dissensions and feuds that disrupt the social lives of young people come into being not because strong natures are vying with even stronger ones, but because weak and unformed natures, too weak even to do honor to their own strengths, see no particular reason why they should honor those of others. Just as clearly, only the adult has lived long enough to recognize just how psychically powerful envy and resentment really are, and to understand that only by keeping these in check can we hope to preserve that sense of gratitude which alone sustains us in life.

While some teachers will perhaps concede that the concept of spiritual jealousy is indeed too lofty to be within the reach of the average young person, they probably will go on to assert that adolescents are just as capable as anyone of recognizing and relating to romantic jealousy of the type Othello suffers from. Yet even this assertion is, in my opinion, open to attack. For while presumably quite a few young people do suffer Othello-like torments when they see a former sweetheart walking arm-in-arm with someone new, adolescents are less likely to be goaded to madness by the sense that a potentially great love has gone awry than to be beleaguered by doubts and fears as to the nature of true love itself, and by misgivings about their own ability to really be "in" it. It is precisely that more generalized love-sickness that afflicts Troilus and Cressida, and adolescents would be sure to empathize deeply with that unhappy couple if only they were given a chance to read the play that bears their names.

If then the theme of jealousy really is less teachable at the secondary level than many perhaps have supposed it to be, we are left with two major themes as possible sources of interest to the secondary student. As for the first of these, that of a black man suffering injustice at the hands of white men, I can only state my own belief that this theme, as it is played out throughout the drama, is too subtle in its implications and ramifications for the teenage reader to be able to analyze it with much profit. For while some aspects of racism in *Othello* are quite blatant — for instance, the taunts and insinuations of Iago and Brabantio — others, such as the whole relationship between Othello and Desdemona, are far more subtle and problematic. Surely these could be analyzed far more ably and authoritatively by an adult writing in the *Shakespeare Quarterly* than by an adolescent throwing his weight around in a banal and cliché-ridden classroom discussion of racism.

All of those who find *Othello* an attractive text precisely because it helps them to "integrate" an otherwise lily-white curriculum will doubtless find the above judgment a disappointing one, and they may even suspect that some ulterior motive has prompted me to render it as I have. I can only respond by saying that I am as keenly alive as they to the importance of convincing "minority" young people that the Western tradition is preeminently a *human* tradition, and I have nothing to say but "More power to you!" to any and all teachers who have found that this play helps them to do that. However, it seems to me not special pleading but the voice of common sense when I say that the rather unsubtle intellect of the adolescent could only have far better success analyzing and discussing racism as it rears its ugly head in *Black Boy* or *I Know Why the Caged Bird Sings* than as it furtively conceals its features in *Othello*.

Lastly, I would note that there couldn't possibly be a worse way of going about "integrating" a curriculum than by deciding to teach a work solely because it features certain racial characters and situations. If a work has been deemed — as I deem *Othello* — both morally unwholesome and artistically meretricious, then we should keep that work out of the hands of young people, be they black, brown, white, or green.

It would seem, then, that only one of Othello's three major themes — that of the battle between romantic idealism and Machiavellian pragmatism — is likely to pay much of an intellectual dividend to the student who invests his time in the analysis of it. A number of teachers, in correspondence with me, have made it clear that a close scrutiny of both the actions and the language of Othello and Iago can indeed lead the student to an understanding of this romantic/pragmatic split.

Yet I hope those correspondents will forgive me if I contend that, in praising this one indisputable pedagogic strength *Othello* does possess (beyond the obvious ones of plottiness, readability, etc.), they are unintentionally damning the pedagogic *Othello* with faint praise. For not only does this single theme strike me as being of insufficient intellectual substance to, in and of itself, earn this work a place in the syllabus, it also seems to me a theme that is almost beside the point when the play is viewed more comprehensively. Surely there is something almost ludicrous about affixing to the brow of so demonic a "demi-devil" as Iago the faded and colorless label PRAGMATIST, and surely we deceive ourselves if we pretend that the battle between Othello and Iago is anything less than the battle between Good and Evil.

That in this case Good (represented by Othello, but in this connection even more so by Emilia and Desdemona) should be almost inconceivably gullible and passive, and Evil preternaturally diabolical and cunning, tells us far less, in my opinion, about Othello, Emilia, and Iago than it tells us about the spirit that animates the play in which those characters appear. That spirit, to repeat, is one of a cowardly fatalism in the face of Fate, a Fate infinitely more menacing in certain works of fiction than in the real world — a world where the sun, even if it does shine on the good and evil alike, *does shine.*

I can only hope that the reader who has followed my arguments thus far, and who is willing to concede that there is a good bit of truth to them, will find my overall conclusion about the pedagogic *Othello* a convincing one as well: While *Othello* can be read and understood readily enough by an intelligent young person, its more subtle themes are as sure to elude him as its general ethos is sure to depress and confuse him.

Surely we teachers have a duty to remind ourselves that while Youth is indeed the age of doubt and insecurity it is also proverbially the age of Hope, and no work of literature — not even those more designedly depressing ones by the Becketts and the Sartres — could be more inimical to the spirit of Hope than *Othello.* When we steer clear of a work such as *Measure for Measure* because we find it "dark" — whereas in fact the whole point of that work is that its protagonists stumble through the darkness of sin and moral confusion, only to emerge at last into the half-light of grudging social reconciliation and a disquieting but morally redemptive self-knowledge — but fervently embrace a work such as *Othello* — which is one long dizzying plunge into an abyss of darkness — in effect we curse the darkness, rather than light the candle that should guide both us and our students to happier days and a better world.

HAMLET

As we set out to analyze this the most analyzed of plays, we can ensure that our first steps will be taken on solid ground if we make our initial assertions inarguable ones: *Hamlet* is a very popular play even with the unintellectual reader or theatergoer, and *Hamlet* is also the play best loved by intellectuals, in that its many problematic elements lend themselves to brilliant explication.

While there can be no doubt that the popular *Hamlet* — with its superb characterizations, marvelous plot, and richly philosophic poetry — will always win over good students, our first concern here must be with the intellectuals' *Hamlet*. For if we wish to assign this great work to its proper grade level, and also hope to arrive at a clear conception of what lessons we can and cannot expect secondary students to be able to draw from it, we must first sort out in our own minds some of its intellectual implications. If this means that in this case more than in some others we must devote a large portion of our time to a discussion of the play itself, drawing our pedagogic conclusions somewhat summarily therefrom, so be it.

Undoubtedly we must begin where all commentators on *Hamlet* begin, with the endlessly debated question as to the nature of Hamlet's "irresolution." Of course if one doesn't particularly care to analyze this matter too closely, one can always fall back on the words with which Olivier begins his filmed version of the play. As the camera descends on Elsinore, the voice-over tells us, "This is the tragedy of a man who could not make up his mind." While most of us would be willing to accept that in one sense or another that statement is true — if we could enter into the record a hundred provisos, there being no space here for the listing even of one — the deeper question is, in *what* sense? Our answer to that question will to a great extent determine not only our attitude toward Hamlet and his dilemma, but our judgment as to the best pedagogic uses to which his play can be put.

For generations, Coleridge's view of Hamlet was blithely accepted as being too axiomatic to merit further analysis: Hamlet is a typical "intellectual," i.e., someone in whom the preference for reflection over action has grown so pronounced that the capacity and will for action have atrophied almost to nothing. All those critics who over the years have reared their theoretic edifices on that bedrock position tend to be extraordinarily severe in their attitude toward Hamlet. They seem to take little account of the genuinely unique and complex difficulties besetting him, and they foolishly accept Hamlet's own false estimation of himself (typically adolescent in the undue severity and outright inaccuracy of its self-censure) as a mere "John-a-dreams," when they should see in him a young man who has very good reason for cursing the spite that has thrust him into a world so monstrously out of joint.

Most remarkable of all, these critics reveal an astonishing bloodthirstiness in the way in which they urge Hamlet on to the taking of a life (Claudius's) and seem to dismiss out of hand any scruple anyone (including Hamlet himself) might feel about committing the act of murder (always tidied up by the word "revenge" in such analyses). To listen to such critics, one would think that the Almighty had fixed his canon 'gainst *self*-slaughter, while at the same time gaily proclaiming open season for slaughter itself.

For those of us who wish to be kinder to Hamlet than he is to himself, and who have always been suspicious of theories that invoke the word "irresolution" to explain Hamlet's inability to cope with a well nigh un-copable situation, a more recent generation of theorizers has arrived on the scene to free us from Coleridge's essentially unimaginative and uninteresting conception of Hamlet. They have done so, first, by pointing out that while Hamlet is indeed an intellectual in some senses — he's a university man, and he plainly has a taste for reflection — he is by no means a mere bookworm or shrinking violet. He is in fact the well-rounded Renaissance gentleman par excellence:

> The courtier's, soldier's, scholar's eye, tongue, sword,
> The expectancy and rose of the fair State,
> The glass of fashion, and the mould of form,
> The observed of all observers...

a man who has kept up his fencing practice even during this confused and melancholy period and who, as Fortinbras eulogizes, "was likely, had he been put on, to have proved most royally."

Yet while the scholars have made it abundantly clear that there is nothing in Hamlet's nature per se that renders him unfit for action (indeed, the stabbing of Polonius and the grappling in the grave with Laertes reveal him as being at times all too youthfully impulsive), they have done even better service by making us aware of the very good grounds Hamlet has for proceeding with that degree of deliberation and caution he does in fact show. While numerous scholars have done brilliant work in this area, I have found no one analysis so succinct and convincing as that of George Lyman Kittredge in his Introduction to the play.[17]

Kittredge makes clear to us that the the question of whether the Ghost is "a spirit of health or goblin damned" would have seemed by no means an idle one to an Elizabethan audience, and that it certainly is not so to Horatio, the sentinels, and Hamlet. If my reader wishes to corroborate Kittredge's assertion, she can simply do as I have done and track down every mention of the Ghost throughout the play. She will find that the Ghost, whether seen or merely thought on, never fails to arose genuine dread and awe in the viewer or speaker (and why not?). One might cite as examples Horatio's "It harrows me with fear and wonder," Hamlet's "I'll speak to it, though hell itself should gape/And bid me hold my peace," or Hamlet's appeal for heavenly intercession when the Ghost appears to him in his mother's bedroom: "Save me and hover o'er me with your wings,/You heavenly guards!"

Once one has understood that the Ghost in *Hamlet* is closer, in its dreadfulness, to the Sphinx in *Oedipus Rex* than to the troubling but reliable oracle at Delphi, one quickly apprehends two additional facts: that Hamlet is entirely wise in his decision to somehow try to corroborate what the Ghost has told him, and that, far from being irresolute, he in fact shows remarkable promptitude in devising two stratagems to achieve that end. Immediately after his first encounter with the Ghost he hits upon the idea of putting "an antic disposition on" (obviously on the theory that someone might divulge vital information when in the presence of a man assumed to be mad), and then the sight of the First Player moved to tears by his own declamation — giving Hamlet as it does visible proof of the power of drama to bring to the surface strong latent emotion — convinces him that "the play's the thing." The words that immediately precede those make clear, more than any others in the play, how vitally important to Hamlet is this whole issue of the Ghost's uncertain reliability and doubtful beneficence:

[17]George Lyman Kittredge, ed., *Hamlet* (Waltham, Mass: Blaisdell Publishing Company, 1967), pp. ix-xxii.

The spirit that I have seen
May be a devil, and the devil hath power
T'assume a pleasing shape; yea, and perhaps
Out of my weakness and melancholy,
As he is very potent with such spirits,
Abuses me to damn me. *I'll have grounds*
More relative than this. . . .   [II, ii]

Yet if in fact we can no longer characterize Hamlet in the Coleridgean fashion, as a man who thinks too much and acts too little, how are we to conceive of him? While it may seem an idle paradox to assert as much, we would adhere much more closely to the facts of the case if we said that Hamlet is a man who acts too much — or at least too impulsively — and who thinks too little — or at least too ineffectively. The real tragedy of *Hamlet* is not that of a man who cannot "make up his mind" in the traditional sense, i.e., who weakly vacillates in times of crisis, but of a young man who has not had time to "make up" his mind in the deeper sense of put together a coherent world-view. For while some men and women seem quite capable of going through life without troubling themselves overly with thoughts as to "ultimate reality," Hamlet is not one of these. He is a great man desperately in need of some genuine convictions as to the relation of this world to "the next," the correct response to evil, and so on.

Seen from this point of view, Hamlet's agonized uncertainty as to the "spiritual status" of the Ghost makes perfect sense, in that it is the exact analogue of his deep anxiety over the spiritual status of himself and the rest of humankind: Is man not merely the "paragon of animals" but in some ways even angel- and god-like, or is he a kind of vermin "crawling between heaven and earth"? Is death a consummation devoutly to be wished, or an invitation to perpetual nightmare? And so on. Needless to say, many critics have taken note of the fact that Hamlet seems to be caught between the rock and hard place of two disparate world-views, and go on to assert, with David Bevington, that "the play's hero stands between a Christian, medieval world of faith and one of skeptical uncertainty."[18]

While at first glance such an assessment might appear to

[18]David Bevington, ed., *Twentieth Century Interpretations of Hamlet: A Collection of Critical Essays* (Englewood Cliffs, N. J.: Prentice Hall, Inc., 1968), p. 12.

account for Hamlet's situation admirably, in fact it can only fail to do so, in that it routinely accepts the false notion that the medieval era was preeminently an "Age of Faith." While of course there were countless individuals in that period who were filled with genuine faith, we would come closer to the truth if we referred to it as being an Age of Credulity. It was a time when pious, circumspect Horatios gratefully accepted and subsisted on their dollop of received truth, not an age when ardent, inquiring Hamlets gave free play to every skeptical impulse until at last they arrived at a faith that both includes and transcends reason.

For strange as it may seem to assert as much, if we wish to behold the image of true faith (so that henceforth we always will be able to distinguish it from mere orthodox belief), we need only direct our gaze to Hamlet as he appears in Act V. Hamlet's newfound faith that "there's a special providence in the fall of a sparrow" brought has him a quiet confidence — and a patience with underlings such as the gravedigger and Osric — he has never before evinced, but it has not made him a dogmatist, or a prig, or a cold fish (witness the scene at Ophelia's grave), and it certainly has not endowed him with some less-than-human spiritual sangfroid. (As this remark to Horatio makes clear: "But thou wouldst not think how ill all's here about my heart — but it is no matter.") Genuine faith is always like Hamlet's — tentative, human, fitful — yet none the less real or precious for all that.

If then the theory that Hamlet is a man unable to choose correctly between two mutually exclusive world-views strikes us as being a plausible and attractive one, yet we wish to avoid the common critical error of designating these "faith" versus "skepticism," we need only choose our world-views more wisely in order to make our theory more serviceable. The fact is that Hamlet is not caught between an Age of Faith and an Age of Skepticism, but between an age characterized by vengeance and that inadequate code of morals known as chivalry — call it the Feudal Age, since man has indeed been feuding for as long as he has been man, and indeed before — and that age of genuine morality and forgiveness of sins that was born with the teachings of Buddha, Jesus, Confucius, Socrates etc.[19] and is still little more than a

---

[19]Although a feminist might argue, with very good reason, that it actually was born the first time a woman talked a man out of committing some violent and/or foolish action.

toddler even in our own day.[20] To realize this is to discover, to our delighted amazement, that those two utterly dissimilar masterpieces composed on or about the same year — *Hamlet* and *Troilus and Cressida* [21] — share at the deepest level the same theme: "modern" man's struggle to free himself not only from his age-old lusts and stupidities but also from that chivalric code (itself only a somewhat upgraded version of the Code of Hammurabi) under whose iron law he has fared perhaps worse than if he had had no moral code whatever.

If we are indeed right in thinking that below the surface of *Hamlet* a battle is raging between the feudal and ethical principles for the possession of its hero's soul, we should be able to find evidences of it wherever we turn. Such "evidences" can never be such in any scientific sense — for it can always be debated whether a symbol has been interpreted correctly, or indeed is a symbol at all — but when one has accumulated a great number of these the likelihood increases that they all do

[20]This whole line of inquiry, a very promising one in my estimation, never would have been opened up to me had it not been for the following comments by Bernard Shaw. Let it be noted, by the way, how unfortunate it is that so many dismiss Shaw as a Shakespeare critic, knowing as they do that Shaw rates Shakespeare too low only so that he may rate himself that much higher. For despite that fact, Shaw is without doubt one of the handful of truly *essential* Shakespeare critics. Herewith the passage: "What happened to Hamlet was what had happened fifteen hundred years before to Jesus. Born into the vindictive morality of Moses he has evolved into the Christian perception of the futility and wickedness of revenge and punishment, founded on the simple fact that two blacks do not make a white. *But he is not philosopher enough to comprehend this as well as apprehend it* [italics mine]. When he finds he cannot kill in cold blood he can only ask 'Am I a coward?'. When he cannot nerve himself to recover his throne he can account for it only by saying 'I lack ambition.'" Edwin Wilson, ed., *Shaw on Shakespeare* (New York: E. P. Dutton & Co., Inc., 1961), p. 80.

[21]Dissimilar, certainly, but with at least two points of superficial contact that I've been able to note. First, the speech that the First Player declaims for Hamlet concerns itself, of course, with the Trojan War. It is interesting to speculate on which came first, *T & C* or this speech; perhaps both came into being as a result of Shakespeare's having read Chapman's translation of the *Iliad*, published two or three years earlier. Second, Hamlet's response when Polonius asks what he is reading — "Words, words, words" — is almost exactly the disillusioned Troilus's response to Pandarus when the latter asks what Cressida has had to say in her letter to Troilus: "Words, words, mere words, no matter from the heart." Hamlet's reply is flippant and whimsical, Troilus's bitter and heartbroken.

indeed subserve the same great theme.

One might begin by noting that the Ghost appears in full armor. The theory advanced by Bernardo to account for this, that it is in some way related to the squabbles between Denmark and Norway, leaves us utterly unconvinced. The reader knows that all such petty affairs of state can only mean less than nothing to the Ghost, who has returned to earth on entirely different and more pressing business. Surely a more plausible hypothesis is that the Ghost, having come in search of vengeance, has armed itself as it goes in pursuit of its quarry. While one might assert as much with reasonable equanimity, I would go further and say that the figure of a man in armor is the very image of the Feudal Age, and by extension all those ages when man has staked his honor, or someone else's, on the death of a foe.

As an addendum of sorts to this armor issue, one might also note that Hamlet demands of Horatio et al that they swear *on his sword* not to tell what they have seen. While this practice arose from the fact that a sword's hilt forms the shape of the Cross, a sword is a martial implement nonetheless, and surely we will not go far wrong if we assert that those who take an oath on it are in effect pledging themselves to serve the false gods of chivalry and vengeance. Indeed, given the manner of Hamlet's death, and our cognizance of the fact that ultimately he is offered up in sacrifice to those gods, we might risk the quip that those who swear by the sword (or force others to do so) die by the sword — or the rapier. The appearance of Fortinbras at play's end — also fully armed — surely signifies the triumph of the feudal ideal, as it exultantly lords it over the dead body of Hamlet, a man who had tried and failed to fully incarnate in himself the "new age" virtues of gentleness and forgiveness of sins. Seen thus, Hamlet is the natural son of Hamlet senior, but the Ghost's true spiritual heir is Fortinbras.

Let us now look at two passages — two of the great soliloquies in fact — that reveal as clearly as can be Hamlet's inability to distinguish between the feudal and ethical ideals, much less choose between them consciously and wisely. The first of these is the "rogue and peasant slave" soliloquy (II, ii), in which Hamlet upbraids himself for being a mere "pigeon-livered" "John-a-dreams," and compares himself unfavorably in this respect with the First Player, who has just been reduced to tears by his own declamation.

Is there the slightest logic in such a comparison? Of course not. The player is in fact the genuine John-a-dreams, Hamlet a potentially great man of action stymied at the moment by an impossibly complex set of circumstances. There is in fact a real lesson to be drawn from the player's tears — that of the power of great literature to exalt the spirit and soften the heart — but as Hamlet is a man already imaginative and empathic to a fault he has no need of such a lesson and thus twists it — as he twists everything — into a reproach of his failure to take decisive action. Rather than see the player as a man cut from essentially the same cloth as he, an artist and a thinker, Hamlet makes him out to be almost another Fortinbras, capable of reducing himself to tears as expeditiously as Fortinbras can reduce a foreign populace to slavery.

Speaking of Fortinbras, when his and Hamlet's paths cross in Act IV, scene iv, Hamlet performs precisely the same conjuring trick we have seen him pull off with the player, but in this case he reverses it: Instead of turning an artist and thinker into a man of action, he turns a man of action into a thinker. The sight of Fortinbras's army marching off to conquer "a little patch of ground/That hath in it no profit but the name" inspires in Hamlet, of all things, an utterly sublime statement expressive of his faith in both God and Reason:

> Sure he that made us with such large discourse,
> Looking before and after, gave us not
> That capability and godlike reason
> To fust in us unused.

Assuredly not — but what on earth does any of this have to do with that thoughtless, godless muscleman Fortinbras, the sight of whom has exalted Hamlet to these poetic-philosophic heights? Not a thing. If Hamlet had that self-knowledge he so clearly lacks, he would heed his own words and concentrate on developing his analytical powers, not on flailing himself for his supposed inadequacies as a man of action.[22] As it is, only moments later the same man who had just thought and spoken as few human beings are capable of doing is talking utter rot of the kind all the

[22]A passage from Emerson's journal seems to speak directly to the issue we are addressing here: "How imbecile is often a young person of superior intellectual powers for want of acquaintance with his powers; bashful, timid, he shrinks, retreats before every confident person, and is disconcerted by arguments and pretensions he would be ashamed to put forward himself."

macho Fortinbrases — true knights of the feudal spirit — are constantly spewing forth in barracks and beer hall:

> Rightly to be great
> Is not to stir without great argument,
> But greatly to find quarrel in a straw
> When honour's at the stake.

Now if we have spent this much time in pursuit of that most elusive of quarries — the "real" meaning of *Hamlet* — we have done so only so that we might ask one probing pedagogic question: How likely is it that the average — or even the brilliant — seventeen- or eighteen-year-old will be able to follow our tracks, and stand by his teacher's side when the truth at last seems ready to be flushed out? For while I will stand by the assertion I made in the course of my commentary on *As You Like It* — that the "moral" of a work, if it is organic and not engrafted from without, will always take root in the reader's subconscious, if not always his conscious mind — surely most if not all of the works we assign to juniors and seniors (as opposed to 7th- and 8th-graders, in the case of *AYLI*) should be ones that test these students' ability to *consciously* recognize and analyze these works' deepest intellectual implications.

Were I to try to answer my own question, I would begin by suggesting that even the brilliant secondary school student is unlikely to be able to plumb *Hamlet* to the depths. I would quickly add, however, that in my view it would almost be a shame if he or she *could* do so on first reading. For although it has been the business of many of these pages to suggest that when a teacher seeks to arouse in his students only an "appreciation" for literature he may fail to do even that, there are certain works — *Hamlet* preeminent among them — so rich and intellectually appetizing that the mere savor of them nourishes us, long before we have committed ourselves to the chores of mastication and digestion.

Yet while no one could be more of a "booster" for *Hamlet* as a staple of the secondary school curriculum than I, and while I certainly have no intention of committing the same error Plato did (when he banished music from the Republic) by banishing *Hamlet* from the syllabus as mentally or morally destabilizing, I do feel enough concern and even anxiety about precisely what kinds of lessons our students are learning (or *think* they are learning) from *Hamlet* to ask my colleagues to ponder well these two questions.

One: While I have no doubt that the papers on *Hamlet* you have received over the years from the brilliant students have been exceptionally brilliant, have the papers from the confused students perhaps been exceptionally confused? Two: Even among the brilliant papers, have there been many that have challenged or seen beyond the standard Coleridgean interpretation of *Hamlet* as a play about a dreamy, wishy-washy intellectual who is congenitally incapable of action (i.e., a person remarkably similar to S. T. Coleridge)?

I pose those two questions because they correspond to the two chief fears I have about *Hamlet* in the classroom. First, that *Hamlet* is a work more likely to prompt in the student a myriad of relatively unrelated *thoughts* than it is one that will school her in the rigorous art of *thinking*. Second, that while the "real" moral of Hamlet may indeed be tunneling through her subconscious, to bore its way upward into consciousness many years later, the moral the average student probably takes away from *Hamlet* — that in the battle against life's ills, reflection and deliberation are weapons best left unhefted — is not only simply the wrong one, but an immensely dangerous one as well.

If it should prove to be the case that there are indeed grounds for these fears, it would seem that we are confronted with a paradox, or rather a flat contradiction: *Hamlet* is an indispensable part of every secondary school Shakespeare syllabus, but *Hamlet* is probably in certain key respects a far from ideal pedagogic tool. Is there any change we teachers can make in the Shakespeare syllabus that will allow us to continue teaching *Hamlet*, but also minimize the confusion this great work may engender in immature minds?

In my view, our best option in this tricky situation is to move *Hamlet* from the senior to the junior year (at present almost twice as many schools teach it to seniors as those that teach it to juniors). By thus freeing the senior year for the study of a different Shakespeare play, we can ensure that that work is one that a) the slower student can feel he has mastered, rather than been mastered by, and b) sends every student out into the world convinced that reason and morality are not such as "make livers pale and lustihood deject" (which, although the words are Troilus's, is what *Hamlet* is probably teaching most of our young people at the moment) but the key to the life more abundant.

Many sensible objections will of course be made to my

"demoting" *Hamlet* thus (and many passionate voices raised when it is heard that I plan to put *Troilus and Cressida* in its place), so allow me to respond to a few of them in advance.

To those who may say that *Hamlet* will be a tougher reading experience for juniors than for seniors, I would say that the real difficulty in studying *Hamlet* is trying to figure out what on earth it all *means*, and that seniors aren't much better equipped for that task than juniors. So too, *Hamlet*'s difficulties of language, while relatively formidable, are unlikely to seem much less so to seniors than to juniors.

Others will object that it's absurd to give any thought at all to what work "crowns" a Shakespeare syllabus, suggesting that, after all, the large majority of secondary school students go on to college, and therefore those four years and the four of high school should be looked on as a seamless continuum. Perhaps so, but my personal conviction is that secondary education is far more important in molding character and mind-set than is college education, and that we do best — if we believe passionately that a particular work is one that can change lives and affect conduct, as I do about *Troilus and Cressida* — *not* to assume that our students will "run into it" in college.

In making my case both for moving *Hamlet* to the junior year and for putting *T & C* in the senior-year slot that move has opened up, I would also ask that the jury of my peers admit as evidence a couple of facts about the junior and senior years themselves. As all teachers at those grade levels are aware, keeping seniors interested in their studies is by no means an easy task, their thoughts often being hundreds of miles away at the colleges of their choice. Might it not make more sense, then, for so involuted and problematic a work as *Hamlet* to be studied by students who are feeling as introspective and uncertain about what the future holds as Hamlet himself — which is to say, by juniors?

By contrast, *T & C*, a work at once more openly didactic and less convoluted than *Hamlet*, is likely to be precisely the kind of "breezy" read that seniors, with one foot already on the open road, are in the mood for. I'm well aware that the prevalent opinion among my colleagues (as revealed by the survey) is that *T & C* is a work as far from being "breezy" in any sense as could be imagined, and to whatever extent "breezy" connotes "easy" I would agree with them. Nonetheless I do indeed contend that there is a strong breeze blowing across the plains of Troy that will never insinuate its way into any of the chambers of the castle at Elsinore, and that its name is Hope.

If I had written this book for no other purpose than to draw my colleagues' attention to their preemption of *Troilus and Cressida* from its rightful place at the very crown of the Shakespeare syllabus, my every effort would have been well expended. Living as we are in an educational era when many are demanding a greater attention to values in the classroom, and asserting that students should be required to do more thinking about thinking, it is high time we put to its proper use a play containing a "lofty... didactic eloquence"[23] rivaled only by Milton or the Bible, a play in which a master thinker displays for our edification the myriad of ways in which unsound thinking and rash acting lead to human folly and misery.

While I will try in a moment or two to account for the unaccountable — the failure of teachers to take advantage of a pedagogic resource of unparalleled richness, and the failure of critics to recognize *Troilus and Cressida* for the masterpiece it is — let me begin simply by reminding my colleagues what they — and, far more to the point, their pupils — are missing. As they read the passages I have selected, I would ask them to consider well whether the student who has once come in contact with such Olympian wisdom will ever be quite the same again. I would also have them keep in mind, as they read, that this is a play many critics have execrated, calling it "cynical"[24] and even "the most degrading and filthiest of Shakespeare's plays."[25] For one who believes, as I do — passionately — that *Troilus and Cressida* is in fact the most profoundly moral work ever to come from Shakespeare's pen, such wildly erroneous judgments can only lead one to weep — as Thersites laughs — at "the common curse of mankind, folly and ignorance."

[23]William Hazlitt, *Characters of Shakespeare's Plays* (London: Oxford University Press, 1962), p. 64.

[24]The word appears everywhere in *T & C* criticism, but here it will perhaps suffice to cite this comment: "[*T & C*] is permeated by a cynicism about human beings immersed in Time that is destructive of every value." Wiley Sypher, *The Ethic of Time: Structures of Experience in Shakespeare's Plays* (New York: Seabury Press, 1976), p. 137.

[25]A survey respondent passed on to me this comment, one he had dug up from his notes of a professor's lecture at one of this country's most prestigious graduate schools of English.

Herewith the passages.

Ulysses on the average sensual man's contempt for thought and preference for action:

> They tax our policy, and call it cowardice,
> Count wisdom as no member of the war,
> Forestall prescience, and esteem no act
> But that of hand. The still and mental parts
> That do contrive how many hands shall strike,
> When fitness call them on, and know by measure
> Of their observant toil the enemies' weight,
> Why this hath not a finger's dignity.
> They call this bed-work, mapp'ry, closet-war;
> So that the ram that batters down the wall,
> For the great swinge and rudeness of his poise,
> They place before his hand that made the engine,
> Or those that with the fineness of their souls
> By reason guide his execution.   [I, iii]

Helenus, rebuking Troilus for his preference for passionate polemic over reasonable deliberation:

> No marvel though you bite so sharp at reasons,
> You are so empty of them.
> Should not our father
> Bear the great sway of his affairs with reason,
> Because your speech hath none that tell him so? [II, ii]

Ulysses on the perniciousness of pride:

> Things small as nothing, for request's sake only,
> He makes important. Possessed he is with greatness,
> And speaks not to himself but with a pride
> That quarrels at self-breath. Imagined worth
> Holds in his blood such swollen and hot discourse,
> That 'twixt his mental and his active parts
> Kingdomed Achilles in commotion rages,
> And batters down himself. What should I say?
> He is so plaguy proud that the death-tokens of it
> Cry "No recovery."   [II, iii]

Ulysses warning Achilles of the dangers of solipsism and quietism:

> I do not strain at the position,
> It is familiar, but at the author's drift;
> Who in his circumstance expressly proves
> That no man is the lord of anything,
> Though in and of him there be much consisting,
> Till he communicate his parts to others;
> Nor doth he of himself know them for aught
> Till he behold them formed in th' applause
> Where they're extended; who, like an arch,
>   reverb'rates
> The voice again, or, like a gate of steel
> Fronting the sun, receives and renders back
> His figure and his heat.   [III, iii]

Now while most readers of those lines probably have been duly impressed by their majesty and wisdom, and some perhaps have also noted how extraordinarily relevant to adolescence are the counsels contained within them (insisting as they do on the need for right thought as the indispensable prerequisite of right action, and of self-knowledge), it seems likely that many still harbor serious reservations about the appropriateness of teaching *T & C* at the secondary level. After all, it may be objected, good "philosophy" does not necessarily a good play make, and besides, all of this may be over the heads of young people. Let's begin by considering the first objection.

For all of those who find *T & C* a troubling play — and their number is legion, if one may judge by much of the criticism and by the survey results, which reveal that it is taught only at a very few independent schools — the easiest way of demoting this play from its rightful rank of masterpiece has been to kick it upstairs. That is, to insist that *T & C*, while it's all very fine in its way (or would be, if only "rank Thersites" somehow could be expunged from it), is in fact *too* fine for most readers; this, after all, is what the editors of the quarto edition did when they affixed a preface to this play that exults in the fact that it has "never [been] clapper-clawed with the palms of the vulgar" (i.e., performed before the general public).

Yet while it is all too tempting to think of *T & C* as fare fit only for an elite, the kind of play Hamlet describes to the players as having "pleased not the million, twas caviare to the general," the fact is that it *does* possess, and plentifully, what that other play was said to lack, "sallets in the lines, to make the matter savoury." For could any work that encompasses the railing wit of Pandarus and Thersites, the scandalous doings of Achilles and Patroclus or Helen and Paris, and the self-deluding vanity of "blockish Ajax" really be accused of lacking spice, or a zesty salad to garnish its sublime main course, Ulysses' and Hector's great speeches of moral and intellectual counsel? The fact is that whenever the reader feels himself in danger of disappearing into the empyrean, borne upward by drafts of Ulysses' lofty discourse, rank Thersites clamps him in his "mastic jaw" and drags him back to earth with his honest cynicism; or when he feels himself about to swoon along with Troilus at the thought of the bliss that awaits him in in Cressid's arms, Pandarus is on hand to snap him out of it by means of a salacious jest.

Thus while there is no point in denying that *T & C* is one of Shakespeare's "talkiest" dramas, it is worth noting that even the seemingly unphilosophical talk of the characters who in this play take on the role usually assigned to some Clown or Fool — Thersites and Pandarus — is far more full of "matter" and genuine wit than the labored wordplay of a typical Shakespearean clown (say, Lavatch in *All's Well*). Then too, one would have to go to Kate and Petruchio, or to Falstaff and Hal, to find banter so full of energy and passion, so thoroughly uncontrived, as that between Pandarus and the lovers, or between Thersites and Achilles/Patroclus/Ajax. Pedagogically, this means that students are as little likely to find Pandarus and Thersites boring as they are very likely to find Touchstone or Feste unfunny.

If we do indeed have Pandarus and Thersites on our side, to help us debunk the false conception of *T & C* as being merely long-winded or highbrow, we also have — need it be said? — the lovers themselves to help us hold young readers' attention. In my opinion the love story in *T & C* has a real-life quality that *R & J* lacks, and as a result I grieve far more genuinely at the separation of the Trojan lovers than I do at the stagy deaths of their Veronese counterparts. Yet while each of my readers is free to have her or his own opinion as to that, what cannot be gainsayed, I feel, is the fact that the young reader is certain to see his or her own insecurities about "relationships" mirrored far more truly in *T & C* than *R & J*.

Two examples. Almost every girl has thought, at one time or another, as Cressida does when she confesses in soliloquy (I, ii) that she loves Troilus and has only been playing hard to get,

"Men prize the thing ungained more than it is." So too every boy (and girl?) has felt Troilus's "performance anxiety": "This is the monstrosity in love, lady, that the will is infinite, and the execution confined; that the desire is boundless, and the act a slave to limit."

Let it also be noted here that while one survey respondent mentioned *T & C*'s "sexual sensitivity" as a reason for avoiding it at the secondary level, its treatment of sexual matters is in fact remarkably forthright and free of prurience. With the possible exception of Cressida's remark to Pandarus that she lies "upon [my] back to defend my belly," there is actually no more bawdry here than elsewhere in the canon, perhaps even less. And lest it be thought that all the great speeches in this play are stilted and declamatory, let it also be proclaimed that *T & C* offers us love poetry every bit as rich and sensuous as anything *R & J* has to offer:

> O, that her hand,
> In whose comparison all whites are ink
> Writing their own reproach; to whose soft seizure
> The cygnet's down is harsh, and spirit of sense
> Hard as the palm of ploughman.   [I, i]

> No, Pandarus, I stalk about her door
> Like a strange soul upon the Stygian banks
> Staying for waftage. O, be thou my Charon,
> And give me swift transportation to those fields
> Where I may wallow in the lily beds
> Proposed for the deserver! O gentle Pandar,
> From Cupid's shoulder pluck his painted wings,
> And fly with me to Cressid!   [III, ii]

Having thus, it is hoped, completely exploded the notion that *T & C* has nothing to offer an eager and passionate young reader but togaed figures declaiming, Demosthenes-like, to the four winds, we must now try to overrule the second of our possible objections to teaching *T & C* at the secondary level, that insofar as it is a "philosophical" play it is probably over the heads of most high school students. Needless to say, we have here neither the time nor space to debate fully the question of whether students have a natural liking for, or antipathy to, philosophical speculation per se, so all I can do is state that some of my own classroom experiences strongly suggest that the former is true. Students are not only wise enough to disdain the niceties of literary criticism that so absorb the attention of many adult academics, they also seem to know as if by instinct that the freedom to speculate about the eternally contested questions of philosophy is part of every human's distinctively human birthright.

If we are right in thus assuming that philosophizing and young people do indeed go together, then the question before us is really quite a simple one: Is there anything in the "philosophical" speeches of *T & C* that is beyond the reach of high school seniors, either by dint of language or of content? As to the issue of language difficulty in *T & C*, it can only be said that this is an extraordinarily easy play to read. The number of footnotes is relatively low, and most of these are of the type that give synonyms for archaic terms or explain classical allusions, rather than those that give the gist of entire passages whose original wording is syntactically complex or poetically "dense." While its language is not so thoroughly trouble-free as that of *Richard II* it is surprisingly close to it, certainly far closer to it than to *R & J*, *Hamlet*, *Macbeth*, and so on.

As to possible problems students may have with its philosophic content, I can only ask my colleagues to look for a second time at the passages from the play excerpted earlier, passages that (along with many others) I myself have perused time and again in my struggle to see this play not from my own point of view but from that of a seventeen-year-old of below-average intelligence. I feel confident that their reappraisal will bring them to the same conclusion I have come to: There is no reason in the world why anyone equipped with common sense — and prepared to *think*, or to be *compelled* to think by a teacher — should be debarred from a full appreciation of passages such as these. Indeed, I would stake all of my modest pedagogic experience and any critical ability I might possess on the truth of an even bolder proposition: Passages such as these are not only *easier* for the student to get a handle on than much of the complex verse confronting her in *Hamlet*, *Othello*, et al, but, when she gives that handle a pull, a treasure chest is laid open before her that contains countless gems of moral wisdom: "precepts that would make invincible the heart that conned them" (*Coriolanus*, IV, i).

For ultimately there is no more important duty for anyone who sets out to put together a Shakespeare syllabus than to compute a strict cost/benefit ratio for each play, one that contrasts the investment of time and effort a student must make to come to terms with Elizabethan English with the long-term intellectual dividend she can hope to receive for her investment. For instance, to my way of thinking that student receives a very poor return on investment who, in reading Act I, scene iii of *Twelfth Night*, must first figure out what a "kickshaw," "galliard," "caper," and "back-trick" are, then struggle to envision what kind of men Sir Andrew and Sir Toby are (figures in most respects wholly hidden from an immature mind by the mists of time) and why they are talking about dancing at all, then perhaps vaguely perceive that Shakespeare is having some fun with a vain coxcomb and a pompous drunk, to be rewarded at last with a very slight smile at a joke that still substantially eludes her.

In marked contrast to this kind of tortuous treasure hunt, one that generally leads to very little philosophic treasure but only to some comic Elizabethan counterpart of cheesy old Ben Gunn, the student who is grappling with, let us say, Ulysses' magnificent "Take but degree away" speech will not have to journey far at all — if she has a good teacher to guide her — to arrive at the gist of what Ulysses is saying. Rather she will have to stay right where she is — in her seat — and ponder the *significance* of his words, i.e., *think*.

Ulysses tells us that things are screwed up because people no longer know their place, whereas in the cosmos (and here the teacher can discourse profitably for a moment on the Ptolemaic vision of the universe, and on the Renaissance conception of a great Chain of Being) everything stays in its own groove and thereby produces not discord but the music of the spheres. What does the student think about this, both as it relates to her own world — do we suffer today because our social roles are less clearly defined than they were in feudal times, or is our freedom an unmixed blessing? — and as it relates to the Greek army's predicament — is it really only because Achilles and Ajax have grown proud and self-willed that Troy "yet upon his basis" stands?

Thus while I willingly concede that the discussion of any one of the great speeches in *T & C* could fill up a whole class period and more, I insist that this should be a cause for jubilation, not handwringing. Surely teachers never have a more perfect right to exult than when they discover that a text they have chosen is causing students to struggle not to *understand*, but to *think*. And when that text gives students the opportunity not merely to think but to think about thinking, something has gone profoundly right in education.

Take for instance that extraordinary scene (II, ii) in which the Trojan leaders are debating whether to bring the war to an end by returning Helen to the Greeks. Hector superbly rebukes the vainglorious Troilus and the glib and self-absorbed Paris for having "on the cause and question now in hand... glozed but superficially," and numbers them among those "young men whom Aristotle thought unfit to hear moral philosophy." (Yes, Shakespeare is guilty of an anachronism here, in placing Aristotle pre- rather than post-Trojan War!) Then, to our profound shock and dismay, Hector turns traitor to the very Reason he had until then proved himself so worthy a servant of, as he decides to "keep Helen still;/For 'tis a cause that hath no mean dependence/Upon our joint and several dignities."

Need it be said that the student who has followed with delight Hector's defense of reason against Troilus's charge that "reason and respect make livers pale and lustihood deject" only then to see Hector let his liver (passion) usurp his brain (rational function) has had to do some long and hard thinking abut thinking? Nor could he have failed to draw the proper conclusion: Reason can do much to guide us in life, but only if our wills consent to be thus guided.

Although this discussion has already gone on too long, I cannot bear to send back out into the world a work I love so well until I have tried to scour it clean of two other calumnies with which it has been blackened. The first of these baseless accusations is one that I would guess many women bring against it; to wit, that there is something unwholesome, or at least unfeminist, in its portrayal of Cressida, in that by virtue of her weakness she, like Eve, seems to have been made the scapegoat for all the foibles of humankind.

Two answers might be made to this objection. First, if ever there was a play that set out to expose the almost pathological weaknesses of the male sex — particularly its fondness for masking its passions in the guise of philosophy (*vide* Troilus) and its undisguised fondness for itself (Achilles lolling on his bed, Ajax pluming his ego in preparation for his combat with Hector) — it is *Troilus and Cressida*.

Second, a strong case can be made, and indeed has been made in a brilliant analysis of this play by Joseph Papp, for seeing not Cressida but Troilus as the more faithless of the two lovers. Papp accuses Troilus of having "a double standard in honor,"[26] and by means of that telling phrase reminds us of the

---

[26] Joseph Papp, from his Introduction to the Festival Shakespeare edition of *Troilus and Cressida* (New York: Macmillan, 1967), p. 37.

true theme of *T & C*, that of the huge discrepancy between genuine honor — whose real name is morality — and that degraded macho travesty of it whose name is chivalry. All of Troilus's speeches as he imagines what it will be like to be at last in Cressid's bed and "taste indeed/Love's thrice-repured nectar" are frankly sensual both in thought and in imagery, whereas by contrast Cressida's soliloquy is notably sober and full of cautious self-analysis.

Even more to the point, Papp points out that, on the morning after their night together (IV, ii), Troilus seems as eager to get away from Cressida as a ladies' man after a one-night stand ("Dear, trouble not yourself; the morn is cold"; "To bed, to bed"; and, most shocking of all, "Sleep *kill* those pretty eyes"), while it is Cressida who remonstrates with Troilus thus: "Prithee, tarry; you men will never tarry." So too Troilus seems to accept almost blithely the news that Cressida is to be conveyed to her father in the Greek camp ("Is it concluded so?") and to be thinking less of Cressida herself than of the bitter irony that all of this should be transpiring just when he has finally "scored" ("How my *achievements* mock me!").

Another highly sexist note here, which Papp points out but a careful reader could make note of herself, is the manner in which Pandarus, with the sobbing Cressida only a few feet away from him (and note that she has been desolated by the thought of being separated from *Troilus*, not Troy) can think only of the effect all this will have on Troilus, and has only contempt, not comfort, to offer Cressida ("Would thou hadst ne'er been born! I knew thou wouldst be his death. O poor gentleman!").

As Cressida arrives in the Greek camp her manner is one of sexy, saucy impudence as she banters with the sex-starved generals and barters with them in words and kisses. Papp sees this as evidence that Cressida is now a woman who has lost her innocence in every sense, and has learned like every beautiful woman of the world to use her sex appeal as a tool and weapon.

Certainly a production that chose to portray Cressida as a girl transformed by a first night of lovemaking into a lustful woman could do so without raising too many eyebrows. Nonetheless, I would contend that this is still in many ways the old innocent, appealing Cressida, and that Cressida among the Greeks is less a sexual adventuress taking her pick from a tempting array of "hunks" than what she had envisioned herself as being: "A woeful Cressid 'mongst the merry Greeks!" I would cite two facts in support of that contention.

First, while Papp is perhaps correct in seeing a new, sexually knowing Cressida here, and while almost any production would want to get at least a hint of that from the actress portraying her, one might cite another of Papp's own fascinating insights in arguing against him. He himself points out that Cressida's sexual banter with Pandarus earlier in the play (I, ii) by no means convicts her of being licentious by nature; rather, such wordplay might well be the pose adopted by a sexually wary young girl, living in a sexually loose era, to mask her deep insecurities. Should this be true, what is to prevent us from seeing her banter in the Greek camp as only a somewhat more genuinely sexy "update" of her usual pose?

Second: The most convincing evidence I've been able to glean in support of this theory that there is really only one Cressida, not two, comes from her relationship to Diomedes. It is surely worthy of note that Cressida refers to Diomedes not once but twice as her "guardian"; clearly, "woeful Cressid 'mongst the merry Greeks" feels the need for a protector at least as much as she feels desire for a man. Then too, while I'm sure many a production has had Cressida perform this scene (V, ii) exactly as Diomedes would have insisted it be played if he were director — with Cressida as a coy "tease," pure and simple — it seems far more likely that what *appears* to be sheer sexual provocativeness in her is in fact a genuine vacillation between, on the one hand, her need for a protector and desire for a lover, and on the other, her sense of moral scruple and her guilty remembrance of her oh-so-recent protestations of constancy to Troilus.

Ultimately, of course, this whole question of whether one perceives the Cressida of the Greek camp as a kind of second Helen, gladly adapting to a life of semi-harlotry, or as a thoroughly wretched, heartbroken young girl, is moot. The only points really worth making about Cressida and her fate are two: 1) Cressida as we first meet her is not only without question an attractive and honorable person (and none the less so for some sexiness of speech, manner, and person), but in many respects a more thoughtful, sensitive, and caring person than is Troilus; 2) whether Cressida adapts to her fate grudgingly and in despair, or willingly and full of lust, she is a genuinely pathetic figure, a woman infinitely more sinned against than sinning. More specifically, Cressida embodies all of those graces and rather fragile virtues that are the first to be offered up in sacrifice to Mars whenever men revel in war, that deadliest emanation of man's o'erweening pride and bestial stupidity.

Let us be certain, before we take leave of this whole issue of the sexism, or lack of it, to be found in *Troilus and Cressida*, that we make two crucial pedagogic observations. First, let us note that *T & C* not only is *not* sexist in any real sense, but that it is in fact a work almost certain to appeal to female students even more than male ones, and to inspire them to do some very fine critical thinking and textual analysis in their effort to prove that Cressida is far more than the "slut" she is too often taken to be. Indeed, I will risk provoking my female readers by saying that the subtleties and moral ambiguities of a *T & C* seem to me far more likely to put budding feminists on their best mental mettle than the cut-and-dried banalities of all the *Doll's House*'s ever written!

Second, let it be stated that, in my opinion, the general sexiness of *T & C* — which, a number of survey responses seem to indicate, is one of the major factors causing teachers to shy away from teaching it (and probably *Measure for Measure* as well) — is an unalloyed pedagogic *plus*. For while I myself have been surprised to discover just how awkward and tongue-tied I become when it is time to discuss a "sensitive" passage with a class, both I and my colleagues owe it to our students to untie our tongues and banish our blushes and get on with the teaching of such material. Sex is, after all, Hot Topic # 1, 2, and 3 with adolescents, and a work such as *T & C* — one that is not of course obscene, nor even (as one discovers if one takes the trouble to look at the text itself, and not simply allow one's memories of it to make one skittish) all that suggestive — is a work as certain to provide the young with catharsis for their deep sexual anxieties as it is to titillate them just enough so that all drowsiness will be banished from the classroom.

Having at last, it is hoped, cleared *T & C* of the charge of sexism, we can now turn our attention to the second of the calumnies that has been been allowed to tarnish the luster of this masterpiece: the imputation to it of cynicism, and pessimism. I confess I can hardly bring myself to conduct the defense during this part of the case for *T & C*, for I have read so many utterly wrongheaded criticisms of this play, all of them accusing it of cynicism, that I've begun to wonder whether I inhabit the same critical universe as those who have penned them. Suffice it to say that the one play in the canon that many critics find morally offensive (*Titus Andronicus* turning the stomach more effectively than it shocks the conscience) is for me the one place in the canon where the generally unassuming "sweet Will" rises to the dignity almost of a Buddha, and with one hand held high softly intones the words "I give you sorrow, and I give you the ending of sorrow."

The ending of sorrow can be achieved, of course, by taking seriously and putting into action the great moral counsels of Hector and Ulysses, and yes, even by lending an ear to the harsh but highly tonic truth-telling of Thersites and Pandarus. Yet while the morally fastidious person is always highly willing to heed such counsels of perfection, generally he also wants to turn his head from all proferred evidences of human error and evildoing. The great teacher knows that the pupil who does so has no chance of achieving the moral progress he seeks, for there can be no ending of sorrow without an intimate and detailed knowledge of all that leads human beings into its clutches. Hence the supreme and savage irony we are presented with here: Shakespeare fulfills his highest duty as both teacher and artist by depicting for us the thousand and one ways in which human beings can go wrong, and for his pains we brand him and his work "cynical" or even "immoral."

For the record, let us take note of some of these erring mortals in *T & C*, and the errors by which they are distinguished: Agamemnon, eloquent but essentially vacuous, and perfectly willing to let the more thoughtful and purposeful Ulysses usurp his command; Nestor, another Polonius, well-meaning but old and ineffectual; Ulysses, a gentleman of the old school, full of wisdom and political savvy but quite blind to the fact that the feudal order of things he rhapsodizes has irrevocably passed away; Achilles, "so plaguy proud, that the death-tokens of it/Cry 'No recovery'"; the beef-witted Ajax; Hector, the intellectually inconstant; Cressida, the sexually inconstant; Troilus of the empty bragadoccio; Thersites, the pure (or rather, decidedly impure) cynic and misanthrope.

The name of Thersites is an appropriate one to linger over for a moment, because it is without doubt the presence in *T & C* of so grotesque a figure that provokes the revulsion of so many readers, and convinces them that any work containing such a demon can only be as immoral and cynical as he. Interestingly enough, no one objects thus to Thersites' closest relative in the canon, Caliban, and for an obvious reason: Caliban, however much he may be said to *represent* evil tendencies in man's nature, is himself clearly a piece of fiction and hence unthreatening, like some theme-park Frankenstein we might even dare to reach out and pat on the head. Thersites, by contrast, is all too real for the average reader. Yet it is his very reality that makes him, in my

view, a creation a good bit more interesting than the merely pic-
turesque Caliban.

At any rate, it would seem likely that if we can properly
answer "the Thersites question" we will at last have some solid
basis for our assertion that, just as *Merchant* is not an anti-
Semitic play but a play about an anti-Semitic world, so too
T & C is not an immoral or cynical play but an intensely moral
play about a world brought low by immorality and cynicism. And
the answer to the Thersites question is a remarkably simple one:
Shakespeare has placed at the center of this work an ugly and
disturbing truth-teller, a figure in the great tradition of the Old
Testament prophets, to remind us that the truth is often ugly
and disturbing, and that nothing so actively fosters evil as vanity,
sentimentality, and every form of self-delusion.

For while Thersites suffers from the sickness of Diogenes and
all "tough-minded" individuals — a tendency to see things much
blacker and more menacing than they really are — and while
Shakespeare is entirely aware of his sickness and of how it has
deformed him spiritually, Shakespeare also knows that for every
Thersites who looks too much on the dark side there are a hundred thousand humans who every day unwittingly aid and abet
stupidity and evil by refusing to admit that there are any such
things. (Or who, when they do grudgingly acknowledge these,
either insist that they are mere anomalies of human existence, not
to be taken seriously, or point them out only as they flower
grotesquely in the Richard IIIs and the Iagos, never as they qui-
etly bloom and thrive in average folks such as themselves.) The
presence of a Thersites in their midst — or a Socrates, or a
Jesus, or a Van Gogh — is socially indispensable, in that these
individuals are the salt of the earth, without whom a bland, complacent humanity would quickly lose its moral savor.

Surely it is one of the truest hallmarks of Shakespeare's
genius, attested to by the constant juxtaposition throughout his
work of the terrible and the comical, that he can do two things
at once that most human beings have difficulty doing separately:
recognize the fact of evil, but at the same time (and unlike
Thersites) not let that recognition so mentally unbalance him that
he makes evil into a far bigger bugaboo than it is, or so frighten
him (as seems to happen with so many of *T & C*'s critics, Mark
Van Doren for one) that he represses the original recognition.
Those of us who reverence this ability in Shakespeare feel no
need, like so many of the nervous Nellie critics, to embarrassedly
explain away Thersites, or the play in which he appears, but

rather point to him with pride as one of Shakespeare's greatest and most *meaningful* creations. I would add that, unless I'm very much mistaken, the iconoclast that lives and smirks within every adolescent will revel greatly in Thersites, and share none of his elders' squeamishness about being in his company.

While the preceding remarks perhaps have caused a few readers to revise their assessment of *T & C* as being a cynical work, many will continue to assert that only a master whitewasher could pretend that it is anything other than pessimistic in its view of human life and human beings. This is a charge I of all people am forced to take very seriously, in that I feel very strongly, and have stated as much in these pages, that the Shakespeare syllabus as a whole tends too much toward the lugubrious.

The simple fact is that, while the world of *T & C* is certainly a bleak one, bleakness has nothing whatever to do with pessimism. The central message of *T & C* is not the base and cowardly one of *Othello* — "As flies to wanton boys are we to the gods. They kill us for their sport." — but a stern and unsentimental one, precisely the kind we have a duty to impart to young people before they begin to imitate their elders and become slobbering sentimentalists, willing to embrace any fiction about human nature that will leave them to their physical comfort, their intellectual torpor, and their moral complacency. In essence this message is identical to that implicit in the Eastern conception of *karma*: All that each of us thinks and does comes back to us, so that a world of poor thinkers and lazy and dishonorable actors will inevitably be a bleak one. There is of course nothing "pessimistic" about such a message, in that as soon as men and women decide to cast off the spiritual sloth they wrap around themselves like a security blanket, and walk forth to become cogent thinkers and genuine do-gooders, they will get precisely the world their thoughts and actions have merited them: a just and happy one.

Having mentioned *Othello* in passing, I might note, in closing, that in my view there is a whole world of difference, intrinsically but above all pedagogically, between the honest bleakness of a *T & C* [27] and the Sturm und Drang of an *Othello* or a *Richard*

---

[27] As Shaw notes in a number of different contexts, the Shakespeare who penned this play was the highly conscientious artist, not the fashionable dramatist cranking out *Winter's Tale*'s to give his rich audience the bucolic pipe-dreams they craved, and himself wider property holdings in Stratford.

III, even a *Lear*. (After all, if *Lear* doesn't offer us "Storm and Stress," what work does?)

The latter type of play — one which, students doubtless recognize almost intuitively, is (like so much of Eugene O'Neill) far too full of ranting and raving to bear much resemblance to real life — is likely simply to overawe the student, rather than force him to take a long look at the dark side of human life. A balanced syllabus, in my view, would be one that contained many works which are affirmative or even downright cheery (something it is quite possible to be while still being morally serious) and others that take a hard look at real, unglamorous, banal human evil, not at the hokey, overwrought, *Richard III*-ish dramatic parodies of it. Needless to say, in my opinion *Troilus and Cressida* is preeminent among works of the latter type.

Postscript: Two other reasons teachers might cite to back up their decision to teach *T & C*: 1) If, as I believe is the case, far more of today's students are encountering the *Odyssey* than the *Iliad*, it is certainly better that they should become acquainted with Shakespeare's version of the story that is in many ways the first and greatest (secular) tale of Western civilization than with none at all; 2) if one were to teach Shakespeare's version of the story in conjunction with Chaucer's, there would be endless opportunities for students to "compare and contrast."

KING LEAR

While critics are free to disagree as to whether *King Lear* is Shakespeare's greatest or most successful play, if they are responsible they can hardly fail to acknowledge that it contains speeches and scenes — notably Lear's mad divagations in Act IV, scene vi, surely one of the most extraordinary things in literature — so superlative that they transform the critic who sets out to praise them into yet another "poor Tom," stammering and sputtering but finding no words with which to praise so great a Maker.

It should hardly surprise us, then, given the fact that for most of us *Lear* is *Hamlet*'s only possible co-claimant to the title of greatest play in all of Shakespeare, that teachers do seem to throw caution to the winds and attempt to teach it to secondary students. While I'm sure that so great a work must have at least some effect on the student who studies it, I do have the gravest doubts as to whether secondary students are likely to a) cope well with this work's *very* considerable difficulties of language, b) grasp the real import of its protagonist's torment (rather than merely compassionate with him in a general way), or c) learn as much about parent-child relationships as some might suppose one could from a play in which all events and emotions are set in motion by filial ingratitude, both supposed and real. Let us first take a brief look at the "logistical" problem — *Lear* as a problematic reading experience for the secondary student— and then see if we can determine whether this is preeminently a play about hard-hearted young people or about insufficiently wise old people, and — if such a distinction can indeed be made — whether it is likely to prove a pedagogically idle one.

Of course one of the chief glories of *Lear* is the Fool, and this not so much because he talks glorious nonsense as because his seeming nonsense masks the profoundest sense (and sensibility). In this he stands in marked and blessed contrast to many another fool in Shakespeare, whose nonsense is all too often truly nonsensical or, when it does convey a deeper sense, a relatively paltry sense, unendowed with any of that tragic and moral resonance that distinguishes that of Lear's Fool.

Yet it is precisely because virtually every one of the Fool's utterances is fraught with moral meaning, and even the intelligent adult reader has to ponder long and hard the deepest significance of each (generally only after he has first consulted the explanatory note), that his riddles, rhymes, and conundrums are certain to give the adolescent pause — a pause that may well lengthen into a considerable break in his concentration, or indeed his reading. And when we consider as well that the Fool is the most straightforward man alive in comparison with poor Tom, whose sublime gibberish sends every reader scurrying to the notes for explication, and that the ravings of the mad Lear — inexpressibly delightful though they are to the mature mind — are sure to perplex the immature one, one has some idea of the reading difficulties a true madman, a feigned madman, and a jesting mad man can pose for the student reader.

Given what a daunting gauntlet of wordplay our students must pass through if they are to seize the pedagogic prize held out for them at its end — some revelation of truth — we, the teachers who send them through it by having them study *Lear*, ought to be able to assure both ourselves and them that the prize is one a young person will very much benefit from possessing. If we are to be in a position to do that, we must first arrive at some agreement as to whether one of the two readily apparent themes in *Lear* is in fact more potent and predominating, and if so whether it is this theme that has the most to "say" to adolescents.

At first glance one might assume that *King Lear* is about exactly what Lear himself would tell us it is about, "filial ingratitude." Yet while of course this *is* to a certain extent what *Lear* is about, and while it is Lear's mistreatment at his older daughters' hands that elicits the viewer's pity, what seizes the viewer with "terror" (i.e., fascinated mental interest), and what really makes *Lear* the world's foremost tragedy, is the specter of a rash and choleric old man being schooled by the elements in judgment and mercy.

By contrast, Regan and Goneril (and Edmund as well) are dramatically necessary but humanly improbable and intellectually uninteresting. Shakespeare the dramatist needs such stage villains to move the action along and to mesmerize the groundlings (always convinced that they are seeing "absolute evil" depicted with uncanny accuracy), so that Shakespeare the poet-philosopher may be free to lavish all the care and attention of a doting father on Lear, Cordelia, Kent, the Fool, Edgar, and Gloucester. The reader who expects to learn something of value about the moral ambiguities that dog parent-child relationships when she studies the relationship between Goneril and Regan and their father surely will be disappointed, particularly if she has heeded well that between Hal and King Henry, Jessica and Shylock, Miranda and Prospero, Hamlet and Gertrude, Imogen and Cymbeline, Juliet and Capulet.

Now if we are right in thinking that *Lear* is not really an examination of the how and why of filial ingratitude, but rather a kind of extended meditation on Blake's maxim, "If the fool would persist in his folly he would become wise," it can only be plain that the latter theme has far less to offer the young than the former might have. Every adult, however intelligent, often has had cause to lament his deeply ingrained foolishness, and to suffer from his seeming inability to learn any lesson once and for all. The young, by contrast, have not gone far enough down the road to self-knowledge to know how often one must sit by the side of the road, head in hands, bewailing the high number of obstacles one has placed in one's own path. Even if it did have some experience of how rocky this road can be, Youth, always cocksure to the point of arrogance and beyond, would be utterly loath to confess as much, and even less willing to acknowledge that the stumbling steps of another sojourner there bear a remarkable resemblance to its own.

It should also be noted that the young are in no position to learn the chief lesson the school of hard knocks teaches both Lear and Gloucester, that of the world's crying, undying need for social justice: "distribution should undo excess,/And each man have enough." For while it is true that the young — to their infinite credit — are keenly aware of life's inequities, and feel tenderly for the outcasts of our society, the compassion that is native to youth all too often suffers eclipse when advancing years and the need to make a living come between us and our better selves. It is not the kind-hearted but ethically untested youth, but rather the worldly middle-aged man or woman — financially secure but spiritually underdeveloped and therefore morally at risk — who is likely to be rocked to the core of his or her being by Lear's words, some of the simplest and mightiest in all of literature:

> O, I have ta'en
> Too little care of this! Take physic, pomp;
> Expose thyself to feel what wretches feel,
> That thou mayst shake the superflux to them,
> And show the heavens more just.   [III, iv]

I can only conclude by saying that, while the pedagogic energy expended in teaching *King Lear* to young people could never be entirely wasted, the level of waste is, almost certainly, prohibitively high. Our chief task as educators should be to make our students as wise as young people can be, so that as few as possible will find themselves (forty years hence), Lear-like, striking their foreheads and cursing themselves for their stupidity. That even the wisest of us adults spend an extraordinary amount of our time in forehead-striking is no real argument for asking the young to witness such a spectacle, or to write down on paper their reactions to this most bizarre of adult pastimes.

THE TEMPEST

For the adult, and particularly the adult who has an extensive knowledge of the life and works of Shakespeare, the viewing of a superb performance of *The Tempest* can only be a deeply moving experience. This is the Swan of Avon's swan song, a mature artist's bittersweet valedictory to his art, and its prevailing mood is one of pathos. The question before us here is whether the adolescent is likely to savor as well as his elders this work's distinctly autumnal flavor, or to be moved almost to tears, as they are, by Prospero's final speeches. Should we harbor any doubt on points such as these, we would do well to entertain even graver doubts as to our wisdom in having made *The Tempest* a cornerstone of our curricula.

Yet before we can arrive at any sober judgment as to the pedagogic wisdom of asking young people to study a work whose central theme is that of the artist's role in society (or even, one might say — given this play's grandeur of vision — in the cosmos), we as teachers must first arrive at a consensus that this is in fact the work's deepest theme, and one that has been set to work there by a masterful and fully conscious artist — a Caliban entirely at the service of its Prospero. This is likely to prove more difficult than one might at first have imagined, and for two reasons.

First, many academics have been taught to scream bloody murder at the slightest sign of encroachment by the allegoric into the domain of the purely fictive. They are likely to resist the commonsensical notions that a) Prospero is at least as much Shakespeare's alter ego as he is any autonomous, full-blooded "creation," and that b) *The Tempest*, while it is certainly not allegory proper, *is* a kind of quasi-allegory, or fable. This is unfortunate, in that the mature mind, more disposed to revel in truth wherever it finds it than to fastidiously reject all works that fail to fall into its favored categories, can accept with perfect good humor the allegoric elements in *The Tempest* and never dream of demoting it to a lesser artistic rank merely on their account.

Second, doubtless there are at least a few teachers out there who are also bardolators of a very curious stripe, those who feel that they are exalting their Bard by conceiving of him as a "natural," a naif warbling his native wood notes wild, who was scarcely conscious of the deepest themes at work throughout his plays. One can only demand of such readers whether they honestly think a genius of Shakespeare's stamp could have written a line such as "And deeper than did ever plummet sound / I'll drown my book" without being fully aware of its relation to his own situation, that of a veteran artist retiring to live the life of a gentleman farmer. All those who think of Shakespeare as "sweet fancy's child," a kind of barefoot boy of genius, would be well advised to heed Emerson's far more telling assessment:

> It takes an ounce to balance an ounce, and deep
> thought and the keenest insight into all parts of society and
> all the acts of life cannot be evinced by a profligate and a
> buffoon.[28]

At any rate, let us assume that we teachers have concurred
— at least tentatively and for the time being — that this theme
of the artist in society is indeed at the core of *The Tempest*, and
let us assume as well that we are willing to take up the task,
however onerous, of revealing this theme to our students. Surely
it is worth pausing a moment to weigh just how heavy a burden
that may prove to be, lest we discover too late that it is we
rather than our students who are doing all of the intellectual
heavy lifting.

The primary point to be made in any argument against
teaching *The Tempest* to adolescents is that the figure of the
artist, which looms so large in the inner vision of the middle-
aged academic, is an almost invisible one to the average young
person. For while he may to some limited extent be consciously
aware that writers, painters, musicians, etc. constitute a class routinely referred to as "artists," it is almost certain that none of
these intrigues him as much as the businessman, the athlete, or
the entertainer. Of course many an academic, while admitting that
there is truth in such an observation, will go on to insist that this
only makes it all the more imperative that we teach works such
as *The Tempest* (and *Portrait of the Artist*, etc.) in order to make
our students vividly aware of the artist and his social significance.

The problem with such a position is that it asks the student
to show an interest in someone who provides a certain social service long before he has gained any clear conception of what that
service is. Seeing as he reveres the businessman simply because
he (the student) knows the value of a dollar, the athlete because
he admires physical grace and courage, and the entertainer
because he loves a good laugh or a good song, it seems certain
that he will come to genuinely respect the artist only when he
has been deeply impressed by one or the other of his artistic
feats. We teachers should be wise enough to realize that a young
person must ponder long and hard (throughout the secondary
years) the social significance of many a cultural artifact, before he

[28]Emerson, op. cit., p. 315.

can at last (in the college years and beyond) direct his gaze to the face of the artificer himself.[29]

Thus far it has been suggested that many teachers will be loath to analyze too closely, or at all, *The Tempest*'s central theme, and that even those who are willing to do so may find their task a lonely and thankless one. The question before us now is this: If we are still determined to teach *The Tempest*, even suspecting as we now do that its loftiest theme will soar over our students' heads as swiftly and invisibly as another Ariel, what exactly will we be teaching? Perhaps it would be prudent, before we attempt to answer that question, to pose and answer a far simpler one: Why is *The Tempest* one of the firmest fixtures in many a syllabus, the seventh most commonly taught play nationwide?

Surely *The Tempest* is taught so widely for essentially the same reasons as *Midsummer* is taught widely, i.e., because both are intensely charming fairy tales, and because it is assumed, probably with good reason, that such plays will have an immediate appeal — at least of a superficial sort — for young people. After all, any play containing Ariel and Caliban, a man mistaken for a fish, love at oh-so-first sight, bad men restrained from their badness by magic spells, etc. etc., could hardly fail to arouse at least *some* interest in today's video-glutted young person.

Now as I hope I have made clear, I am not so foolish as to underrate the importance of choosing plays that tickle a young person's fancy, nor so obdurate as to close my ears to the Bard's words of good counsel: "no profit grows where is no pleasure ta'en." Yet I continue to insist that as educators we have a duty to ensure that wherever pleasure is being taken there is indeed also some profit growing. Let us pause for a moment to see just how much intellectual significance we can discern in two of those crowd-pleasing elements of *The Tempest* glanced at above, Ariel and Caliban, and then go on to ask ourselves (proceeding along exactly the same route of inquiry as that we followed in the commentary on *Hamlet*) just how much of that significance the average seventeen-year-old is likely to be alive to.

Ariel and Caliban are of course two of Shakespeare's most memorable creations, and any human spirit who aspires to the former's sensitivity or the latter's bluntness of speech could do naught but speak highly of them. Nonetheless, I do take gentle

---

[29]Of course secondary students do research and write about the lives and works of favorite authors, but I'll stand by my generalization as being, in the main, an accurate and useful one.

issue with Hazlitt's assertion that "nothing was ever more finely conceived than this contrast between the material and the spiritual, the gross and the delicate."[30] None would deny that this contrast has indeed been finely conceived and even more ably executed, but is Hazlitt right to imply that it is the fineness of the conception he describes that makes Ariel and Caliban two of Shakespeare's most sublime creations? For if it is merely a question of creating and contrasting a feminine spirit, all grace and sensibility, with a masculine demon, all brute power and earthiness, we might find that there is less to choose than we had at first supposed between an Ariel/Caliban and a Cathy/Heathcliff or an Esmerelda/Quasimodo.

No, what makes Ariel and Caliban figures as fascinating to the mind as they are fantastic to the eye is not the fact that one of them is an air-spirit and the other an earth-spirit, but the extraordinary uses to which Shakespeare — and Prospero — has put them. The real significance of Ariel is not that she is an air-spirit, or even the spirit of delicacy and spirituality, but that she represents, in her relation to Prospero, the (potential) ability of the artistic imagination to serve as a kind of courier (or Hermes) for the fully awakened moral faculty (Prospero being a kind of regenerated Zeus).

So too, Caliban's relation to Prospero is far more complex and problematic than that of mere primordial beast to fully evolved man. On the one hand, Caliban surely represents — and one need not be a Marxist to assert as much — the downtrodden proletariat. For while to a certain extent we are willing to take at face value Prospero's estimation of him ("Filth as thou art"), we cannot help but see in Prospero's exploitation of him ("We cannot miss him. He does make our fire,/Fetch in our wood, and serves in offices/That profit us.") a clear parallel with the polished but iniquitous world of ancient Greece, where an acropolis of fine words and thoughts was reared up on the backs of all-too-human caryatids: women and slaves.

Then too, as much or more as Caliban symbolizes all that segment of society that does our dirty work and receives for its pains our dirty looks, so too he is the living embodiment of all that moral insensibleness, rank stupidity, and base ingratitude that exists within all of us, whether we be Prosperos or Antonios. It is precisely because Caliban represents *both* our intractable social ills — made intractable largely because of our protracted failure to

[30]Hazlitt, op. cit., p. 93.

face up to them — *and* the "old Adam" within each of us that we also are too cowardly to look in the eye, that Prospero's final acceptance of him is one of the monumental things in the literature of the world: "this thing of darkness/I acknowledge mine."

Let us remember that we have lingered thus long on Ariel and Caliban only in order to determine, if we can, whether *The Tempest* — even when stripped of its central theme — still has a good deal to offer the student that she is in a position, intellectually, to accept and make good use of. While our discussion has made it clear that Ariel and Caliban are indeed figures of intense intellectual interest to the adult mind, to me at least it seems certain that the adolescent who beholds in Prospero only a wizard on the order of Gandalf rather than an artist on the order of Shakespeare will also be she who sees in these two not the complex and symbolically significant spirits we have managed to descry, but only the rather banal air-spirit and earth-spirit we spoke of a moment ago.

Nor is the reason for this far to seek. Ariel and Caliban being, in essence, simply emanations of Propero's — the artist's — spirit, it stands to reason that the student who is too immature to recognize an artist when he sees one will also never be struck by the distinct likeness between the artist and his creations. When one goes on to consider that these three — Prospero, Ariel, Caliban — have, between them, a virtual monopoly on *The Tempest*'s store of intellectual significance, one is driven to the conclusion that, for the student whose incomprehension of these three has effectively locked him out of that store, *The Tempest* can only be a rather amusing little fable — a fable without even a moral to boast of — not the great, resonant work of art it is for his elders.

Are his elders content that this should continue to be so? That our juniors and seniors should go on frittering away their time on a — *to them* — amoral tale, when they should be toning their moral muscle on a *Hamlet*, a *Cymbeline*, a *Troilus and Cressida*, a *Measure for Measure*? If in fact that thought troubles my colleagues more than a little, then the pedagogic writing is as clear as graffiti on a classroom wall: Painful as the process certainly will be for those who love it well, *The Tempest* must be banished from the syllabus. In order that my colleagues may better steel themselves to do that which, in my view, has to be done, I now offer them a few additional thoughts as to the inappropriateness of teaching *The Tempest* to *today's* youths in particular.

There can be little doubt that one of the chief functions of secondary education should be to introduce young people to moral complexity as a fact of life — in most respects, *the* fact of life — and to make them aware that life's evils — while always, it is to be hoped, of lesser importance and influence than the goods — are all too real, and demand of us all the courage and conviction we can muster if we are to vanquish them, or at least keep them indefinitely at bay. The need for such an educational emphasis on the seeming intractability of both social and personal ills has never been greater than in our own day, and this for two reasons.

First, modern life is so surfeited with pleasures and comforts — any one of which our overworked and underfed ancestors might well have given a right arm for — that the tendency to dismiss all of life's ills (petty and great) as things of no consequence, to be dismissed with a shrug and a smile as we pop another tape in the VCR, has never been so pronounced. (This remains roughly true, in my judgment, even with the recent rise of "compassion chic" in pop and rock culture.)

Second, this tendency to dismiss all of life's unpleasantness as mere illusion has been immeasurably exacerbated by the way in which our movie and video culture — an enormous influence on all of us, but particularly the young — is perpetually suggesting to us that all of life's ills will miraculously disappear if we will only consent to regress to the moral and intellectual level of four-year-olds, sucking our thumbs in the complacent conviction that, because we are "good at heart," we can do no evil nor have evil done to us. (Some films that spring to mind in this regard are *E.T.: The Extraterrestrial* and *Field of Dreams*, as well as the book *Everything I Really Need To Know I Learned in Kindergarten*.) In other words, Huxley's brave new world, in which the sybaritic and the insipid feed on and foster each other, is in most respects very definitely upon us, and today's movies (with their Dolby sound etc.) are nothing if not his "feelies."

Thus I would suggest that if we wish to follow Neil Postman's advice in his *Teaching as a Conserving Activity* and seek always to counteract in the classroom the specific negative influences acting upon students in the culture at large[31], we can ill afford to present Prospero to them as merely the most recent in

---

[31]Neil Postman, *Teaching as a Conserving Activity* (New York: Delacorte Press, 1979), p. 131.

a long line of intergalactic wizards, whisking them off in his spaceship (the *U.S.S. Ariel*) to an amoral paradise where the good never suffer (or at least only suffer retrospectively, like Prospero, or very temporarily, like Ferdinand) and the bad perpetually amuse us by playing the role of funny drunkards up to their noses in a smelly swamp.

If I appear merely churlish in wresting so pleasant a fable from the hands of the young before they have a chance to misinterpret it as being only a pleasant fable, I would simply remind my reader that Prospero himself, in his relation to Ferdinand, is a model pedagogue, insisting that he struggle, and come to terms with pain and sacrifice, in order that he may thereby prove himself worthy of — and more capable of appreciating — the divine Miranda.

Postscript: In offering my colleagues so many rather highfalutin reasons for refraining from teaching *The Tempest* at the secondary level, I have perhaps neglected to state one rather simple one. To wit, while of course all of the Shakepeare plays are *plays*, meant to be performed, some are more clearly "performance pieces" than others, and these tend to just lie there on the printed page, like fish very much out of water. In my estimation *The Tempest* (despite, or perhaps because of, its inherent difficulties of production — Ariel, etc.) is the "performance piece" to top them all. For instance, a seemingly slight but actually rather central scene (II, ii), that in which Trinculo creeps under Caliban's garberdine (speaking of fish out of water!) packs a punch only about one one-hundredth as powerful when it is read as when it is seen.

Given these considerations, I would here enunciate a principle that I will have cause to invoke more than once before the final page of this book: While of course students should always see a performance of the play they are studying whenever that is possible, if a play absolutely *has* to be seen to be even *partly* appreciated, it is probably not the right work for classroom study. Thus, while no one would deny that *Hamlet, Merchant,* or *Henry IV* (to take a few examples more or less at random) are never truly themselves until they have been given life on the stage, the fact remains that with them the average reader can get by quite well, and even enjoy staging the play in his or her own imagination. By contrast, a farce such as *Shrew* or *Merry Wives,* or a spectacle such as *Henry VIII*, are all but unstagable within the "wooden O" of one's cranium.

Twelfth Night is in some respects one of the most genuinely comic of Shakespeare's "comedies." At its center stands that formidable three-headed fool — "Have you seen the picture of we three?" — Malvolio, Sir Toby, and Sir Andrew. In performance it is a delight, and the smile-ridden Malvolio is without doubt the single funniest bit of business Shakespeare ever put on the stage. Surely, then, the teacher who introduces her pupils to so zany a crew will be doing them a favor?

Not necessarily, by any means. Not only is it truer of *Twelfth Night* than of most of the other "comedies" that it must be seen to be heartily laughed at (particularly the dressing down of Malvolio by means of some garters and yellow stockings), but the student who reads this play is likely to have other difficulties of visualization as well. Whereas he can readily identify with, for instance, the protagonists in *As You Like It*, in that those characters have a certain universality about them, his attempts to summon up an accurate image of the chief comic characters in *Twelfth Night* may be thwarted by the fact that all three are figures notably of one time — the Renaissance — and one place — England. He will be able to appreciate both the characterizations and the humor in this play far less fully than the adult, simply because he has not had the adult's opportunity to store up mental images of various medieval and Renaissance "types" through years of reading and picture-viewing.

For instance, the educated adult knows that Malvolio is buoyed up in his pompous pride by the rising tide of Puritanism in England, and she understands as well that Sir Toby's seemingly casual confrontation with Malvolio ("Dost thou think because thou art virtuous, there shall be no more cakes and ale?") is in fact a moment of genuinely epochal significance: Merrie Old England confronting sober New England. So too a cultivated adult can call up the image of Sir Andrew at a moment's notice: thinner than a rail; sallow-skinned and dim-witted from too much beef and sack and not enough fresh fruit and vegetables; something unwholesome about the thin, lank hair — in short, a rake, but one too ugly, stupid, and thin-blooded to cut much of a figure, much less a caper. While it might be argued that a dedicated teacher could supply the student with enough historical information to allow him to appreciate the rising hostility between Puritans and Cavaliers in English society, and Malvolio and Sir Toby thereby, Sir Andrew's is a figure that simply cannot be sketched in a day or even a week — it must slowly take shape in a cultured mind over a lifetime.

Doubtless many of my readers are perplexed by the fact that I seem to be confining my analysis to the comic butts in this work, and utterly neglecting the romantic leads: Viola, Olivia, the Duke, et al. Alas, I must confess that I wish I could go on neglecting them indefinitely, for I am one of those heretical few for whom the mismatched lovers in this tale have almost no appeal. In my view *Twelfth Night* stands or falls on its farcical elements, let the mood music of love play on as it will. For the fact is that the romantic figures in this play not only aren't very likable, they're downright annoying: Orsino, the walking basket case; Olivia, "the marble-breasted tyrant"; and Viola, the — dare I utter the dread word? — *perky* . . . .

At this point my critics may be crying out, and quite rightly, that the above paragraph should be stricken from the record, as being utterly at variance with the stated first principle of this book, to wit, that a curriculum should reflect the predilections of its student users, not its adult makers. The objection is sustained, but if the reader will give the prosecution a chance it now will endeavor to supply proof somewhat more positive that there are indeed aspects of the romantic side of *Twelfth Night* that make it a work notably less suited to adolescents than, for example, *As You Like It.*

Chief among these must be the mood of muddled yet potent eroticism, and the confusion as to sex roles, that pervades this play. As we know from the Sonnets and from aspects of some of the other plays (for instance, the relationship between Antonio and Bassanio in *Merchant*), the cultivated Elizabethan pushed his conception of ideal male friendship to the brink of pederasty, and perhaps beyond. While I am not such a prude or a "homophobe" as to suggest that young people observing the rather odd relationship between Orsino and Cesario/Viola are in any danger of being morally tainted by it, I would assert that this kind of Platonic sensualism meant far more to a cultivated Elizabethan than it can ever mean to us moderns. To an adolescent, of course, it probably will mean precisely nothing, and seem far more silly than risqué.

The reader who wishes to dismiss the above speculations as so much highbrow tosh could point to Rosalind/Ganymede in *As You Like It* (or for that matter Imogen/Fidele in *Cymbeline*, Portia/Balthasar in *Merchant*, etc. etc.) and demand of me what right I have to grow so Freudian in my analysis of the play I like less but not at all in that of the one I like far more. To this I can only say that a comparison of the two plays clearly reveals that in the one play Shakespeare fitted a woman with a man's clothes so that he might create an atmosphere of androgyny, in the other to allow her to exult, by means of some very conscious play-acting, in that sense of moral authority and dominating physical presence that thitherto only the male of the species had had the opportunity to revel in.

Note, for instance, that the attraction Olivia feels toward Cesario/Viola is largely a physical one ("I do I know not what, and fear to find/Mine eye too great a flatterer for my mind") whereas what Phoebe loves in Rosalind is the moral fervor that animates Ganymede whenever he upbraids her for her arrogance ("I had rather hear you chide than this man woo."). Then too, while Rosalind seems to have been transformed spiritually as well as physically when she became Ganymede, suddenly being full of passionate joy ("What said he? How looked he?"), triumphantly mocking irony ("Men have died from time to time, and worms have eaten them, but not for love"), and moral imperiousness ("Who might be your mother,/That you insult, exult, and all at once,/Over the wretched?"), Viola is the very soul of unliberated womanhood: All she can do is mope over Orsino and "let concealment, like a worm i' th' bud,/Feed on her damask cheek."

Now if any of the preceding speculations should prove to be on the mark, and if it is in fact the case that students have difficulty understanding, not to mention appreciating, both the farcical and the romantic aspects of *Twelfth Night*, what are we to make of the fact that, according to the survey, it is the ninth most commonly taught play nationwide? Surely it will come as no surprise to my reader what *I* make of it: *Twelfth Night* is a work that is of great appeal to the middle-aged academic (it ranks sixth in the survey's "teacher favorites" category — p. 235), and therefore, like the boy who presents his mother with a new train set on Christmas day, he insists on bestowing on his students an intellectual gift quite certain to mean far less to them than it does to him. If this is true, it might be worthwhile to pause for a moment longer, so that we may explore two of the more plausible reasons for the popularity of this play with teachers.

One of those reasons, almost certainly, is that teachers, like all adults, have learned over the course of an often harried and worried lifetime how rare and precious a tonic laughter is, and they in particular are in a position to know that in all of literature there are few moments of merriment more pure and refreshing than those in *Twelfth Night* featuring Malvolio. Yet surely one can savor these moments every bit as fully as one's colleagues and still suggest that, if one is indeed going to present a play to students primarily so they can share some laughter with their teacher (questionable as such a rationale is, in and of itself), one has a professional obligation to calculate very precisely the odds in favor of the student's being able first to get the joke, and then to genuinely appreciate it. As I have gone to some lengths to demonstrate, those odds may be by no means as good as some innocently have assumed them to be.

My guess as to the other reason *Twelfth Night* is so popular a play with the middle-aged may strike some as outlandish, but I will be so bold as to offer it to them nonetheless. To wit, the weltschmerz in which this work is steeped is essentially identical to that particular form of world-weariness all of us over thirty-five begin to feel, when we wake up one morning with a start to the discovery that sex basically means reproduction, not passion (preeminently the male delusion) or love (the female delusion). Laughable as it may sound (and in most respects is), it is in fact no easy thing to look back over twenty or so years of life and face the fact that for a good part of it one has been little other than the dupe of one's hormones. In our effort to avoid having to do so, we of the "thirtysomething" crowd are apt to adopt any and every stratagem that will aid us in our effort to reinstate the erotic impulse as our rightful sovereign and banish that pesky pretender to the throne, Right Reason. Seen in this light, *Twelfth Night* is clearly the *thirtysomething* of Shakespeare plays: It is populated by whining melancholics, trying desperately to jump-start their run-down sexual batteries by applying the various shocks of music, sexual role-playing, and emotional binging.

I can only conclude from all of this that the teacher who envies her students both their innocence and their passion will be doing them a favor if she keeps both her middle-aged blahs and her love for *Twelfth Night* to herself. (As to the former, she may be more inclined to listen to Falstaff's words of wisdom on the subject than mine: "You that are old consider not the capacities of us that are young: you do measure the heat of our livers by the bitterness of your galls.") What young people need to absorb from great literature is not angst but a sense of the awesome power of human passion and of the grave dangers attendant upon its misuse. Given the fact that the canon is rich in works that trade in precisely that theme — *Antony and Cleopatra*, *T & C*, *Measure for Measure*, *R & J*, *Cymbeline* (to mention only those that are, in my opinion, pedagogically suitable) — the wise teacher would do well to stick to these, resting assured that her students will indeed make the acquaintance of *Twelfth Night* some moonlit summer-stock evening twenty years hence, to laugh and sigh in equal measure at what fools these lovers be — and were.

MUCH ADO ABOUT NOTHING

It is a striking and amusing fact that two of Shakespeare's best-known works — *As You Like It* and *Much Ado About Nothing* — are also his best titled. *As You Like It* really is Shakespearean "comedy" as we (or at least I) like it, but about *Much Ado* we can never quite shake the feeling that, for all of its surface attractions, it is hollow and lifeless at the core. Two of those numerous defects in this work which, when added together, go to form that empty zero, come immediately to mind.

First, and most importantly, *Much Ado*'s central plot element — the disgrace, "death," and "resurrection" of Hero — is, for me at least, one of those exceptions that prove the rule: Yes, Shakespeare usually can transform even the tritest bits of melodrama into something magical and significant, but no, he hasn't succeeded in doing so here. This is, in the main, banal and tedious stuff.[32] Second, this play's villain, Don John, is entirely a *stage* villain (one can almost picture him twirling a handlebar mustache between his fingertips), a man who does his dirty deeds almost perfunctorily, with none of that devilish delight in evildoing that so endears to us a Iago or Richard III.

If then the "intrinsic" *Much Ado* is something of a dud, being unable to offer the reader even the wacky humor and pathos of a *Twelfth Night*, not to mention the high spirits and moral energy of an *As You Like It*, does the pedagogic *Much Ado* have much more to offer? I doubt it, and it would seem, judging by how relatively rarely this play is being taught (see survey, p. 227), that

[32]While I rarely find myself in total disagreement with any judgment of William Hazlitt's, I can only think Hazlitt has fallen victim to sentimentality when he asserts that "Hero is the principal figure of the piece, and leaves an indelible impression on the mind by her beauty, her tenderness, and the hard trial of her love." Op. cit, p. 235.

most of my colleagues doubt it as well. For while this play is of course a joy in performance, it is simply too weak intellectually for us to ask our upperclassmen to devote any time at all to the study of it, and a number of factors make it unsuitable for the junior high school student. Let's look at a few of them.

Let it be noted, first of all, that if an appropriate subtitle for *As You Like It* would be "Lessons in Love for Beginners," then *Much Ado*'s would have to be "Last Chance for Love." Beatrice and Benedick strike one as being the forerunners of Tracy and Hepburn, or the stars of the TV show *Moonlighting*: bickering middle-aged "lovers" who are not at all sure they have the time for, or much interest in, love. The audience for such comedy-dramas is largely made up of all of us real-life Benedicks and Beatrices, grad student types who appreciate a good quip better than good sex (or so we keep telling ourselves...). Junior high students are still too full of life, bless them, to have our genius for sublimation, which is only another way of saying that they are not Benedicks and Beatrices but Orlandos and Rosalinds.

Yet even if the passionate young reader had a real interest in tracing the trajectories of the lethal barbs shot back and forth by the hero and heroine of *Much Ado*, he or she almost certainly would have a great deal of difficulty in doing so. For instance, pretend that you're an early teen and train your gaze on this volley from Act I, scene i:

> *Beatrice.* I had rather hear my dog bark at a crow, than a man swear he loves me.
>
> *Benedick.* God keep your ladyship still in that mind, so some gentleman or other shall 'scape a predestinate scratched face.
>
> *Beatrice.* Scratching could not make it worse, an 'twere such a face as yours were.
>
> *Benedick.* Well, you are a rare parrot-teacher.
>
> *Beatrice.* A bird of my tongue is better than a beast of yours.
>
> *Benedick.* I would my horse had the speed of your tongue, and so good a continuer. But keep your way a God's name, I have done.
>
> *Beatrice.* You always end with a jade's trick; I know you of old.

This is the kind of repartee which, when bandied about onstage to the accompaniment of much mugging and posturing, wins an audience over, but which is of very limited charm when met with on the printed page. The jokes are few and strained, the occasions for consulting the notes to puzzle over this or that double entendre many. It seems certain that the adolescent reading these words will be very much nonplussed by them, and just as certain that if he sees the play in performance his interest will be entirely in the actors' body language, not in their language proper. In short, the more he enjoys *Much Ado* in performance the less likely it is he will learn from it, and the harder he tries to learn something from the text the more certain it is he will not enjoy it.

If then the prognosis for the pedagogic *Much Ado* seems a gloomy one, perhaps we shouldn't be so surprised to see two of Shakespeare's most amusing rude mechanicals — Dogberry and Verges — driving the final nails into its coffin. For it does seem to me that the early adolescent is no more likely to see the humor in a bumbling malapropist such as Dogberry than he does in a bombastic thespian such as Bottom, and for the very same reason. As I pointed out in my commentary on *Midsummer*, the thirteen- or fourteen-year-old is himself too consummate a rude mechanical to see anything funny in the conduct of his fellow guild-members. To do so he would have to be able to do the one thing he cannot do: see himself as adults see him.

THE TAMING OF THE SHREW

I had a good bit of fun one year teaching *The Taming of the Shrew*, yet I can't help but wonder if students really enjoy it as much as we teachers have supposed they must, or if we have been right in assuming that "farce" spells surefire classroom winner. While I'm not surprised that so accessible and entertaining a work is the eleventh most commonly taught play nationwide, I would suggest that it deserves to keep that relatively high ranking only if we are convinced it is bringing our students a good deal of unalloyed pleasure. Seeing as I have no way of knowing for certain whether it is in fact doing so (although its seventh-place finish in the survey's "student favorites" category suggests that it may be), perhaps the best I can do here is play devil's advocate, and bring to my colleagues' attention certain aspects of this work likely to detract from student enjoyment.

The most salient fact about *Shrew* is, as we have mentioned, that it is a farce, and all logic would suggest that farce, far from being ideal for the classroom, would be the form of comedy least suited to book-study. I well recall the look of stunned disbelief on my students' faces when, their long slog of reading through the play in class at last over and done with, they set eyes on the Burton-Taylor movie. Clearly they were dumbfounded by the discovery that somewhere within all that Elizabethan verbiage (rhymes with garbage?) they had stumbled over for so long, there had lurked all along this riotous world of color, buffoonery, sex, and laughter. As they feasted their eyes on all of this, and as I feasted my eyes on them as they at last got some pure enjoyment out of Shakespeare, I couldn't help but wonder if the payoff had really made the long slog worth it, from their point of view.

If there is a moral to the above tale, doubtless it is that a farce such as *Shrew* not only *must* be seen in one form or another, but must be seen *before* the student has read too far into the play and concluded that the whole thing is a colossal drag. Thus, either the Burton-Taylor, the John Cleese (BBC), or some other video must be gotten ahold of and shown either before reading or after each act or scene. (In my case I had to pay for the video rental out of my own pocket, in that the public school where I was then teaching hadn't "authorized" me to show the film at all. I mention this fact not to prove what a great guy I am, but to underscore my deeply held conviction that students have a *right* to see every Shakespeare play they read, a right we teachers probably too often trample on, citing lack of time, etc.).

One aspect of this farce that gave my students — and, I confess, myself — a great deal of trouble as they were reading it, and that the viewing of one of the videos before or during reading doubtless would have made less vexing, is the swapping of identities between Tranio and Lucentio, with the furthur complication that Lucentio masquerades as one Cambio, Hortensio as Licio. For while in performance a character is always clearly himself, however many names he might assume, the student who is reading the play, and who has none of a character's physical features before her eyes to help distinguish him from all other characters, is compelled to continually make mental computations along the lines of "Lucentio" = Tranio, "Cambio" = Lucentio, "Licio" = Hortensio. These, as far as I can determine, distract the student mightily, and go a long way toward making the reading of *Shrew* a chore rather than a joy.

Another slight cause for pedagogic concern when teaching *Shrew* is, of course, the Induction, a framing device that Shakespeare inherited from a previous version of the play but left without its closing bracket in his version. While perhaps my colleagues have found ways of making the Induction at least moderately interesting to their students, I found it to be little more than a nuisance, particularly given its murderously high level of archaisms: in the first few lines alone, "pheeze," "paucas pallabris," "Sessa," etc. If one of our best reasons for teaching *Shrew* is to show students that Shakespeare was no mere bookworm or fuddy-duddy but a man of raucous and zesty good humor, we might do better to razor-blade the Induction pages out of every student copy of the play (joke!) than to throw such a wet gray of blanket of words over our students' heads before the party has even begun.

Needless to say, none of the negative pedagogic factors I have thus far enumerated is so formidable that it need dissuade the teacher intent on teaching *Shrew* from doing so. It is one of the most purely fun of Shakespeare's plays — at least if one takes its sexism, as surely one must, with a boulder-sized grain of salt — and we could do worse than prove to our students that the Bard was the very reverse of a killjoy — as long as we remain committed, elsewhere in the syllabus, to doing even better by teaching more morally rigorous plays.

RICHARD III

It seems clear, from comments made by quite a few survey respondents, that many teachers think it prudent, when charting a Shakespeare course, to steer well clear of the history plays. Nor can one begrudge them their circumspection if, as one suspects, it is *Richard III* that looms largest in their mind's eye, a huge and jagged rock closing fast just off the port bow.

For this play is in many respects *Henry VI, Part Four*, and only the reader who has read the earlier play (or at least Part

Three) can hope to make heads or tails of *Richard III*'s many references to the events that led the House of York to the English throne, or to appreciate where a character like Old Queen Margaret is (in the most literal sense) "coming from." In marked contrast to *Richard II* or *Henry IV*, where the student whose teacher has supplied him with a bit of background information can manage to fit into a chronological pattern the far fewer allusions to earlier events, the student studying *Richard III* has been given the unenviable — yea, virtually impossible — task of making some sense of a sequel without ever having read the work it succeeds. That that student has hardly relished the task is perhaps attested to by the fact that *Richard III* received not a single vote in the survey's "student favorites" category.

Yet even if *Richard III* could somehow be transformed into a play easy for the student to understand (and of course I'm not suggesting for a moment that *Henry VI* should be taught merely in order to make such a transformation possible), nothing could make it a play worthy of study at the secondary level. For, far from being the completely successful depiction of absolute evil that so many insist it is, in many respects *Richard III* is, as Shaw states[33], nothing more than Shakespeare's particularly brilliant rendition of the Punch drama, in which all of life's manifold and complex evils have been condensed, for our viewing pleasure, into one all-too-obvious hump on a puppet's back.

While one can of course get an intense, rather childish delight from watching Punch belabor his wife with a stick or Richard pile corpse upon corpse (and let there be no mistake, *Richard III is* spellbinding theater), there is about as much genuine intellectual interest in the one as in the other. For we teachers to ask our students to pay serious heed to so overly theatrical a creation as Richard makes about as much sense as demanding that they write a detailed psychological analysis of Punch, in his relation to Judy.

Of course some will continue to insist that Shakespeare's portrait of Richard is indeed an absolutely accurate likeness of absolute evil, and that as educators we have an obligation to make our students aware of the existence of such evil so that they may be in a better position to recognize and fight it throughout their lives. Let's begin by subjecting to closer scrutiny this notion that Richard is a credible super-villain, capable of arousing within us our deepest moral outrage, then go on to

[33] Wilson, ed., op. cit., p. 164.

examine the question of whether "absolute evil" is the evil we have the highest obligation to bring to our students' attention.

While one might wish to believe that, in studying a Richard III or an Iago, one is by implication studying a Hitler or a Stalin, one need only apply a simple test to prove that these stage villains are in fact as dissimilar as could be from their real-life counterparts. The salient characteristic of great evil, and of greatly evil men and women, is, as Hannah Arendt has made clear to us, banality. The reason Mel Brooks can send up Nazidom so uproariously in *The Producers* is that Hitler and his ilk are always completely humorless; were they otherwise, they would never provide such perfect fodder for the satirist.

By contrast, the Iagos and the Richard III's are always intensely alive to the black humor inherent in their black deeds, and love nothing more than to provoke the audience to a genuinely mirthful laughter, and to a rubbing of the hands together in glee, by protesting to it (with a gigantic wink to the gallery) that (like Troilus) they are "weaker than a woman's tear;/Tamer than sleep, fonder than ignorance,/Less valiant than the virgin in the night,/And skilless as unpractised infancy." A typical such protest is that made by Richard in Act I, scene iii:

> Cannot a plain man live, and think no harm,
> But thus his simple truth must be abused
> With silken, sly, insinuating Jacks?

While life might be more amusing than it is if life's real villains consented to be so cheery and boldfaced in their blackguardism as a Richard or an Iago, the historical evidence — and the evidence of our own eyes and ears — suggests to us that they are generally humorless, brooding, and secretive.

Even if Richard III and Iago really were adequate pedagogic stand-ins for Hitler and Stalin, we certainly would err if we decided that the best way to introduce young people to the evil life does contain is by pointing out to them those few supremely wicked individuals in whom such evil has reached its apotheosis. For while of course false messiahs and charlatans of every description will always plague the human race to some extent, and while education can do a limited service in helping us to recognize them whenever and wherever they appear, education can do an almost unlimited service when it instills in young people two beliefs.

First, that while many of life's ills can indeed be traced to a relatively few genuinely evil, or at least thoroughly benighted individuals, ninety-five percent of them spring directly from the unglamorous, day-in, day-out follies and sins of all of us average folks. In this connection it is worth noting that there is all the difference in the world, in terms of the quality of a moral education, between the thought young people are likely to find themselves thinking as they read a work such as *Richard III* — "We have met the enemy and he is (thank God!) someone as different from us as could be imagined" — and the one they will be thinking as they read a *Troilus and Cressida*, a *Merchant*, a *Measure for Measure*: "We have met the enemy and he is — Oh my God! — *us*." Second, that precisely because evil is invariably human rather than superhuman in size, and because we humans are — thank God — always at least a little bigger than our sins and stupidities, we could wrestle it to the ground whenever we chose if only we would first a) turn to face the enemy, b) become conscious both of its strength, and of the fact that we are stronger still, and c) decide that it's time to get off our lazy rear ends and start to grapple with it.

As if it weren't enough that *Richard III* is a play full of historical allusions certain to perplex the student (or indeed, any) reader, and not so much a serious investigation into evil as a rather cheerful cavalcade of carnage, it is also of course a historical whitewash. The Richard Shakespeare gives us is the Richard of the Tudor historians, eager to prove that the Yorkist slain on Bosworth Field by the future Henry VII had been an incubus draining the lifeblood from the English nation. The real Richard bore not even the faintest resemblance to his evil Shakespearean twin, having been one of England's better kings (something perhaps not so hard to be, considering the quality of the competition!), without a humpback, and very likely unsullied by the blood of the two princes.

At this point the objection could be raised that Shakespeare's business as an artist was to draw from his own imagination a fascinating and believable creation, not to sketch a historical figure from the life. Two things might be said in response to this.

First, one of the real charms of the history plays in general is that we feel we are reading about real people and about events that actually occurred. Although the "histories" are of course rarely at all accurate as history, few are such whole-cloth fabrications as *Richard III*.

Second, if we are to accept Shakespeare's Richard as a valid creation quite distinct from the historical figure, we must feel that although he did not exist he *could* have existed. While human history has by no means been deficient in murdering monsters, it seems certain that villains who have combined utter moral depravity with an insouciant spirit have been rare. (Witness our own sense as modern Americans that there was something quite specially horrific about Ted Bundy, with his turtlenecks, his grin, and his purely evil nature.) And as we have seen, even such figures as have existed are not the proper focus of study for secondary school students, in that they delude the young person into thinking a) that evil is never petty and banal, but always rather exotic and entertaining and b) that evil is something that happens to — or rather *in* — the other guy, never in us.

ANTONY AND CLEOPATRA

For sheer delight, perhaps no other play in the canon can match *Antony and Cleopatra*. This play's variety of incident, marvelous characterizations, and above all its highly evocative poetry make it a joy to read, and certainly neither the teacher nor the student given the chance to share it in the classroom would have any reason to complain. As I see it *A & C* is one of the three relatively "amoral" Shakespeare plays (*Shrew* and *Midsummer* being the other two), plays that teach us little but delight us much, that we should always be pleased to invite into our classrooms — on the strict condition that more morally rigorous plays be on hand to greet them. Yet while I certainly would not spurn any opportunity to share *A & C* with students, I doubt whether I'd actively seek one out. Let's look at two of my reasons.

First, *A & C* is not as morally important a work as some might insist it is. Although the critic who finds himself in the presence of this most sensual and tantalizing of plays may be overcome with the desire to throw his pen and reading glasses into the fire, so that he can join Cleopatra on her couch, when and if he gets the better of himself he will concede that *T & C* — strumpet though she may appear to much of the world — would in fact make him a better wife.

While in name at least *A & C* is a "tragedy," and while there is — in theory, at any rate — a lesson to be learned here about the danger of neglecting duty and eschewing common sense in the name of love and passion, it seems safe to say that none of us is in much of a mind to learn it. We are so besotted by the sheer glamour of our title heroes that, like a drunk irritably shrugging off the bar owner's hand on his shoulder, we are in no mood to listen to counsels of moral sobriety. We know full well (as we knew when we followed with rapt interest the doings of the Liz and Dick who once portrayed these two) how much sheer weakness and folly there is to be found in a "great love affair," but we are not likely to follow Enobarbus's example and convert our knowledge into moral wisdom: "I see still a diminution in our captain's brain/Restores his heart...."

Second, *A & C*'s disregard of the dramatic unities (well nigh legendary, owing to the problems it has posed for generations of theatrical producers), which we are no longer disposed to think of as weakening the "intrinsic" play, may perhaps weaken the pedagogic one. This is not a *Macbeth* or an *R & J*, where events build steadily and relentlessly to great climaxes, but a rather discursive, episodic work, in which Shakespeare seems content to follow wherever his Plutarch leads him. (It might be objected that *Troilus* is equally episodic, but its intense moral dynamism charges each of its episodes, and the work as a whole, with an electric tension *A & C*, in its sleepy, sensual languor, can claim not a volt of.) The average student may be as content to mosey along with Shakespeare, glorying in the poetic and dramatic wildflowers crowding both sides of the path, as Shakespeare has been to follow Plutarch, but then again she may remember wistfully how a play such as *Macbeth* seemed to hurtle her forward toward its harrowing conclusion.

Perhaps the only way to bring this very inadequate assessment of *A & C* in the classroom to a close is to repeat that, for the most part, this is a work that brings its reader joy, not wisdom. While there can be little doubt that *A & C* eminently deserves the chance to prove itself in our classrooms, the only way we will ever be able to determine whether it deserves to remain there as something of a curricular fixture is first to give it that chance, and then to monitor closely just how much delight our students seem to be taking in it. If a great deal, then all is well; if only a moderate amount, then we owe it to our students to replace *Antony and Cleopatra* with a work of greater moral consequence. In this regard it must be noted that, in the survey's "most popular with students" category, *Antony and Cleopatra* (like *Richard III*) received not a single vote.

There is no doubt whatever, at least in my mind, that *Measure for Measure* is precisely the kind of play — precisely *the* play — that a good Shakespeare elective should concern itself with. For while this is a play of unquestionable moral seriousness it is also a fairy tale of sorts, and like all fairy tales it is redeemed from its essential grimness (Grimm-ness?) by much charm, humor, and excitement. Pedagogically, this means not only that *Measure* has a good deal to teach students, but also that it offers them a much-needed break from the standard tragic Shakespearean fare they now get more than their fill of in four years of study. It should also be noted that the question this play poses and then answers is one that the adolescent is perpetually puzzling over: How does one walk the fine line not only between chastity and licentiousness, but also between a priggish self-righteousness (with Angelo) and an overly familiar gregariousness (with Lucio)?

The major potential drawback of teaching *Measure* is the difficulty of much of its verse: Even the adult reader can find it annoyingly precious and elliptical. Nonetheless, juniors and seniors who have *elected* to study it are almost certain to find it even more fascinating than it is daunting. Also on the debit side here, at least in terms of the "intrinsic" if not necessarily the pedagogic *Measure*, is the fact that there is almost certainly less to *Measure* than meets the eye, when it comes to either philosophically profound reflections on the subject of hypocrisy and a double standard in morals, or to genuine (as opposed to rather stagy) emotional power in the confrontations between its protagonists.

As to the latter, for instance, as far as I'm concerned that extraordinary and moving scene (III, i) in *Henry VIII* in which Katharine magnificently denounces the two cardinals as hypocrites and false comforters, makes us feel the egregiousness of all double-dealing in a way Isabella's exquisitely fashioned but essentially lifeless tirades against "man, proud man" in Act II, scene ii of *Measure* do not. (Isabella's speeches there do of course contain some of Shakespeare's very greatest poetry; it is the dramatic impact of these, not their value as verse, that is here being called into question.) Ironically enough, however, the very staginess of *Measure* is probably a pedagogic plus rather than minus when it is being taught at the secondary level (as is its absurd but nonetheless entirely winning plot).

As for the suspicion that there may be less real "philosophy" in this play than one had at first decided there was, even those of us who are inclined to disagree with Hazlitt's judgment that "this is a play as full of genius as it is of wisdom"[34]— altering his equation to reflect the fact that this is a play which, in the last analysis, is far more brilliant and charming than it is "wise" in any strict sense — would concede that this matters little from a pedagogic point of view.

For it is, after all, only rarely that we think of Shakespeare as being a "thinker" in any formal sense (*Troilus and Cressida* being the hallowed exception to the rule), simply because he is usually that much higher, more Emersonian thing, Man Thinking. Thus while we walk away from *Measure* with no speeches worthy of being chiseled in marble and mounted on the walls of a philosophy department (although the "man, proud man" speech might look rather nice adorning those of a department of political science), nonetheless we walk away exhilarated, feeling that we have been made to do our *own* thinking. Need it be added that any play having such an effect on its reader should be deemed by the enlightened pedagogue to be worth its weight in gold?

If then we have here both a fairy tale to delight the student and a "problem play" challenging her to make sense of its many problematic elements, why is *Measure* so little taught?

Of the three reasons teachers doubtless would cite for avoiding *Measure for Measure* — its sexiness, its gloominess, and its obscurities of language — in my opinion only the third holds up at all. Yes, *Measure* is a difficult play to read, and yes, it may well be out of reach of the slower student. Yet for the average and the above-average student there should be all the fun and intellectual excitement of doing a good crossword puzzle in attempting to decode this play's cryptic verse. More importantly, the "message" of that verse, once decoded, makes a great deal of moral sense indeed, as a superb passage such as this one from Act I, scene i, amply attests:

> Thyself and thy belongings
> Are not thine own so proper as to waste
> Thyself upon thy virtues, they on thee.
> Heaven doth with us as we with torches do,
> Not light them for themselves; for if our virtues
> Did not go forth of us, 'twere all alike
> As if we had them not. Spirits are not finely touched

---

[34] Hazlitt, op. cit., p. 25.

> But to fine issues; nor Nature never lends
> The smallest scruple of her excellence
> But, like a thrifty goddess, she determines
> Herself the glory of a creditor,
> Both thanks and use....

As for this work's sexiness, I can only repeat two of the points I made in my discussion of *T & C*. First, that every teacher in his right mind simply has to acknowledge that all sexiness in a work, this side obscenity, is a pure pedagogic boon at the secondary level. Second, that the moralist who objects to *Measure for Measure* because it features unsavory characters and delicate situations is no moralist at all. As Chesterton reminds us in his great essay *"Tom Jones* and Morality,"[35] the most moral works of literature invariably concern themselves with the least moral of humans. It is only by gazing long and hard at wrong conduct that we can we ever hope to learn any lessons about right conduct.

Those who shy away from this play on account of its perceived gloominess make, I believe, the biggest mistake of all. For while I suggest in Appendix I that the term "comedy" has a nasty habit of misleading even those scholars who are most convinced they are using it properly, if any work *is* a comedy in the scholars' sense of one that has at least a relatively happy ending, it is *Measure*. What matters in this work is not so much the thick fog of moral confusion and sexual turpitude the characters often lose their way in, but the fact that they do at last emerge from it and find, if not the high road, at least *a* road, to personal and social betterment.

What also matters, pedagogically, is that (as I see it) that fog corresponds nicely to the uncertainties and anxieties that darken and disorient the inner vision of the adolescent. Should such be the case, whenever we deny young people the right to ride through the dimly lit House of Horrors that is *Measure* we deny them not only many intellectual thrills but many moments of catharsis-inducing terror as well. Not to mention that most cathartic of moments when they, along with Angelo and all the rest, emerge from the spook house into the light of a tolerably sunny day.

---

[35] G.K. Chesterton, *All Things Considered* (London: Methuen & Co. Ltd., 1925), pp. 197-198.

CYMBELINE

Nothing could make more plain the lamentably imperfect state of the present Shakespeare syllabus than the fact that, of the last three plays from Shakespeare's hand (*Henry VIII* and *Pericles* excluded here as being, in certain acts and scenes at least, of doubtful authorship) — *Cymbeline, The Winter's Tale,* and *The Tempest* — *Cymbeline,* a play at least as great intrinsically as *The Tempest* (and, for me at least, morally far weightier), and in another league entirely from *The Winter's Tale,* is being taught virtually not at all.

One might be able to remain sanguine about this situation if one could convince oneself that this play had been banished from the syllabus because it was in some way unsuited to adolescents, yet the plain fact is that *Cymbeline,* particularly when it is contrasted with the elegaic *Tempest* or the soporific *Winter's Tale,* has the passion, the exalted poetry, and the plottiness to make it a surefire winner with young people. When one goes on to consider that this play is moral through and through, and that the moral wisdom it has to offer is of precisely that sort certain to capture the fancy of all genuinely noble young men and women, our failure to have made it the jewel in the crown of our Shakespeare electives seems all the more shocking.

Let us begin our examination of the pedagogic pluses and minuses of *Cymbeline* with the only conceivable minus, its style, which Van Doren rightly describes as "the richest and most elaborate of Shakespeare's styles thus far."[36] Certainly one would never venture to teach *Cymbeline* at any grade level other than the 12th (or perhaps in an elective open to both juniors and seniors), and it's sure that even seniors will need to mull over many a passage.

Yet of *Cymbeline* it might be said, even more truly than of *Measure for Measure,* that its poetry is well worth the mulling. The poetry of *Measure* is metaphysical — austere and studied in its conceits. By contrast, the complexity of *Cymbeline*'s verse seems more akin to the complexity of interweaved capillary, cartilage, and tissue — it is organic, not contrived. Those readers who suppose such meaty verse is certain to blunt the student scalpel, or who imagine that *Cymbeline* must be unsuited to secondary education in some other way, would do well to listen to

[36]Mark Van Doren, *Shakespeare* (New York: Henry Holt and Company, 1939), p. 305.

the comments of this department chairperson (seemingly the only person in America, or close to it, who recently has taught *Cymbeline* at the secondary level):

> Yes, *Cymbeline* is very rewarding to teach. The poetry is no more beyond the students than that of *Hamlet* and *Lear*, which we regularly teach. Also, and very important for me because I work in a girls' school, Imogen is a wonderful heroine — strong, intelligent, resourceful, witty and generally winning.
> I taught the play first from curiosity, and later because it proved very successful. There are just so many marvelous effects and a top-notch heroine. No, it wasn't over folks' heads — at least not in the very select prep school where I taught. I think it would work most places. It gives the students a lot to enjoy (and write about) at different levels — pure sensation and, as you said, some weighty ideas. Yes, I would do it again; and yes, I would recommend it.

In speaking so glowingly, and so very aptly, about Imogen, perhaps Shakespeare's most winning female protagonist, this department chairperson has given us our first strong incentive to include *Cymbeline* in our syllabuses. Yet I would perhaps even broaden my colleague's encomium to include Imogen's true love, Posthumous, and to suggest that these two noble young people (in the company of Guiderius and Arviragus, and with Cloten along as their butt and foil) set an example of human greatness the morally ambitious student would joy to observe and to emulate, were he or she given the chance.

For while the egalitarian and aristocratic principles are always in a state of dynamic tension and equilibrium in Shakespeare, as they are in any great spirit, in this play Shakespeare the natural aristocrat is in the ascendant, and he sings the praises of sheer human quality: "clay and clay differs in dignity,/Whose dust is both alike." This sense of the deep and abiding value of natural aristocracy emerges from his descriptions of the two lovers (as in this description of Posthumous, made by one of the two gentlemen in the opening scene: "I do not think/So fair an outward, and such stuff within,/Endows a man but he.") but above all from Belarius's wonderment at the way Nature triumphs over Nurture as the kingly impulses keep asserting themselves in his foster sons:

> O noble strain!
> O worthiness of nature, breed of greatness!
> Cowards father cowards, and base things sire base.
> Nature hath meal and bran, contempt and grace.   [IV, ii]

If the example of native nobleness set by the young protagonists in *Cymbeline* stands out as the most conspicuous reason for including it in our syllabuses, there are a number of others scarcely less compelling. One might note, for instance, that there are two valuable lessons to be learned — and taught — from the play's central incident, the sundering of the bond between Imogen and Posthumous by the Iago-like Iachimo.

First, there is a genuinely feminist message here as to the evil consequences that inevitably ensue when men treat woman's love and fidelity as a commodity to be bartered or wagered for. Second, the manner in which each lover, when convinced that the other has been untrue, proceeds to categorically condemn the entire opposite sex, reminds young people that genuine tolerance and understanding between the sexes is as needful as it is difficult to come by.

Then too, there is much that is both moving and morally weighty in the whole subplot involving Belarius and the king's two sons. To my way of thinking this part of the play is a sort of somber reprise of *As You Like It*, (just as *The Tempest* might be seen as an austere reworking of *Midsummer*): Cymbeline is another Duke Frederick; Belarius, exulting in the rough but morally untainted life of the great outdoors, is another Duke Senior; the cave of Belarius is a more elemental Forest of Arden; Imogen/Fidele is a far more grave and dignified Rosalind/Ganymede; and the intergenerational loyalty between Belarius and his lads brings to mind that between Adam and Orlando. Above all, however, the earlier play's youthful sense of gratitude for existence has here been exalted to a genuine piety, a piety that pervades Shakespeare's later works:

Belarius. A goodly day not to keep house, with such
      Whose roof's as low as ours. Stoop, boys, this gate
      Instructs you how t'adore the heavens and bows you
      To a morning's holy office. The gates of monarchs
      Are arched so high that giants may jet through
      And keep their impious turbans on, without
      Good morrow to the sun. Hail, thou fair Heaven!
      We house i' th' rock, yet use thee not so hardly
      As prouder livers do.

Guiderius. Hail, Heaven!

Arviragus. Hail, Heaven!   [III, iii]

Lastly, one could hardly fail to mention as one of *Cymbeline*'s most attractive features precisely that scene some of the play's critics feel there is a need to apologize for. I refer to the "masque" in which Jupiter, much in the fashion of Jehovah speaking out of the whirlwind to Job (except that this deity brings to mortal man, in this case the long-suffering Posthumous[37], not cosmic riddles but words of comfort and peace), descends to utter words so sublime only a Shakespeare could have penned them:

> Be not with mortal accidents opprest:
>   No care of yours it is; you know 'tis ours.
> Whom best I love I cross, to make my gift,
>   The more delayed, delighted. Be content:
> Your low-laid son our godhead will uplift;
>   His comforts thrive, his trials well are spent.   [V, iv]

Whether one endorses or rejects the theism intrinsic in that speech, one can hardly fail to be moved by the scene of which it is a part, or to feel that young people living in our get-it-while-you-can, quick-fix culture could only benefit later in life, when troubles have begun to besiege them, from their memory of the sight of the exhausted, half-dead Posthumous stoically hanging in there until redemption at last is his.

I would also take this opportunity to note for the record, and to right the critical wrongs that have been done to this masque, that in my estimation it not only is not the hack-work the undiscriminating take it to be, but is in fact in every way superior to its far more famous counterpart in Act IV of *The Tempest*. The latter owes its great fame not to any intrinsic merit (it's something of a bore, and as strictly aesthetic and Nijinsky-like as the masque in *Cymbeline* is deeply moral and *Job*-like), but to those immortal words with which Prospero breaks the spell that had created it, words that seem to break

---

[37]Technically speaking, the words quoted here are directed not to Posthumous but to the apparitions that surround him as he sleeps. One assumes, however, that this whole scene actually transpires within Posthumous's dream, and that therefore he is privy to these words as well.

our hearts along with it. The masque in *Cymbeline* brings the reader real spiritual food, whereas that in *The Tempest* brings only, as we know, a ghostly banquet.

This much having been said about the play's pedagogic pluses and its one conceivable minus, some words now must be spoken as to its intrinsic merits and defects, if only to stir up debate about a play most teachers seem to consider unworthy even of debate. (See my comment following survey question number eight, on page 238.)

As to its defects, those who know the play at all well perhaps will take a position akin to Dr. Johnson's, and lambast *Cymbeline* as a work too wildly farfetched to merit any kind of serious attention.[38] In my opinion, those who follow Dr. Johnson in this matter only commit themselves to an overly rationalistic position of an eighteenth-century stripe, and thereby prove themselves to have none of the modern critic's ever-increasing respect for the vast poetic power — the ability to speak truth through fable — of the myth and the fairy tale.

Clearly the world of *Cymbeline* is a fairy tale world, a world where wicked queens poison cats and dogs in their spare time and where men routinely spend the night in trunks in order to win wagers. If we wish to be poets and not pedants, in our criticism as much as elsewhere, all we can demand of any work depicting such a world is that it be a) internally consistent and b) rich in that mythopoetic quality that surrounds every action and character with an aura of heightened rather than diminished reality. And the fact is that *Cymbeline* responds to these demands admirably. Almost certainly, the critic who dismisses *Cymbeline* as merely unreal shows an unfair selectivity in his critical targets, and probably becomes far more annoyed at the death-feigning potion in *Cymbeline* than he does at the same dramatic device as it is put to similar use in *R & J*.

When it comes to arguing this play's many claims to greatness others can probably do so more effectively than I, and in doing so clear me of any accusation of special pleading. Note then that that marvelous man, William Hazlitt, not only spurns a chronological approach and places *Cymbeline* at the very beginning of his seminal work, *Characters of Shakespeare's Plays*, but speaks of it as being "a favourite with us."[39] Or consider this eloquent

---

[38] W. K. Wimsatt, Jr., ed., *Samuel Johnson on Shakespeare* (New York: Hill and Wang, 1960), pp. 107-108.

[39] Hazlitt, op. cit, p. 10.

early nineteenth-century verdict, with every word of which I am in agreement:

> This play, if not in the construction of its fable one of the most perfect of our author's productions, is, in point of poetic beauty, of variety and truth of character, and in the display of sentiment and emotion, one of the most lovely and interesting. Nor can we avoid expressing our astonishment at the sweeping condemnation Johnson has passed upon it; charging its fiction with folly, its conduct with absurdity, its events with impossibility; terming its faults too evident for detection and too gross for aggravation.
>
> Of the enormous injustice of this sentence, nearly every page of *Cymbeline* will, to a reader of any taste or discrimination, bring the most decisive evidence. That is possesses many of the too common inattentions of Shakspeare, that it exhibits a frequent violation of costume, and a singular confusion of nomenclature, cannot be denied; but these are trifles light as air when contrasted with its merits, which are of the very essence of dramatic worth, rich and full in all that breathes of vigour, animation, and intellect, in all that elevates the fancy and improves the heart, in all that fills the eye with tears or agitates the soul with hope and fear.[40]

THE WINTER'S TALE

For those of us who dearly love the Bard but are not bardolators (i.e., *uncritical* lovers of the Bard), the fact that there are one or two more or less unqualified duds in the canon is cause not for lamentation but for rejoicing. Given the fact that this one mortal, Will Shakespeare, has left humankind a cultural bequest more bounteous than those of a hundred other artists and thinkers combined, we would have an even harder time than we do picturing him as a creature of mere flesh and blood like ourselves had he not been so thoughtful as to leave us

---

[40]Nathan Drake, M.D., *Shakespeare and His Times* (Paris: Baudry's European Library, 1838), p. 562.

Timon of Athens and *The Winter's Tale*.

I'm aware that most critics, when putting together their short list of Shakespeare's very weakest works, place *Timon* at its head, with *Titus*, *Pericles*, and perhaps *Two Gentlemen* somewhere below it, but that they don't include *The Winter's Tale* at all. Doubtless their rationale for excluding *WT* and including those other plays is that the others are positively offensive in some way, whereas the worst that can be said about *WT* is that it is a colossal bore. Yet to the critic keenly alive to what it is that makes Shakespeare Shakespeare — a spirit that quickens, arouses, thrills, but *never* bores — his lapse into sheer somniferousness in *WT* is infinitely more embarrassing than the lapse into gore in *Titus*, unrestrained punning in *Two Gentlemen*, or mad ranting in *Timon*.

That *The Winter's Tale* is indeed Shakespeare at his very lowest ebb is attested to by the fact that there is hardly a single moment here sufficiently lively or interesting to redeem the whole. The first two and a half acts, in which Leontes' paranoia — even more strictly theatrical, and even further from human motivation or probability, than Othello's — results in his queen's death, outdo even *Timon* for sheer unredeemed (and unredeeming) unpleasantness. Of course, given so thoroughly dreary a first two and a half acts, the bardolatrous critic feels it incumbent on himself to wax ecstatic about the fabled "sheep-shearing" scene (IV, iv) and to sing the praises of that "lovable rascal" Autolycus (some even committing the unspeakable sin of uttering his name in the same breath as Falstaff's).

In fact the "sheep-shearing" scene is nothing more than Shakespeare, ever the practical playwright and the man of business, giving his courtly, Blackfriars audience the chance to envision themselves (eighteenth century-style) living the utterly denatured "bucolic life." Could anything be more depressing than the sight of literature's greatest nature painter — he who gave us the blasted heath of the three witches, the cave of Belarius, and the shipwreck that begins *The Tempest* — reduced to painting theatrical backdrops? It is as if Turner had thrown it all over to mass-produce lederhosened little shepherds and shepherdesses!

As for Autolycus, he is as much the mere "stage rogue" as Don John in *Much Ado* is the stage villain. Or to look at him from a more modern perspective, he is the kind of thoroughly sanitized "bad boy" that might win the hearts of millions in a sitcom. When one compares his relentless cutesiness with all that is truly morally unsavory about Falstaff, one feels compelled to borrow some of Hamlet's words and use them to reproach the critic who had dared to think of Autocylus as another Falstaff: "What judgment would step from this to this?"

The last best hope of *WT* is its final scene, the "coming to life" of the "statue" of Hermione, but alas, this hope is dashed like every other. To realize just how perfunctory and spiritless this "recognition" scene really is, one need only compare it with Pericles' slowly dawning recognition of Marina. In the latter, the mastery with which Shakespeare (and it clearly is the Master at work here, regardless of who wrote the first few acts) ushers in that dawn, altering its pigments ever so slightly to mirror each advance in certainty in Pericles' mind, makes us feel that here the old nature painter is not only on the job, but — like the aged Monet — more firmly in control of his craft than ever. By contrast, the scene in *WT* makes one wish he had never forsaken painting for sculpture.

Yet the real miracle, in comparison with which the awakening of Hermione is but a cheap conjuring trick, is that despite its (to me, at least) absolutely patent weaknesses, *The Winter's Tale* has been taught more often in the last five years (in independent schools) than fifteen other plays. A few survey respondents even went out of their way to speak highly of it, asserting that its vision of death and rebirth somehow makes it well suited to young people. (Although why young people, who are still in the process of being born, should have any interest in being *re*born, is an utter mystery to me.)

Struck speechless as I am by all of this, all I can think to say is that if *WT* really does succeed in the classroom, then statues really must come to life. How any young person, on fire with life and love, could do other than grow chilly and pale when given the ice-cold shoulder by Leontes for two long acts, is more than the mind of this man can conceive. Yet of course, I must concede that the student who manages to get through the first two and a half acts without frostbite does then have the golden opportunity of warming herself before the roaring fire that is the "sheep-shearing" scene....

It must also be mentioned, before I bid a fond adieu to one of the only two Shakespeare plays I am always genuinely glad to see the last of, that while *WT* is every bit as boring, in its characterizations and plot, as *Cymbeline* is scintillating, so too its poetry, when compared with that of *Cymbeline*, is as arid and devoid of scenic peaks and valleys as that of the latter play is almost unbelievably lush and variegated.

CORIOLANUS

While I'm sure so "ideological" a play as *Coriolanus* is not to every taste, there is no doubt in my mind that it is top-rank Shakespeare. Although the Bard who writes so peerlessly about man the political and military animal could hardly be described as "sweet fancy's child," and although we do miss the romance and the whimsy to be found in many of the other plays, we are more than compensated for this lack by some of his most virile and straightforward verse. This latter, it should be noted, represents (along with its gripping plot) the chief pedagogic strength of *Coriolanus*, in that a play so blessedly free of idle wordplay is also a play relatively easy to read.

Yet while *Coriolanus* is genuinely great Shakespeare, and while the average student could certainly make at least some sense of it all, a number of factors militate against making it a curricular staple, or even a play to be used in electives. One might begin by noting that, although voices are often raised in this play and tempers do flare, it remains in many respects as emotionally cool as its protagonist. While surely we err if we imagine that every play young people read must be as white-hot in its passion as *R & J*, or as satisfyingly gory and creepy as *Macbeth*, *Coriolanus* does seem simply too far at the other end of the emotional spectrum to make it a satisfying read for most young people.

More importantly, *Coriolanus*'s vast treasure trove of political insights is one that the average young person is intellectually unequipped to explore, and too emotionally undeveloped to recognize the value and significance of. For while the play's central theme — an examination of the conflicting claims to sovereignty of the few, the strong, and the lucky versus the many, the weak, and the unfortunate — is as timely today as it ever was, one has to have observed and pondered for many a year this struggle for dominance between the aristocratic and egalitarian principles — in the headlines, in the schools, and within one's own heart — before one is likely to find the viewing of *Coriolanus* every bit as wrenching (or even, for me at least, more so) as that of *King Lear*.

I might also take this opportunity to suggest that, even if the average adolescent were in a position to appreciate the almost earth-shaking significance of the struggle being waged in this play between, on the one hand, common humanity and justice, and on the other, uncommon humanity and its claim to special privilege by dint of exemplary social service, we might have good reason to feel qualms about offering the privileged

independent school student a play in which — when all is said
and done — the aristocratic argument receives a far fairer hearing than the populist one.

For while so steady and sane a mind as Shakespeare's can
always be counted on to see both sides of an issue more or less
impartially, and while it is even plausible that in this play
Shakespeare really is "concerned with debunking certain upper-
class conceptions of honor,"[41] the fact remains that Coriolanus,
however contemptible and even loathsome he often strikes us as
being, is always something of a hero in our eyes. We see the
tribunes of the people, on the other hand, less with our own
eyes than with those of Coriolanus and his aristocratic faction,
and needless to say we are not pleased by what we see: two
rabble-rousers, as short-sighted as they are smug and self-serving.

That so unsavory a character as Coriolanus should somehow
be able to wring from us every last drop of our pity, leaving us
none to shower like a gentle rain from heaven on the Roman
masses, is of course a cause for wonderment, but we have had
much less to wonder about ever since William Hazlitt explained
the phenomenon as follows, in what must surely be one of the
most brilliant and suggestive passages in all of criticism:

> The cause of the people is indeed but little calculated
> as a subject for poetry: it admits of rhetoric, which goes
> into argument and explanation, but it presents no immedi-
> ate or distinct images to the mind, "no jutting frieze, but-
> tress, or coigne of vantage" for poetry "to make its pen-
> dant bed and procreant cradle in."
>
> The language of poetry naturally falls in with the lan-
> guage of power. The imagination is an exaggerating and
> exclusive faculty: it takes from one thing to add to anoth-
> er: it accumulates circumstances together to give the great-
> est possible effect to a favourite object . . . . The principle
> of poetry is a very anti-levelling principle. It aims at effect,
> it exists by contrast . . . . Poetry is right-royal. It puts the
> individual for the species, the one above the infinite many,
> Right before Might . . . .
>
> There is nothing heroical in a multitude of miserable
> rogues not wishing to be starved, or complaining that they

[41]Sir Tyrone Guthrie, "On Producing *Coriolanus*," from the Laurel
Shakespeare *Coriolanus* (New York: Dell Publishing Co., Inc., 1962), p. 23.

are like to be so: but when a single man comes forward to brave their cries and to make them submit to the last indignities, from mere pride and self-will, our admiration of his prowess is immediately converted into contempt for their pusillanimity.... Wrong dressed out in pride, pomp, and circumstance has more attraction than abstract right.[42]

HENRY V

Henry V is of course a marvelous work, with many stirring and memorable speeches, and there would be no reason to rebuke the teacher who chose to teach it. One might put it to particularly good use if it were taught from a "Shakespeare on film" angle, in that students could compare various key scenes and speeches in the two film versions and the BBC video (which holds its end up quite nicely, given its confinement to a sound stage). Yet despite all of this, I probably would choose not to teach it; let's look at a few of my reasons.

If I were to succumb to the temptation to teach *Henry V* it would probably be because the opportunity had arisen to position it in chronological sequence, hard on the heels of *Henry IV* and (if it had been studied also) *Richard II*. Yet while to do so might to some extent broaden the historical panorama and give the student an even wider angle of social vision, in most respects it would serve little real purpose. For the best reason for teaching *Henry IV*, as we have seen, is to allow the student to follow the odyssey of a young person who, like herself, has strayed for a time into the amoral, youthful world of fun- and pleasure-seeking, only to return to the social fold all the more confident and fully human for having wandered. The whole point of *Henry V*, however, is that the king is *not* the Hal we once knew; the "Reclamation of a Profligate Prince" has been fully achieved, and therefore we waste our time if we seek to study that theme in this work.

King Henry does of course continue to learn and grow throughout this play, particularly in the play's most compelling scene, scene i of Act IV. Here, like another becloaked sovereign curious to hear what his subjects have to say about him — the

---

[42]Hazlitt, op. cit., pp. 53-54.

Duke in *Measure for Measure* — Henry suffers his final moments of weakness and doubt before at last coming to full maturity in the subsequent battle. (Has anyone ever been bold enough to compare this scene with that in the Garden of Gethsemane?) Nonetheless, these last steps in Henry's journey toward personhood are for the most part obscured by the trampling of all those horses and men, and it would take a dedicated teacher and much hard work before the student could perhaps come to look on this work as "Prince Hal, Part Three" rather than as an absorbing and self-contained battle epic.

While *Henry V* does lack any readily discernible theme — much less one so pedagogically ideal as that we have discerned in *Henry IV* — to provoke discussion and analysis, it is also deficient in those conflicts between a number of fascinating and strong-willed characters that make the history plays in general such compelling reading and viewing. Needless to say it has numerous attractions that ably compensate for these two deficiencies, but the fact remains that those deficiencies loom far larger pedagogically than intrinsically. For if a class cannot with great profit analyze a work's theme or themes, or at the very least discuss the conflicting aims and motivations of its major characters, they can do little else than appreciate whatever moments of eloquence, pathos, or comedy it has to offer.

Of course *Henry V* has enough eloquence for five plays, and a number of affecting scenes (IV, i, as described above, preeminent among them). Unfortunately, its comic elements are not all a teacher might wish them to be. Not only is it true that, even if we were to consider Gower/Fluellen/Macmorris/Jamy/Pistol /Nym/Bardolph as one composite comic creature, he could never hope to fill Falstaff's gargantuan shoes, it also must be noted that figures such as Fluellen — the professional soldier par excellence — or Pistol — Shakespeare's parody of the fire-eating swashbuckler common on the Elizabethan stage — are every bit as temporal, characters strictly of an age and not for all time, as Falstaff is eternal. The student is likely to be puzzled or downright nonplussed by all of these secondary comic characters, particularly when he also has to contend with the nonstandard spellings Shakespeare employs to approximate their various Welsh, Scottish, and Irish speech patterns.

If the pedagogic cons do indeed seem to be outweighing the pros as we tinker with the scale to see whether we should add *Henry V* to our syllabus, one last consideration should tip it decidedly toward the con side. To wit, of all of Shakespeare's plays *Henry V* is the one which, in this video age, the student is most likely to encounter in later life in one of the two filmed versions (if she hasn't already). If, as Neil Postman suggests, formal education does its job best when it exposes students to intellectual influences they are *not* likely to be molded by in the culture at large, surely in this one instance we teachers can step to one side and let *Henry V* teach itself to our students at some later date.

All's Well That Ends Well

If someone were to ask which of Shakespeare's plays is most purely a moral tale, or fable, perhaps the most accurate response would be *All's Well That Ends Well*. *Pericles* might be considered a co-claimant to the title, although its doubtful authorship probably would lead the judges to rule it ineligible, and *Cymbeline* and *Measure for Measure*, by virtue of their greater weightiness, doubtless would be judged in a different category than the sparer, no-frills *All's Well*.

At any rate, there is something immensely satisfying and morally cheering in the way one of Shakespeare's most capable and intelligent heroines transforms the man of her dreams, by the sheer power and perdurability of her love for him, from an utter boor into something at least remotely human. Even more winning, perhaps, is the way in which a marvelous old gent named Lafew, with a nose for a scoundrel keener than a hound's for a fox, sets about exposing the coxcomb known as Parolles, only to — in a quintessentially sublime Shakespearean moment — grant him sanctuary when that exposure has been fully effected by others: "Though you are a fool and a knave, you shall eat."

Yet what really makes *All's Well* an attractive choice for a Shakespeare elective or AP course (plainly, the only places where one might teach such a morally "dark" and stylistically difficult play) is its first plot element, which might be described as not merely the curing of the King by Helena but the rejuvenation of Age by Youth. Technically, of course, it is Helena's father and not she who cures the King, Gerard de Narbon having passed on to his daughter the "receipt" for that remedy which was "the dearest issue of his practice." Nonetheless we can't help but feel that it is the magic potion the King drinks in from Helena's very presence in his bedchamber that really cures him, a potion composed of one part Youth, one part Hope, one part Courage, one part Beauty, and another part — a part not to be reckoned in drams by mortal man — of Divine Grace. ("It is not so with him that all things knows,/As 'tis with us that square our guess by shows./But most it is presumption in us, when/The help of heaven we count the act of men.")

I have no doubt at all that this scene (II, i) — one that is almost if not quite as moving as its canonical cousin, the scene (V, i) in which another young female healer (Marina) brings another old man (Pericles) back to life — will move the student reader even more deeply than the adult. Nothing is more galling to Youth than the unending condescension it must endure from the adult world, and thus it is likely to take deep solace from the sight of a young person acting so courageously and speaking up for Youth so eloquently: "He that of greatest works is finisher,/Oft does them by the weakest minister./So holy writ in babes hath judgment shown,/When judges have been babes."

Interestingly enough, the same play that shows the spirit of Youth at its best also shows it at its worst, in the figure of that overgrown and *nearly* incorrigible adolescent, Parolles. If young people are sure to be heartened, on an emotional level, by the sight of the lovely and gracious Helena shedding light and healing all around her, it is equally certain that they will be sobered, on the moral level, by the sight of the Wisdom of Age personified — Lafew — bringing this true rapscallion to heel.

Now that I have pointed out to my colleagues some of those aspects of *All's Well* that young people should find either fascinating or morally improving, and suggested that it might well be a good work to try in an elective or with an advanced group, I feel all the more conscious of my obligation to bring to their attention one potentially very troublesome aspect of this play: its language, which runs from the precious and elliptical to the downright incomprehensible. In this respect it outdoes even *Measure for Measure*, a play which, I think most of us would agree, is notably more successful and more charming than its poor relation. For instance when Helena says (in Act I, scene iii)

> I know I love in vain, strive against hope;
> Yet in this captious and intenable seive
> I still pour in the waters of my love,
> *And lack not to lose still.*

the sense of that last line becomes clear enough to an adult reader after prolonged pondering, but it is sure to leave the student reader more or less permanently stumped.[43] And even the adult reader can only throw up his hands over lines such as "whose judgments are/Mere fathers of their garments" (I, ii). One can only assume it was utterly wretched lines such as that one that prompted Ben Jonson to wish his friend had blotted a thousand of them.

In bringing this assessment of *All's Well* in the classroom to a close, I would say this. While I have ranked this play high on my list of elective/AP choices in Chapter 6, if only to make clear to my reader that this is a morally compelling work and one likely to be of interest to the capable junior or senior, my own guess is that teachers will turn to it only when and if they've grown weary of *Measure for Measure* and *Cymbeline*. *All's Well* is, after all, by no means the near-complete success each of those two works clearly is, and its difficulties of language should prove to be the icing on this tasty but still rather disappointing cake.

If those difficulties are the icing, we might go on to say that Lavatch, the clown in this play, is the ornamental figure stuck on top. For my money he is the all too quintessential Shakespearean clown, not only because he is very hard to follow, but because even he who succeeds in keeping up with him can't quite shake the feeling that he is chasing a creature more akin to a wild goose than to the lord Hamlet.

KING JOHN

If candidates for a Shakespeare syllabus had to run for office in the manner of political candidates, *King John* would be in the unenviable position of being thoughtful, articulate, solid on the issues ... but alas, utterly lacking in sex appeal. For this play has in John a genuinely tragic figure, but one not nearly so glam-

---

[43]It might be objected here that the student can always consult the note if he can make no sense of the line on his own. Yet I would assert that the student who perpetually is forced, owing to highly abstruse language, to seek out paraphrasing footnotes, is likely to grow disillusioned and demoralized — and for good reason. After all, he is not reading Shakespeare but "Shakespeare made easy," and this will only serve to confirm him in the conviction that "Shakespeare" is essentially a synonym for "dead language." Then too, if he is at all intelligent and independently minded he will come to question — again with good reason — the validity of many of the paraphrases that are being offered him.

orous or fascinating as Richard II; true moral complexity (John's wrangling with the Pope's legate, and the political and personal ramifications of his attempt to murder young Arthur), but a complexity that interests us more than, like that of *Merchant*, it compels us; in Philip the Bastard a marvelously witty and unpretentious hero, but a hero who is only a supporting player, not the protagonist; and an extraordinary amount of great verse, but verse, one would guess, that few make the journey to the outskirts of the canon to hear, on the assumption that so unsexy a singer couldn't possibly have a good singing voice.

Thus although, if the rest of the canon were to vanish from the face of the earth tomorrow, teachers would consider themselves lucky indeed to have a *King John* available to them, it seems certain that until that apocalyptic day this play will find its way into few classrooms. *Henry IV* has infinitely more to "say" to students and is certain to be more popular with them, and from the teacher's point of view *Richard II* is a far superior play, intrinsically but above all for what it offers pedagogically: its perfect clarity of language.

For if *Richard II* is a play that can indeed be understood perfectly well without footnotes, *King John* emphatically is not. This is not to say that it renders invalid the generalization that the history plays, as a group, pose the fewest language problems for students, but simply that it is perhaps the hardest of these to read. One might make this point more vividly by saying that *King John* sends the reader to the notes more often than the "historical" portions of *Henry IV*, and therefore about as much as the scenes in that play featuring Falstaff.

THE COMEDY OF ERRORS

If one wished to prove that we are indeed failing to make the wisest use of the canon in our present syllabuses, one might simply point to the fact that *The Comedy of Errors* has been taught more often in the past five years than fourteen other plays, among them not only the great *Troilus and Cressida* but also *Measure for Measure* and *Cymbeline*. For while the "intrinsic" *COE* has its very real charms, these are hardly so considerable as to merit our promoting it over the heads of far worthier works, and the pedagogic *COE* would seem to be so utterly problematic that it is a wonder anyone has had the temerity to try to teach it at all. For this is, after all, a work built around confusion and mistaken identity, and even as one watches it in performance one has a good bit of difficulty keeping one's Dromios and Antipholuses straight. How much harder it must be for the poor student, laboring (in vain, one can only think) to sort them out as she reads!

Thus while it is conceivable that those who have been so bold as to teach *COE* never came to rue their decision, and also possible that a class that first sees it in performance can then go on to make at least some minimal sense of the text, one can hardly forbear from presuming that this work is not — *could* not — be a classroom winner.

Given that fact, one can't help but wonder what it is that prompts some teachers to choose to teach it. My guess is that the gremlin who makes his home in every Shakespeare syllabus-in-the-making whispers in their ear, "Kids like comedies, and Shakespeare's comedies are all pretty much the same. Go ahead, pick one — *any* one."

Teachers who have allowed this pesky creature to mislead them before, but are determined to lend him their ear no longer, are referred to Appendix I for some thoughts on how best to flush him out and send him packing.

LOVE'S LABOR'S LOST

Considered in the abstract, a play that satirizes the pretensions of pedants and overzealous students might seem likely to be a surefire winner in the classroom, and perhaps even teach a valuable lesson about the necessity of balancing the cerebral with the intuitive and instinctive. Unfortunately the real *Love's Labor's Lost*, if more of us were to choose to teach it, would almost certainly confound our expectations. For while the intrinsic *LLL* has much going for it, including a vast amount of exquisite poetry and a few uproariously funny send-ups of pedantic affectation, its chief defects — two-dimensional characterization and virtually nonexistent plot — are just those certain to bother a student considerably more than they affect the adult lover of Shakespeare. Worst of all, however, this play's satirizing of scholarly pretensions is sure to leave the student cold, and this for two reasons.

First, the pedant, as he has existed as a stock comic figure on the European stage for hundreds of years, is not one the modern adolescent is likely to recognize well enough even to want to bring him down a peg or two. With the rise of universal education in our day, every man or woman with a college diploma in his or her possession has taken on a bit of that humorless pomposity with regard to learning that used to be the badge of office of a chosen few, so that now the distinction between the "average sensual man [or woman]" and the average intellectual man or woman is neither so marked — nor so funny — as it used to be.

Second, the actual business of satirizing pedants and pedantry in this play is carried out by means of a good bit of abstruse wordplay, much of it in Latin, no less. Rare indeed would be the student who bothered to consult every note in her desire to get the jokes, and far rarer still she who was then moved to genuine laughter. Nothing seems more certain than that the generation weaned on the MTV video — with its invariable portrayal of teachers as dim-witted fools who respond quite nicely to a guitar over the head — will flip right past the Shakespeare channel to a comedy or music channel when it goes in search of cheap laughs at a teacher's expense. Inevitable as this is, it is also, of course, regrettable, in that a scene such as IV, i, that in which Boyet reads to the Princess and her ladies Don Adriano's sidesplittingly funny letter, exhales a far sweeter and purer hilarity than the average young person has ever known.

It seems clear, then, that LLL's lack of interesting characters and exciting plot, along with its rather obscure jests at the expense of historically rather obscure figures, provides us with our warrant for barring it from the classroom. Yet if we were to need more sufficient grounds than these for doing so, we might well cite the potentially adverse effect of introducing young scholars to so anti-intellectual a work. For while Shakespeare is of course more concerned here to point up the woeful inadequacies of the formal learning of his day than to mount a frontal assault on intellect per se, and while the adult reader can both revel in the satire and borrow words from the King in order to exclaim about the satirist, "How well he's read to reason against reading!", the young man who has been thrilled to the marrow by hearing Berowne ask the very same question his hormones are demanding of him on a daily basis — "For where is any author in the world/Teaches such beauty as a woman's eye?" — may well never be sighted in a classroom again!

Henry VI

Although the scholars may be right in asserting that *Henry VI* can never hope to measure up to a *Hamlet* or *Macbeth* in the height of its style or the depth of its moral seriousness, to anyone who has ever seen this extraordinary work in performance it might almost seem that it makes up for what it lacks in those two dimensions in sheer breadth — has Shakespeare ever worked on a broader canvas, or with so clean and uncluttered a poetic line? Indeed one is almost tempted to say that *Henry VI* is Shakespeare's *War and Peace*, although a more appropriate title might be *War, War, and More War*.

Yet despite its very breadth and staggering dramatic diversity — or rather, precisely because of these — this play clearly is not suited to the secondary classroom. There are far too many characters for the student to keep track of, one incident succeeds another with bewildering rapidity, and there is too little in the way of thematic unity to entice the student toward deep analysis.

Above all, of course, *Henry VI* is less a "work of art" than an extraordinary dramatic spectacle — is it any wonder that it made of Shakespeare something of an overnight sensation? For teachers to demand that their students pore over this work as it appears on the printed page, rather than simply hope that some day they will lose themselves in a performance of it, would be like ordering a hungry person to paint a still life of a mouth-watering feast rather than join the rest of the company at the board.

The Two Gentlemen of Verona

Nothing could be more regrettable, from a teacher's point of view, than the fact that *The Two Gentlemen of Verona* (particularly in its first two acts) is one of the most pun-ridden of Shakespeare's plays. For while there may be little pure gold in the "intrinsic" *Two Gentlemen*, there is pedagogic ore here aplenty: silver, variegated now and then by a thin vein of gold. Unfortunately, before a student could mine the ore Acts III through V are so rich in, she would first have to pick her way with infinite care through the minefield of the first two acts, where a thousand puns and quibbles are likely to go off (rather than to go over) whenever they are trod under foot by the unsuspecting reader, too eager to get on with the story. While an occasional teacher doubtless has made this journey and lived to tell the tale, we can hardly expect many of our students to cross the border into Act III in full possession of all their limbs (not to mention their mental faculties).

Now this is a great pity, because if *Two Gentlemen* could only be run once or twice through some sort of de-quibbling device, it might emerge as a remarkably serviceable work for grades 6-8. Its very slightness might, at those grade levels, work for it as a virtue, in that the student who has quickly grasped a work's basic story line is that much freer to concentrate on its vocabulary, poetry, characterizations, and theme(s). More importantly, this play's moral — that love (or more properly, infatuation) too often leads us to "war with good counsel, set the world at naught" — is one that the early adolescent would do well to heed. Particularly given the fact that young people are keenly aware of the value and importance of friendship, their close attention to the whole process whereby Proteus betrays Valentine — so sordid, and yet so full of marvelously comical rationalizations (as when Proteus tells Silvia first that Julia is dead, and moments later ups the ante by saying that Valentine is dead as well!) — would be sure to reward them with one vital insight: that human passion is at least as likely to destabilize and dehumanize as it is to exalt and integrate.

Yet while many of this play's elements might indeed make it not only a valuable but perhaps even a popular work in the classroom (particularly if it were taught in conjunction with the mesmerizingly lovely BBC video), the fact is that all of its intrinsic merits are, alas, outweighed by its one flaw, pedagogically almost a tragic one: its prohibitively high level of idle wordplay. Shakespeare is never so purely the model Elizabethan, or so little the man for all time, as when he is chasing down every pun that comes within a hundred paces of him, bashing it open to expose its marrow, and then toying with the marrow with a stick. It would be a rank discourtesy, both to Shakespeare and to the first-time reader of Shakespeare, to introduce the latter to the former when the great man was busying himself with this most trivial of pursuits.

PERICLES

Although *Pericles* is in most respects a "fractured" fairy tale if ever there was one, the fact remains that anyone searching through the canon for a fairy tale and a fable of death and rebirth would be far better advised to choose it than *The Winter's Tale*. The former, for all its faults — chief among them, Gower's often excruciatingly (or comically, depending upon one's mood) bad verse — is at least magnificently alive, whereas the latter is, one can only judge, in some sort of frigid state of suspended animation. Doubtless many keep their distance from *Pericles* because its authorship is doubtful, but clearly (in my view, and most of the scholars') many scenes, such as that featuring the fishermen (II, i), and above all all of Act V (in my opinion, one of the most sublime acts in the entire canon), are from the hand of the Master.[44]

Unfortunately, the pedagogic *Pericles* is, to put it mildly, problematic. The chief problem, as I see it, is that while this work, like *Two Gentlemen*, has much to recommend it as a junior high text, it too has a fatal pedagogic flaw. I say "junior high text" because I think younger students would be more likely than upperclassmen to respond well to this work's consistently moralistic tone; its gnomic little couplets, with their fortune-cookie tags, are ones the young student might be able to both enjoy and learn from. Then too, Gower's tetrameter, wretched as it often is, might be easier for the junior high student to get a handle on than the full Shakespearean pentameter, while it would only bore and exasperate the upperclassman.

Alas, the tragic pedagogic flaw I have spoken of is the very racy dialogue in all of the scenes in Act IV having to do with Marina's captivity. These, in my estimation, are just too potent sexually for the tender ears of pre-teens and early teens ("And if she were a thornier piece of ground than she is, she shall be plowed," etc.). Needless to say, the tenor of all these scenes is in fact deeply moral — Marina being a kind or pre-Christian Major Barbara, only a far better hand at conversion — but nonetheless the dialogue is often the salty old Bard at his very saltiest.

Yet while I am forced to throw the pedagogic *Pericles* over-

[44]Anyone doubting this would have to look only at a single utterly sublime figure of speech in this play and then try to pretend that any mind other than Shakespeare's could have conceived it. When Boult wants to assure the Bawd that news of a virgin in their midst will immediately bring them customers, he says, "I warrant you, mistress, *thunder shall not so awake the beds of eels* as my giving out her beauty stirs up the lewdly-inclined." Could any image, with its vision of the subconscious as an ocean and of eels as phallic symbols, be more perfectly Freudian?

board, as a work not well suited either to the younger or the older student, I confess I secretly hope it washes up on some colleague's shore and arises, Thaisa-like, to astonish teacher and students alike. For despite its very real weaknesses *Pericles* is, I have found, a work whose charm waxes rather than wanes with long acquaintance. (Perhaps not so surprising, given the fact that this story, in one form or another, has been pleasing Europeans for centuries.) And when I remember as well that the BBC video is a superb one, and that on video this work's innumerable changes in time and scene bother the viewer far less than they do on the stage, I am emboldened to prophesy that *Pericles* will one day be the "sleeper" hit of some intrepid teacher's elective.

TITUS ANDRONICUS

If it were left up to students to frame their own Shakespeare syllabus, *Titus Andronicus* no doubt quickly would become as perennial a favorite as it is at Stratford-upon-Avon. Indeed, one easily can envision the kind of comical scene that might ensue if students were given the opportunity to "vote in" the Shakespeare plays they would study each year.

The student body having gathered together for an assembly, the plot synopses are being read out one after the other. Although some students seem interested, most are drowsing off. Then the description of *Titus* gets under way and an electric shock passes through the throng, rousing it from its lethargy. As one gruesome incident succeeds another the crowd's first tentative titters crescendo to gleeful howls, and when the time at last arrives for the vote *Titus* carries the day "handily." Looking back on the election, the pundits are agreed that it was the unprecedented size and unanimity of the male vote that accounted for the ample margin of victory.

Yet even if it is indeed likely that, in any such referendum, its high level of gore would win over most adolescents — those eternal denizens of the "pit"! — and while it does contain many arresting scenes and striking poetic passages, *Titus* clearly has too little to offer intellectually to make it a work worthy of study at the secondary level. Perhaps the only exception to this rule I can think of (and in suggesting it I may wrongfully be labeled an "elitist") is that *Titus*, particularly if taught in conjunction with the appropriately gruesome BBC video, might be one Shakespeare play that really could get through to inner-city kids whose lives have been blighted by violence.

TIMON OF ATHENS

Nothing would so satisfy my instinct for the dramatic as to announce to my colleagues that, much in the manner of Timon himself in Act IV, I have stumbled onto gold (mine being of the pedagogic variety) when I had least expected to. Alas, the only ore I have been able to unearth in *Timon of Athens* — the magnificent poetry of Timon's tirades, in the last two acts especially — has long since been laid claim to by many a previous commentator. In other words, making exception solely of its great verse, I have found *Timon* to be every bit the thoroughgoing flop generations of earlier critics have found it to be.

While *Timon* has little enough to offer the reader — not to mention the young reader — in the way of gripping plot or varied and interesting characterization, of course what really makes it so thoroughly *unpleasant* a work is the misanthropy that we find at its very core. Yet while we would be acting prudently if we barred Timon from our syllabuses simply for having so dour a look on his face, and such an excess of vinegar in his soul, what should really make him persona non grata in the secondary classroom is not so much his misanthropy as the severely flawed character that provided misanthropy with so many cracks and chinks in which to take root and grow. Let us inspect it more closely for a moment, by the light of our new understanding of one typical characteristic of adolescents.

The assertion was made, in the course of my remarks on the adolescent character in Chapter 1, that the young person too often suffers from the delusion that all goodness is within him, all badness without, and it was suggested that only life itself — helped along, it is to be hoped, by the best of educations — can cure him of it. That the normal, and in most respects desirable, course of human development is that which takes an individual from a cloistered, rather selfish virtue to full social humility strikes one forcibly when one observes a life such as Timon's, where this progression has been reversed. It would seem that he or she who begins life assuming that other men and women are paragons of virtue is all too likely to end it reviling them as contemptible curs. Thus while the rather innocent solipsism native to young people often makes them unattractive and rather ridiculous, we realize when we compare them with Timon that the virtue of beginning life with a thin skin is that it can be shed long before it has had a chance to harden into a formidable defensive armor of bitterness and misanthropy.

Now the point here is that if it is quintessentially adolescent to cast oneself as the tormented, misunderstood "artist" in a world fraught with back-stabbing philistines, then our students are only temporary adolescents while Timon is an eternal one. Just as the young person tends (charmingly enough, to be sure) to be far too lavish in her praise and unstinting in her generosity whenever she genuinely loves or admires someone, so too Timon throws pearls (or jewels, rather) before his swinish friends. And just as, at the slightest disillusionment with her erstwhile god, the young person often becomes as implacable a foe and as captious a critic as she had before been a devoted friend and an ardent admirer, so Timon rails at others when he should chide himself for having confused prodigality and sentimentality with munificence and magnanimity.

Of course it might be asserted that it is precisely because Timon is such an adolescent in the manner in which, having rated the human race far too high, disillusionment with it cuts him off not only from people but from any hope of achieving self-knowledge and self-mastery, that we should offer his story to the young as a cautionary tale. The problem here is that the young person is far more likely to mistake Timon's acerbity for a Holden Caulfield-like sincerity and un-phoniness, and his eloquence for the expression of great and abiding human truths, than he is to see in him his own highly defensive insecurity.

One can only conclude by saying that, given the fact the adolescent is struggling to walk the tightrope between a wild extroversion and a brooding introversion, niggardliness and profligacy, sentimentality and cynicism, we teachers have no business directing his gaze to so shaky a character as Timon of Athens.

HENRY VIII

Clearly, *Henry VIII* is a work not suitable for study in the secondary classroom. For one thing, this is a play that lacks dramatic unity, telling as it does four stories rather than one:

those of Buckingham, Wolsey, Katharine, and Anne "Bullen." This alone is a fatal pedagogic flaw, in that the student has no one or two protagonists to follow through all five acts (the King hardly engages the reader's sympathy), and more importantly no one central theme to analyze.

Then too, *Henry VIII* is almost as much an historical pageant as it is a drama, suited far better to the stage than to the printed page, and this also makes it entirely the wrong play for book-study by young people. While the "intrinsic" play has of course many merits (above all the stirring confrontation between Katharine and Cardinals Wolsey and Campeius in Act III, scene i), these alone will never win it the right to enter the secondary classroom.

THE MERRY WIVES OF WINDSOR

To view a virtually flawless performance of *The Merry Wives of Windsor*, which is what the BBC video now gives all of us the opportunity to do, is to be swept up to the seventh heaven of pure theatrical joy. For this play is not only a superbly constructed farce, and perhaps the most sublime evocation of Elizabethan village life in all of literature, but also, in its last act, as moonstruck an idyll as *Midsummer*. Indeed for me, as one for whom a bit of fantasy goes a long way, and for whom fairies are all the more lovable when they are quite plainly children with pasted-on wings, the mini-*Midsummer Night's Dream* that is Act V of *Merry Wives* is infinitely more touching, and of a purer lyric beauty, than its more elaborate and carefully wrought counterpart.

Purely delightful as *Merry Wives* is, it is clearly a work to be seen rather than read, to be reveled in rather than to be taught. Like some magical elixir that must be drunk only from its native spring, this play will delight and refresh whoever (of whatever age) sees it in a good performance, but its wondrous properties are sure to evaporate if we are so foolish as to try to bottle it and peddle it in our classrooms. If ever there was a time to invoke the principle enunciated earlier in this book, that the more *essential* it is to see a work in performance the more certain we can be that it is a work best left untaught, it is now.

Nor is this true only because there is a sprightliness and good humor to this piece certain not to rise up off the printed page and take the student by the hand. It is also true simply because in a farce so superbly crafted as this, it is all but impossible for a reader to envision in her mind's eye the agitated comings and goings of Master Ford and the rest with any degree of accuracy. We tend to think of "physical comedy" as invariably meaning slapstick, or the kind of rough-and-tumble antics one might see in a good production of *Shrew*, but the wild and frantic rushing-about that characterizes *Merry Wives* is every bit as physical as those bits of business, and just as certain to go unnoticed by the student reader. Also certain to be nothing but a headache to the student are the phoneticized spellings of the dialogue of the French Doctor Caius and the Welsh Sir Hugh Evans.

One can only conclude from all of this that so pure and blessedly amoral an entertainment as *The Merry Wives of Windsor* has been bequeathed to the intellectual public as a kind of Windsor Park of the mind, a place where we may forever wander and restore our frazzled wits. Virtually every form of amusement is permitted to us here, but we have been warned that the park will be shut down the minute anyone fails to heed its one widely posted injunction: "WARNING: Those who wander here must never give a single thought to entering a building — and above all, a school building."

Postscript: There is only one rather unusual way I can conceive of making use of *Merry Wives* in the classroom. While I do believe that there can never be any justification for having secondary students study the text of this work, and while I doubt whether it's advisable to show the video of a work that hasn't been studied at all, a humanities course striving to make connections between the different disciplines might show students all or some of a video of Verdi's *Falstaff*, which is largely based on *Merry Wives*. (I note that my local video store has two separate listings for this work.) Students might get a real kick out of this joint masterwork by an English and an Italian genius.

6.

THE "IDEAL" SYLLABUS

Before I can share with my colleagues my "ideal" syllabus, I must of necessity give them some idea of what I think is wrong with the typical syllabus as one finds it in most schools today. Needless to say, given all of the judgments of individual plays that I have rendered thus far, the first thing I think is wrong is that too many of the wrong plays are being taught and too few of the right ones.

Yet while I will attempt to codify my thoughts on that subject shortly, I wish at the moment to speak of what kind of impression of Shakespeare the average student is likely to have formed after four-six years of reading the plays the present syllabus offers to her. For given the fact that every student hears Rumor of Shakespeare long before she or he ever makes his acquaintance, and therefore tends to imagine that Shakespeare's work must be a sort of paradigm of all of Western culture, and of book-larnin' in general, we can hardly underestimate the ill effect on the cultural life of our nation as a whole if our students, once they have at last been introduced to this fabled Bard, are only too glad to bid him farewell, in the firm conviction that "this Shakespeare stuff" — and perhaps, by extension, this learning stuff — ain't what it's cracked up to be.

It would of course have been an impossible task for me to somehow process my survey results and see if there is anything like *one* completely standard Shakespeare syllabus out there, and even if there were that degree of uniformity across the country one would only have cause to lament the fact that "independent" schools were independent in name only. Nonetheless, let us look for a moment at a syllabus which, while it ignores the facts that in many schools one grade level, usually the 11th, is given over to the study of American literature, and that many schools offer Shakespeare electives, generally open to juniors and seniors, is at least roughly representative of current practice:

> 8th grade — Julius Caesar
> 9th grade — Romeo and Juliet
> 10th grade — Macbeth
> 11th grade — Othello
> 12th grade — Hamlet

Let me repeat that my concern at the moment is not with whether I believe in each of these plays individually, or feel that they are being taught at the proper grade level, but with the cumulative effect the study of them is likely to have on the adolescent mind.

If there is a single thread running through all of these plays it is that they are tragedies: works full of passion and violence about eminent individuals who come to grief. While I freely admit that I have stacked the curricular deck unfairly, and that at least one of these grade slots probably would have been filled, in most syllabuses, by a *Shrew*, or a *Twelfth Night*, or a *Midsummer*, I have done so to make the point that the average syllabus does indeed rely much more heavily on the tragedies than on the "comedies" or the histories.

Now as to why this should be the case, two answers suggest themselves. First, the tragedies almost certainly are thought by many teachers to be (by and large) intrinsically weightier than the other plays, and therefore they assume that by serving their students a diet heavy on murder, remorse, etc. they must be giving them that which is also the most morally and intellectually nutritious.

Second, the tragedies, more than many of the other plays, have gripping plots and clearly delineated good guys and bad guys, and it is assumed — perhaps rightly, to a certain extent at least — that these are pedagogic assets too valuable not to be invested in class time. Clearly there is at least *enough* validity in the latter line of reasoning that he who wishes to diversify the Shakespeare syllabus, breaking up the present near-monopoly by the tragedies, must seek to prove that there is something in the nature of tragedy itself that unsuits it, except in carefully administered doses, to the adolescent mind and the secondary classroom.

I begin to make the case against presenting too much tragedy in our classrooms by reminding my colleagues that while tragedy may or may not be the most important literary *art form*, we certainly err if we assume that the word "tragic" is necessarily that which best describes human life and destiny. For while all of us would agree that life does contain countless tragedies — events that cut short or severely limit lives that otherwise might have been full of happiness and goodness — many of us would go on to deny the larger proposition that life is "tragic" simply because all men and women must die. Surely it is true to say of most human beings that their days on earth are far more deeply embued with pathos (on the emotional level) and filled with troubles (on both the physical and moral levels) than they are dogged by tragedy.

If it is indeed true that life is far bigger and more troublesome than even that grave and portentous term "tragic" can suggest, and if one has ever suspected that the picture of life offered to us by tragedy of the Shakespearean sort is at best fifty percent representational, the other half having been drawn for the express purposes of a) purging our emotions through pity and terror and b) selling tickets to a satisfying "evening in the theater," then as an educator one has a solemn duty to think through the ramifications of those two facts. For after all, an educator's chief responsibility is to prepare the student for life in "the real world," and if she discovers that she is doing this far less well than she is teaching her students how to appreciate a particular art form called "tragedy" we all have grounds to be concerned. Our concern can only be heightened if we feel that some of the tragedies that are commonly being taught are not giving us even their required fifty percent of accurate social scene-painting, and it is precisely for this reason that I've argued so vociferously against teaching *Othello*.

I'm by no means asserting here that a *Romeo and Juliet* or a *Hamlet*, simply because they are tragedies, have nothing to teach the young about "real life" — clearly they have almost everything to teach. What I'm trying to suggest is that most of the specifically "tragic" moments in these plays — the lovers in the tomb, Hamlet on a corpse-strewn stage — have far more to do with good drama than with good philosophy or with providing the viewer with an unsentimental yet thoroughly moral orientation toward life. To make matters worse, the academic, with his perpetual tendency to take labels too seriously, is liable to take these moments far too seriously and try to "teach" *them* rather than the thousand and one seemingly incidental moral aperçus of which a work such as *Hamlet* has so rich a store.

It should also be noted, at this juncture, that one may accuse tragedy of being unsuitable for study by adolescents on grounds utterly unrelated to those used to support the charge we have thus far been leveling, that tragedy is by no means the mirror held up to Nature that its proponents are so convinced it is. One might cite, for instance, the simple fact that the kings and queens etc. who are so often the protagonists in tragedy are figures adolescents may come to be interested in, but whom they certainly don't "relate to" in any real way. So too, tragedy's high level of passion and violence — with characters seemingly always rubbing blood from their hands (or trying to!), tossing off poison like Perrier, and throwing fits (of the epileptic variety) over lost handkerchiefs — is more likely to cause the student to exclaim, "Wow! Radical!" than "This is uncannily similar to life as my friends and I live it!".

Even more importantly, one can base one's objection to too much tragedy in the classroom on the plain fact that tragedy is inevitably "me"-oriented, and lacks that broader social vision so many of the "comedies" and histories provide us with. A great tragedy is of necessity about an individual's battle *against* external forces. While all of us must of course fight that battle in our own lives, and while the study of tragedy can help us to fight it more ably and with greater dignity, tragedy's tendency to portray life as exclusively an "I against them" struggle may only serve to reinforce rather than to break down the walls of solipsism and pride with which the adolescent — and Everyperson — is continually shoring up her or his ego.

Thus it must by now be clear what the deficiencies of the present Shakespeare syllabus (almost all of them springing from an over-reliance on the tragedies) are, in my view: too much gloominess; a tendency to confute the merely solemn (for instance, the death scene in the tomb in *R & J*) and the merely dramatic (for instance, Edmund's plot against Edgar in *Lear*) with the morally serious (for instance, the seemingly sheerly idyllic *As You Like It*); characters too far removed from the general experience of modern men and women; and an overemphasis on the tormented individual psyche at the expense of unremitting concern for social issues.

The remedy for these ills is, to our great good fortune, ready to hand: certain of the "comedies" to a) instill in our students a sense that life's problems can be approached cheerfully and without inordinate hand-wringing, but that they are indeed complex and require the most delicate thinking and handling, and b) provide them with characters somewhat more recognizable as down-to-earth human beings than a Brutus or an Othello; and certain of the history plays to a) remind students of the great truth that truth is always both stranger than and greater than fiction, b) help them to know what Carlyle knew, that "man must be governed" — whether well or ill being up to us as concerned citizens — and c) make plain to them that human problems are even more widespread and persistent than human tragedies, in much the same way as humankind is, from a cosmic perspective, bigger and more important than any one person.

Having taken this much time to look at a relatively typical syllabus and speak briefly about some of its shortcomings, the time at last has come for me to put up or shut up by offering my colleagues a syllabus demonstrably superior to their own. First allow me to state that when I refer to this as an "ideal" syllabus I am thinking of the adjective in both of its senses. I *hope* that my syllabus, were it to be put to the test in a colleague's school, would prove itself ideal in the sense of "optimal," but both my colleagues and I know well that the student is a very unpredictable customer, and may well refuse to buy these curricular choices even when (or perhaps *because*) she has been told they will be good for her. Thus "ideal" as used here also has a connotation, if only in my own rather wavering mind, of "merely theoretical; untested." I hope and believe that my syllabus could indeed prove itself in the educational marketplace, but I'm well aware that until the product is actually out there on the shelves all hopes are vain.

That said, let it be known that my aim here is to suggest to my colleagues which plays are for all intents and purposes "the unteachables,"[1] which are available to them for required courses (and at which "ideal" grade levels), and which are best suited to electives and/or AP courses. Let's begin with "the unteachables."

In offering my colleagues a list of the plays best left untaught at the secondary level, I do so with an ironic nod and wink both to the immortal Bard and to them. For if I thought for one moment that all my colleagues would take me strictly at my word, and never be so wisely foolish as to say, "Aw, who cares

[1]Like a good Elizabethan I find I just can't resist this pun, but of course I mean by it not just the plays that I feel "can't" be taught but also the plays that *shouldn't* be taught.

what Roberts says, let's throw *Titus Andronicus* at them next term and see whether it grosses them out [or "... *Coriolanus* at them and see what they make of it," etc. etc.], I would never be so bold as to place a good bit of Shakespeare's work out of the reach of students and teachers alike.

And now, my fit of humility blessedly past, I proceed to offer my reader not one but two lists of plays I feel are best left untaught at the secondary level. From my own point of view plays on both lists are equally unsuited to the secondary class-room, but I have thought it politic, and a good way of showing "a decent respect for the opinions of mankind," to give in one list those plays many an analyst might agree with me quite readi-ly about, and in the other those plays that only the reader of my play-by-play commentaries would be in a position to understand my objection to. Because I object to some of these plays strongly and to others far less so (for instance, I feel that if *Two Gentlemen* were an only slightly different play it would be an ideal junior high text), I have ranked both lists from most to least "unteachable."

"Objective" List	"Subjective" List
Henry VI	The Winter's Tale
Henry VIII	Richard III
King John	Othello
Timon of Athens	King Lear
The Comedy of Errors	The Tempest
Love's Labor's Lost	
The Merry Wives of Windsor	
Titus Andronicus	
The Two Gentlemen of Verona	

Assuming as I do that my reader will refer back to the com-mentaries if he wishes to remind himself of why the above works have been proscribed, I now move on to list those works that I feel are not suitable for required courses but might work well in electives or with AP ("honors," etc.) groups. Needless to say, a teacher is also free to choose any of the more standard works (to be listed and discussed in a moment) for use in an elective or AP course. In this case I've ranked the plays from most to least desirable (left, then right column), but the reader should note that I'm really only "lobbying" hard for the first two on the list.

Elective/AP Choices

Measure for Measure	Twelfth Night
Cymbeline	Coriolanus
All's Well That Ends Well	Pericles
Henry V	Much Ado About Nothing

Our dessert menu of electives having now been drawn up, we can at last turn our attention to the main course. Yet before the chef describes his creations, perhaps he should offer his guests a look at them spread out on a buffet table. He reminds them in advance, however, that while he will stake his small share of professional honor on the fact that they are being served in the right order, it will be up to the discretion and good judgment of his colleagues whether they wish to have their students consume all, one, or none of the works listed for each grade level.

[Note: When a play is listed more than once, this simply means that it might work at either grade level. At each grade level the most likely choice has been placed on top, alternates or less likely possibilities beneath it. The reader should note, however, that these rankings have far less significance for me than the similar rankings of the "unteachables" and the elective choices.]

7th grade	As You Like It
8th grade	As You Like It Julius Caesar
9th grade	Julius Caesar Richard II (?)
10th grade	Macbeth Romeo and Juliet The Merchant of Venice The Taming of the Shrew
11th grade	Hamlet Henry IV (with Richard II?) The Merchant of Venice A Midsummer Night's Dream Antony and Cleopatra
12th grade	Troilus and Cressida, *plus any of the above 11th-grade plays other than* Hamlet

Let us now take a closer look at each work in the "ideal" syllabus. As my reader knows by now, I believe passionately that *As You Like It* is *the* work for the young, first-time reader of Shakespeare. Indeed, I feel so strongly about this that I'm tempted to say that the student who reads this work in an 11-12 elective (which is, the survey reveals, where she is most likely to meet up with it in most schools) is doing so "too late."

Julius Caesar is simply too strong, intrinsically but above all pedagogically, to exile it from any syllabus for more than a year or so. If I, like so many before me, have decided that it works best as "young people's Shakespeare," I would offer the following rationale for that decision.

First, its gripping plot, memorizable orations, and above all immense readability make it a natural for the student new to Shakespeare. Second, the element of stolidity and even, to some, boredom in this play suits it to the rather ponderous, un-ironic intellect of the twelve- to fourteen-year-old. Older students deserve to be consistently thrilled and challenged by Shakespeare, and *JC* does neither as well as many another play. Third, there is so much in *JC* that is of extraordinary psychological subtlety — above all, the confrontation between Brutus and Cassius in Act IV, scene iii — that even the adult reader can marvel at its moral ambiguities without feeling himself capable of — or indeed interested in — unraveling their twisted skeins. If this is true, we are probably right in thinking that certain aspects of *JC* would elude seniors just as completely as they will elude 7th-9th graders, and that therefore we have the right to position this play in our syllabus where we feel it will do the most good.

I would take this opportunity, however, to remind my reader of the position I adopted in the course of my commentary on *JC*: As I see it, this play should *not* be the first Shakespeare play a student reads. If this in turn means that most students will end up coming to *JC* no sooner than in the 9th grade, that is probably all to the good.

Before one can decide how best to position *Richard II* and *Henry IV*, one must first decide whether one wishes to teach them together or separately. Let us examine the pros and cons of each approach.

The great pedagogic benefit of teaching these two plays back-to-back (either in the same year or the same term) would be that the student watching the rise and subsequent demise of Bolingbroke could get a sense of history, with all of its grand sweep and its bitter ironies, that no history text could hope to rival. If we have said that the self-absorbed young person stands in perpetual need of wider and more penetrating "social vision," the Bolingbroke saga, as it unfolds across three plays, is the work certain to endow him with it.

If the two plays are to be taught back-to-back, at what grade level will this be most effective? My own belief is that *Henry IV*, whether taught alone or in conjunction with *Richard II*, should be taught only to juniors and seniors, and this for three reasons. First and foremost, its central theme, that of a young person's transformation from reckless libertine to relatively responsible individual, is one that can be fully appreciated only by the student who is undergoing the same metamorphosis. Ninth- and tenth-graders are in most respects pure youths, not youths in transition.

Second, Falstaff's humor can be reveled in, and the heavily footnoted lines in which it finds expression can seriously be grappled with, only by a relatively mature reader. The 9th- or 10th-graders sense of irony is still too dim for him to see Falstaff as the walking incarnation of an absurd portentousness, and no literary sin is more egregious than that of seeing him as a mere Gargantua, a man-mountain.

Third, and most simply, *Henry IV* is one of Shakespeare's greatest and most characteristic productions, and therefore a work under no circumstances to be thrown away on the jejeune. Let it also be noted, in this context, that in my opinion we err greatly when we decide that the secondary student *must* meet Hamlet, Lear, or Othello, but that he will meet Falstaff only if the latter can manage to squeeze his huge bulk into an already tightly crowded syllabus. Doubtless we have in the past been led into this error partly owing to our subconscious sense that so kinetic a figure as Falstaff can't begin to come to life on the printed page. Yet while our error was entirely a forgivable one in the pre-video era, to continue to persist in it would be madness. For at the touch of a button, and whenever we feel need of him, Falstaff (as impersonated brilliantly by Anthony Quayle in the BBC video) can now be summoned, huffing and puffing, into our classrooms.

As for *Richard II*, the teacher who decides to have his juniors or seniors study this play, either on its own or before going on to *Henry IV*, may do so with reasonable equanimity. *Richard II* is a mature work, and the more mature the student who reads it, the better. Nonetheless, I am going to go way out on a limb and suggest that teachers should at least try to teach this work to freshmen, and this for one primary reason.

We have pointed out, as this play's most priceless pedagogic asset, its crystal-clear, footnote-free verse. Surely it should be one of our most important objectives as English teachers to convince our students early, and to keep them convinced for a good bit after that (before they are confronted by the undeniably difficult verse of *R & J*, *Hamlet*, *Macbeth*, etc., not to mention that of *Cymbeline* or *Measure for Measure*) that Shakespeare really does speak their language.

Just as surely, the student who in junior high has studied the genuinely readable *Julius Caesar* and/or the relatively readable *As You Like It* would be in for quite a shock if in my syllabus, as in the current standard one, he suddenly found himself confronted by *R & J*'s more complex verse. Thus while I freely admit that both *Richard II*'s subject matter and the pedagogic problems attendant upon teaching the history plays may be enough to scuttle its chances as a 9th-grade text, teachers who decide to give it the old college try can at least enter their classrooms knowing that this play's reading level really does suit it to this grade level. More importantly, they can enter knowing that if they somehow manage to beat the odds and make this play succeed at this level, many a student who might have been turned off to Shakespeare at a prematurely early age because of the difficulty of his language will perhaps go on in the next few years to develop a genuine love for — or at least a real interest in — the immortal Bard.

While the issue of readability is what first led me to think that *Richard II* might just work in the 9th grade, I have come to think that there is perhaps an even more important case to be made for studying this play at this grade level. I suggested, as a parting thought in my commentary on *Romeo and Juliet*, that while that play doubtless is worth teaching for the passion and excitement it brings into students' lives, it may not be all as a *learning experience* that it should be. Isn't it conceivable that *Richard II* represents that learning experience, and this, ironically enough, precisely because it is certain to be more antipathetic to adolescent taste than *R & J* ?

In an educational essay written near the turn of the century, Harvard professor Barrett Wendell makes the interesting point that the real virtue of the old classical education was that it forced the schoolboy *to pay close attention to things that didn't interest him* (Greek and Latin) and thus fostered the "faculty of voluntary attention" ("voluntary" being used here in its sense of "related to the will," not that of "by one's own consent"), the very faculty "which education, in the broadest sense, can most surely cultivate."[2] Surely Wendell is on to something there, and surely the youths of our own day — they who are evolving, even as we speak, a slot in the skull into which videos can be inserted directly — need to be drilled far more rigorously in the fine art of paying attention than did the youths of 1908. While *R & J* doubtless is still worth teaching, I do think we teachers should acknowledge the fact that it is a work about as little likely to develop in students "the faculty of voluntary attention" as any one can think of.

As for the best grade-level positioning for *R & J*, I can only repeat what I said in my commentary on the play. For reasons both of language difficulty and student maturity I feel we should move this play from the 9th to the 10th grade, and even to the latter half of the 10th grade. I have no real argument with *Macbeth*'s present preeminence as *the* 10th-grade text, so I suppose a teacher intent on following the "ideal" syllabus to the letter would just have to find room for both plays in that year, alternate them from year to year, or find some other arrangement that seemed to work for her.

For me at least, *The Merchant of Venice* is a play somewhat difficult to position in a syllabus, at least on any strictly logical basis. On the one hand, the whole subplot concerning the wooing of Portia seems to me ideally suited to the younger reader. The verse is marvelously mellifluous, and easy to read as well. Then too, the wooing scenes are essentially the stuff of fairy tales, and therefore well suited to the younger reader. On the other hand the whole anti-Semitism issue is almost certainly too much to impose on the junior-high reader, which means that the present (partial) consensus, which seems to be to teach *Merchant* primarily in the 9th grade, is perhaps a sensible one.

Nonetheless, I haven't quite managed to drive from my head a conversation I had with a female 10th-grader who had read *Merchant* at another school in an earlier grade (I don't recall which, but it was either 8th or 9th). Her reaction to having studied the play, when I managed to elicit it from her, was one of the heartiest "Yuck!"'s I've ever heard, and she assured me that her sentiment was precisely that of the majority of her classmates. While of course it would be absurd to base any decision vis-à-vis *Merchant* on one isolated comment, this project

[2]Barrett Wendell, "Our National Superstition," in *The Privileged Classes* (New York: Charles Scribner's Sons, 1908), p. 172.

means nothing if it doesn't mean that every fervid student "Yuck!" must be given its day in court. My hunch is that we should be counseled by this one to move *Merchant* to grade 10 or even 11, where the anti-Semitism issue can be analyzed and discussed by more mature minds.

For me one of the real surprises of the survey results was the revelation that *The Taming of the Shrew* is taught quite a bit more in 11-12 than in all of 7-10 combined. While there is of course no reason why *Shrew* couldn't figure in an elective, I do feel that in general juniors and seniors should be chewing and digesting only the most morally meaty of the plays, taking perhaps an occasional glass of the very best champagne — *Midsummer* — as an antidote to overseriousness and intellectual fatigue. *Shrew* is a saucy dish, but simply too insubstantial to serve to maturing young people, intent on storing up on moral and intellectual energy before entering the great world. All of which leads me to think that grade 10 is probably the right one for this work.

Perhaps those who have thought it best to teach *Shrew* in 11-12 have done so in the conviction that only older students should be exposed to its sexism, or are capable of discussing tensions between the sexes. The objection to this is that *Shrew* is a farce, meant to be enjoyed and laughed at rather than critically dissected.[3] By the same token, while one can understand why many a teacher might balk at teaching so sexist a work, its sexism is as much broad caricature as everything else in the play, and therefore hardly worth boycotting as a matter of principle.

The rationale for demoting *Hamlet* to the 11th grade and promoting a complete curricular unknown — *Troilus and Cressida* — to the top spot in the syllabus has in most respects already been given as part of my closing remarks in the commentary on *Hamlet*. To repeat, the theory here is that while *Hamlet* is doubtless the greater all-round work it is likely to perplex the student even as it stimulates and intrigues him, whereas the supposedly immoral *T & C* — if taught by those who have come to reverence both its intrinsic and its pedagogic virtues — is both a more accessible work in many ways and also a work that can promote genuine moral and intellectual growth in its reader. *Hamlet* can of course do the latter also, and do so splendidly, but

[3]I have no doubt at all that scholars have found much that is morally meaty and intellectually substantive in *Shrew*, but surely most of that subtext is too subtle to be analyzed with any great degree of success by secondary school students.

far more effectively for the mature reader, returning to it for the fifth time, than for the immature one, who finds himself lost without a map in a brave new world of poetic and moral meanings. *Troilus and Cressida* provides its reader with such a map.

While my reader knows by now that I don't believe in *A Midsummer Night's Dream* as young people's Shakespeare, he may be surprised to hear that I would in fact offer it only to the *oldest* of our students (i.e., never to 9th- or 10th-graders). For while I have said that the early adolescent is himself so consummate a "rude mechanical" he will never really see anything funny in Bottom and company, I would go on to suggest that the middle adolescent is in a perfect position, having gone through puberty and lived to tell the tale, to look back in smug self-satisfaction at the rude mechanical he used to be, and to laugh triumphantly.

In theory at least, *Antony and Cleopatra* is a play that could work well at a few different grade levels, and equally well as a required text or as part of an elective. However, it is certainly of interest that this play totally struck out in the survey's "most popular with students" category. Those who do decide to give it a try in the classroom probably won't want to assign it to anyone younger than a 10th-grader, for as engaging as the story is the verse is by no means Shakespeare's simplest (although it *is* some of his greatest).

In closing out our look at the "ideal" syllabus, let us pose and answer one final question: In having perpetually banished 14 out of the 34 Shakespeare plays (*Henry IV* and *Henry VI* each being counted here as one play) as "the unteachables," and in placing another 8 off-limits for any but elective or AP courses, thus leaving only 12 of the original 34 for teachers to draw on for their required courses, have I put an intolerable constraint on teachers, and unduly limited the scope of Shakespeare studies in the secondary school?

If I am in fact wrong about any of the 12 plays I have proscribed — a strong likelihood, given my lifelong penchant for the fallible — the answer from my reader can only be an angry "Yes!" Yet as I see it the net effect of my proscriptions would be to widen rather than narrow the intellectual and emotional scope of Shakespeare studies in the secondary school. In purging the syllabus as a whole of the Sturm und Drang of *Othello*, *Richard III*, *Lear*, etc., we would in effect "ventilate" it, allowing the sunny cheerfulness of an *As You Like It* and the hastening, chastening wind of a *Troilus and Cressida* to sweep some of the portentous clouds away.

It is also worthy of note, I think, that for virtually every work I have banished I have granted full citizenship to some relative newcomer to the realm: Richard III has haled his hump elsewhere, but that overly handsome man, Richard II, has joined us; Othello is throwing a fit at being excluded, but Imogen, that faithful and virtuous woman, has promised to stay with us if we will abide with her; Caliban has wandered off in a dugeon, but Thersites is very much with us, snapping at our heels and reminding us what rogues we mortals be.

One final and I think very important point in this regard. Think for a moment, if you will, of the heroines to be found in the Shakespeare plays now being widely taught: Calpurnia, Hermia and Helena, Juliet, Kate, Lady Macbeth, Desdemona, Ophelia, Gertrude, Viola, Cordelia, Miranda. What a perfect cross-section of unliberated womanhood! What a choice group of *victims*! And this seems roughly true even when one takes into account the dignity and intellect of a Calpurnia, the brassiness of a Lady Macbeth, the spunk of a Cordelia.

Now think of Rosalind, who dons men's clothing only because it shows off the strength of her womanhood to better advantage; of Isabella, whose true purity finally burns away the dross of her prudishness; of Helena (in *All's Well*, not *Midsummer*) the healer and the mender of broken men; of Portia, that proto-Yuppie outclassing the men assembled with her at the bar; of Imogen, that wisest, strongest, and most constant of women. Surely we find in that listing alone proof positive that the "ideal" syllabus is very much a *feminist* syllabus, a syllabus that offers young women heroines whom they may emulate rather than victims with whom they can only commiserate. Given that fact, I can hardly think that any of my female readers in particular is eager to go back to the bad old days when Viola the Perky, Helena and Hermia the Bitchy, and Miranda the Airy-Fairy were virtually the only women on hand to show the female student around the House of Pain where so many of their sisters lay in bondage.

If then the "ideal" syllabus really is more varied and intellectually interesting than the present syllabus it seeks to transform, what is perhaps all the more remarkable is that it comes so close to holding its own with the old syllabus in terms of numbers of plays available to teachers. If one turns to the data on pages 226–227, one notices that in today's standard syllabus there are 12 plays quite heavily taught (down to *Henry IV, Part One*), 10 plays less so (down through *Measure for Measure*), and 13 virtually not at all. The ideal syllabus, by contrast (or rather, lack of contrast) offers 12 standards (matching today's top 12), and it comes remarkably close to matching the old syllabus's total of 24 basic "teachables" with its own total of 20.

Thus if one is convinced that the thinking and planning behind the "ideal" syllabus make it an immeasurably higher-*quality* syllabus than the sort of syllabus a bardolator might come up with (with his two false assumptions that all Shakespeare is good Shakespeare, and that intrinsically good Shakespeare is by definition pedagogically good Shakespeare) the fact that it comes so close to matching the old syllabus in *quantity* as well surely is rather remarkable.

Envoi

THE TWO-WAY PATH TO HAPPINESS AND VIRTUE

He [the model teacher] will then teach his pupil this new lesson: that the value and height of virtue lies in the ease, the profit, and the pleasure of its practice. . . . "

— MONTAIGNE

The whole process of moral evaluation and choice and directed development is justified in the long run only by the sort of life it facilitates and the sort of personality it produces: but in that process something more than mere goodness is achieved. To live only to be good is to become goody-good. People whose life is confined to obeying the prescribed rules for conduct tend to belittle the very purposes for which ethics exists: that is, a life both more abundant and more significant.[1]

— LEWIS MUMFORD

He [Shakespeare] loves virtue, not for its obligation, but for its grace.

— EMERSON

Given the fact that my reader and I must keep company for many more pages of important appendix material, it seems rather silly that I should be taking this opportunity to bid him or her "farewell." And yet some such final words of evaluation must be spoken of the "moral curriculum" and the revitalized Shakespeare syllabus that should be at its core. For although in earlier sections of this book I have tried to diagnose and provide remedies for some of the weaknesses in current curricular thinking, I have given my reader too slight a sense of precisely what benefits American society — or simply various indi-

---

[1] Lewis Mumford, *The Conduct of Life* (New York and London: Harcourt Brace Jovanovich, Publishers, 1970), p. 155.

165

vidual young people — could hope to receive if all secondary school curricula were more carefully and thoughtfully oriented toward the moral than they are at the moment.

Almost certainly my reader expects to find, at the focal point of my vision of a society regenerated in part by a new moral curriculum, a sober and unsmiling citizen, a puritan who has for so long trod the straight and narrow paths of Right Thinking and Right Conduct that all spring has vanished from his step and all luster from his eye. Therefore it gives me great pleasure to inform him that, while I do think many Americans would be greater and happier human beings than they are if there was less of what Chesterton somewhere refers to as a "harsh and barren frivolity" in their lives and more genuine spiritual elevation and intellectual sobriety, for me the most reliable road to a higher civilization than our own lies not so much down the aforementioned paths as down another that crosses and recrosses them: the path of Right Enjoyment.

For me, a great civilization would be one in which the majority of its citizens — or more realistically, a healthily large "saving remnant" — could make that distinction which, more than any other, distinguishes an adult from an adolescent intellect: that between "having a good time" and living a good — in every sense, not merely the delimited ethical one — life. Quite clearly, vast numbers of modern Americans are incapable of making that distinction, as the get-it-while-you-can, eat-drink-and-be-merry-for-tomorrow-we-go-bankrupt fiscal mentality of the 1980s has proved conclusively. Equally clearly, those who *can* make the distinction owe their ability chiefly to their recognition that life's highest, subtlest, and most enduring pleasures are intellectual ones.[2] For while the Germany of the thirties and forties has

---

[2] My reader will completely fail to grasp what I am on about in this section of the book unless I define with great care two of the terms I've just used in that sentence.

First of all, let it be well noted that by "pleasures" I really do mean "pleasures," not "satisfactions." Most men and women (especially women) find their deepest satisfactions in Love in all its many manifestations — preeminently love of spouse, family, and friends, but also love of community and nation, humanity, and God. This is as it should be. Unfortunately, however, because men and women are so profoundly, and rightly, satisfaction-oriented, when they go in search of pleasure they make the mistake of thinking that life's highest pleasures must resemble its deepest satisfactions. Thus instead of using what little leisure time their lives contain to stimulate new areas of their brains, they are content to endlessly restimulate its Corniness Center, trooping off to Kevin

taught us all too well that the link between a high level of culture and a high level of morality is too often a tenuous one, America in the eighties has been almost as effective at teaching us the "flip side" of the German lesson: that a society which widely abjures book-learning can sink to depths of geopolitical ignorance, cultural insipidity, and personal knavery almost too deep to be plumbed.[3]

Now at this point my reader may well be puzzled. If my long-term pedagogic goal is simply to create a society in which more men and women are capable of recognizing that intellectual pleasure is the highest form of pleasure, why then have I adopted such a sternly moral tone throughout this book, and why have I been so hard on those teachers who seek "only" to arouse in their students a love of literature that will last a lifetime? For two reasons.

I have done so, first, to make the point that the greatest works of literature, and therefore the highest sorts of intellectual pleasure, inevitably revolve around the meditation on moral issues. (After all, if that single noble phrase of Emerson's, "the sovereignty of ethics," seems to say it all about human life, it can hardly fail to do the same about that one small part of life we call "literature.") Until educators become more widely and deeply aware of this fact and, more vitally, of its crucial pedagogic importance, students will continue to be offered works that provide them with only middling amounts of intellectual pleasure.

Second, I have done so because I believe I have faced more frankly than many of my colleagues just how educationally and socially explosive the adolescent's "merciless pragmatism" will continue to be unless we can find some effective method of defusing it. For while that adolescent attitude has certain characteristics all its own — some of them, I have tried to point

Costner movies to shed big greasy tears at the sight of babies (or men with baby faces), rolling grasslands, and true love.
    Second, while by "intellectual" I do of course mean *books*, the term would scare off far fewer men and women than it does if they could be brought to understand that, for instance, playing with a child and carefully noting its actions and comments, watching TV thoughtfully and critically, or making good conversation, are all intellectual pleasures par excellence.

[3]I am of course aware that it's all but obscene to try to compare any other event in human history with the Holocaust, and aware as well that in this context the word "effective" could be misconstrued as being unspeakably insensitive. And yet we must take such risks if we wish to learn from history.

out, relatively charming and educationally beneficent — in many respects it is only the sinfully foolish and short-sighted utilitarianism of our culture writ small. The whole purpose of this book has been to insist that unless secondary education can find a way to counter the young person's already somewhat jaded utilitarianism with an inspired utilitarianism of its own — with the supremely useful lesson, elucidated by work after well-chosen work, that ultimately vice makes for pain and virtue makes for pleasure — our adolescent society's gospel of the "good time" will endlessly prevail over the wise person's gospel of the good life.

All of this leads us directly back to Shakespeare, the man and his work. His work, because there more effectively and less didactically than anywhere else in literature the great point is made again and again that happiness is virtue, virtue happiness. The lesson is of course by no means universal throughout the canon, which has more than its share of Timons and Tituses and Lears struggling to survive in a world where Providence, like Lavinia, seems to lack hands to succor or build, and where Justice, like Gloucester, seems blind indeed. Yet for many of us the affirmative note in Shakespeare sounds all the more sweetly and truly because it emerges from the cacophony of chaos and struggle.

It brings us back to the man, because, if students have gained any sense at all of Will Shakespeare from his plays and/or biographical materials, they have intuited that he is that personally luckiest and socially most valuable of men, an "intellectual" who has forsaken not a scrap of his simple humanity — his love of sex, music, laughter, and people of all ranks and types — as he has gone about acquiring the aesthetic graces of a poet and the dignity of a philosopher. We will recognize just how important it is for young Americans to make the acquaintance of such a man if we remind ourselves that in our country an "intellectual" is essentially the figure Jay Leno brought to life one night (chatting with a guest on the *Tonight* show), as he remembered one of his high school teachers: a dowdy, sexless, chalk-covered creature, the very thought of whom procreating was enough to make his blood run cold. Ridiculous as such a reflection might at first sound, I am entirely serious when I say that formal education can have *no* more important goal than to convince the average sensual man that the average "intellectual" is a creature not less but *more* vibrantly alive than he.

Now the significance for us here of the fact that Shakespeare is at one and the same time a "great man" and a simple man is that only such a person can help his fellow humans to understand that the path of Right Enjoyment is very much a two-way path. The great man insists that virtue really does lead to happiness, but the simple man also reminds us that genuine happiness — something entirely different from that loud and frantic sensualism our culture generally honors with the name — is itself only a step away from virtue. The whole point of this book has been to suggest that when we teach the most pedagogically ideal of William Shakespeare's plays, those in which the signposts along the path of Right Enjoyment are most clearly marked in both directions, we can rest assured that even the student who has missed the signpost pointing from Virtue to Happiness — say, Lucentio's lovely words from the opening of *Shrew*:

> Virtue and that part of philosophy
> Will I apply that treats of happiness
> By virtue specially to be achieved.

will see the post pointing from Happiness to Virtue as plain as day, as in Tranio's response to Lucentio:

> No profit grows where is no pleasure ta'en;
> In brief, sir, study what you most affect.

Once we secondary school teachers have put in place a Shakespeare syllabus that points the student clearly down the path of Right Enjoyment in both directions, can an entire curriculum — indeed, a national culture — that does the same be far behind?

Appendix I

SOME THOUGHTS ON THE TERM "COMEDY"

John Heminges and Henry Condell deserve to be thought of as among history's true secular saints, for the service they performed for humanity in rescuing Shakespeare's works from oblivion. Yet even as one revels gratefully in all they have passed on to us, one can scarcely repress a sigh whenever one considers some of the unforeseen evils that have plagued the academic community ever since the First Folio was divided into comedies, tragedies, and histories.

For while this device was hit upon merely as a way of imposing some minimal amount of order on the vast welter of Shakespearean genius, its chief result has been to provide fodder for generations of pedants. Addicted as the pedantic mind is to the overuse and the misuse of convenient labels, in that they free the mind from the hard labor of considering each work of art or each idea on its own merits and in the light of a myriad of shifting factors and influences, it could hardly have asked for a more potent "fix" than the labels "tragedy," "comedy," and "history" have provided it with.

The pedant's misuse of the term "history" has perhaps wreaked the least havoc, although we always do well to remind ourselves that a "history" such as *Richard II* is every bit as much a tragedy as *Macbeth*; that a "history" such as *Henry IV* contains Shakespeare's greatest scenes of comedy in the standard sense; and that many a tragedy — *Coriolanus*, for instance — is also history. However, virtually all of us fall victim to the same misconceptions as he when we think about the tragedies and "comedies," misconceptions almost certain to make us less wise as we go about choosing plays for a Shakespeare syllabus. While it is primarily the many mental errors the term "comedy" virtually forces us all to commit that I hope to say a thing or two about here, I must first attempt to describe the way in which many people think of the tragedies, for it is to a great extent our exaggerated deference toward the tragedies that explains why we offer such comparatively scant respect to the "comedies."

It seems likely that, in the eyes of many people, academics preeminent among them, the tragedies are the equivalent of the most exclusive of in-crowds, a club to which the ill-mannered comedies and the poor-relation histories will never gain admittance, no matter how often they send in the application form. Regrettable as such an attitude is, an analysis of three factors should at least help to make it understandable.

First, of course, there is the simple fact that Shakespeare's two greatest plays — *Hamlet* and *Lear* — are charter members of this club. These two throw such an aristocratic glow over all of their fellow club members — from the genuinely distinguished Coriolanus right down to reputed crime boss Titus ("The Avenger") Andronicus and Mr. Shabby Genteel himself, Timon of Athens — that many of those admiring them from the other side of the country club's gates probably manage to squelch their suspicions even about the last two, and decide that they too possess the charisma and good looks of the Big Two.

Secondly, and far more importantly, those who overvalue tragedy do so because they have fallen victim to a fallacy that afflicts all uncritical thinkers, that which mistakes the merely solemn or grave for the morally serious — a thing every bit as likely to manifest itself in laughter as in tears.

While of course the critic of drama, far more than any other critic, is repeatedly lured into this error — drama, by its very nature, trading in strong emotion and tragic incident — the discerning critic manages to resist it. He does so by freely admitting that a *Hamlet* or a *Lear* runs on a fuel of more or less pure tragic emotion, while at the same time insisting that what should concern us is not the fuel but the great vistas of moral meaning that the journey itself opens up all around us. In his eyes his more traditionally minded counterpart — he who intones the word "tragedy" in a hushed, reverential whisper — cuts a rather ridiculous figure, particularly when he is busy pouring this fuel into a tumbler, holding it up to the light, and sniffing it, like a true connoisseur.

Thirdly, a fellow by the name of Aristotle once threw out some remarks on the subject of tragedy, including one to the effect that tragedy is superior as an art form to the epic. Ever since then the Western mind, as loath to part company (or, more accurately, even to *seem* to part company) with "The Master of Those Who Know" on this issue as on those of ethics and religion, has accorded those remarks not so much the respect they deserve as a slavish reverence. We would prove ourselves far wiser if we acknowledged that Aristotle's remarks clearly were intended to be suggestive, not prescriptive, and certainly do not constitute some sort of literary statute, as legally binding today or twenty centuries from now as it (supposedly) was in Aristotle's own day.

Having thus, it is hoped, shed some light on a few of the factors that tend to inflate the reputation of tragedy, let us now examine the way in which the very word *comedy* (much like the word *moral* as we earlier assessed its impact on many minds) makes clear thinking about Shakespeare's "comedies" difficult, and perhaps causes us to bar many of them from our classrooms for wholly imaginary offenses.

Academics — this one not excluded — pride themselves on their knowledge that the term "comedy," when it is used to refer to a play, means not "uproarious hijinks" but "a light, amusing drama that ends happily." Yet my suspicion that there is something ironic or even faintly ludicrous about this pride would be confirmed, if it could be shown that the academic stumbles into a far less egregious error than she imagines she does whenever she momentarily drops her guard and conceives of comedy in its usual sense: "something that makes me laugh — loudly!"

We will indeed gain such confirmation if we look for a moment at the way in which the language has made use of the term "comedy" to perform one of its most ingenious tricks. In the course of this trick the language doubles back on itself, so to speak, so that a word's present usage comes to seem almost identical with its original usage, while all of the other variant meanings it has acquired over its two-thousand-year pilgrimage fall by the wayside. Thus, by an irony of linguistic history, when we use the term "comedy" to describe, say, one of the better installments of *Saturday Night Live*, full of song and riotous laughter, we are in fact speaking like true Greeks, drunk with the spirit of Dionysus: the term "comedy" comes from two Greek words meaning "to sing" and "to revel." It is that sternly Apollonian fellow, the literary critic, who insists on our using — or rather, misusing —

this term to describe a work such as *Measure for Measure*, and this for two singularly unconvincing reasons: because it has a relatively happy ending, and because it contains a few scenes (relatively brief, and very much at variance with the dark mood of the work as a whole) of "comedy" in its modern sense — those involving Pompey and Barnardine.

Perhaps the best way of freeing ourselves from the tyranny of this critical killjoy is to remind ourselves that it is only he, and not the Bard himself, who has seen fit to apply this moniker to various plays in the canon. Yet another way is simply to acknowledge with a laugh that, despite our best efforts to pull a long face and play the perfect pedant — "Comedy a laughing matter, my dear fellow? Oh dear me, no! *Comedy*: 'A light, amusing drama that...' " — we do indeed catch ourselves, and often, conceiving of comedy not in its "proper" (one is tempted to say "prim and proper") but its generally accepted sense.

For if all of us do fall into this "error" quite regularly, or at least far more often than we would be willing to confess to our colleagues, this is certain to have a genuinely dangerous effect on our thinking as we go about shaping a syllabus. Convinced as many of us already are that the tragedies are the pick of the canonical litter, if we fall victim even for a moment to the fallacy that there is supposed to be something heartily amusing about a *Merchant* or a *Measure*, we will find ourselves thinking: "The tragedies are supposed to be sad, and they are, but the comedies are supposed to be funny, and they're not. Therefore not only is tragedy the inherently superior art form, it is also the far more successful art form. Why do we bother with the comedies even as much as we do?"

If this is indeed the kind of thinking that goes on, presumably subconsciously, in the heads of quite a few syllabus-shapers, it would certainly help us to account for such otherwise unaccountable phenomena as the minimal use to which *As You Like It* is being put in most syllabuses, or the way in which a few survey respondents, in saying which play they thought worked best at a particular grade level (usually 7-8), simply wrote "Any comedy." Clearly, the assumption at work there is that the difference both in quality and in content between a *Merchant* and a *Comedy of Errors* is no more worthy of noting than that between two different episodes of the same sitcom.

Thus far we have seen that misconceptions about the term "comedy" can lead teachers into two grievous errors, the first conscious and the second subconscious: It can cause them to think that a "comedy" such as *Merchant* must perforce be less rich in moral complexity than a "tragedy" such as *Othello* (when plainly it is infinitely *richer* in that quality), and that as an "unfunny" comedy *Merchant* must be intrinsically a less successful play than the appropriately dreary *Othello*. Yet if we teachers have allowed ourselves to be misled by this term, many a Shakespeare scholar shares with us our folly. For it was he who, troubled by his recognition that many of the "comedies" are such only in the most delimited and pedantic of senses, introduced those absurd terms "problem play" and "dark comedy" in his effort to get everything nicely labeled and back on the bookshelf.

The term "dark comedy" immediately prejudices us against any play so described, for who really wants her comedy "dark"? ("Black humor," in my estimation, being an entirely separate commodity.) As for "problem play," it is a nineteenth-century term coined to describe that sort of play which, Ibsen-like, focuses on some particular social problem. It is therefore patently unsuited to Shakespeare's drama, which even at its most socially concerned is never heavy-handed in its didacticism. It is also worth noting here how ironic it is, particularly given the way in which we subconsciously transmute the term "comedy" from one of its meanings to another more congenial to us, that we do the same thing with the term "problem play." We conceive of the term not in its original sense but as meaning a play that causes us, the pedants, a problem in trying to pigeonhole it!

I would suggest that if we are going to assign a meaning of our own to the term anyway, we would do better to think of the plays thus described as being those that depict life as what it most often is for most of us: a problem. Indeed, perhaps we should have a new mask designed, to take its place between those depicting laughing comedy and weeping tragedy: a mask in the schizophrenic style of Picasso, with one side of the face almost merry and the other side strangely sad. *That*, after all, is the mask most of us go through life wearing, and we know how far from the mingled joys and sorrows of day-to-day existence the scholars have strayed when they are driven to devise laborious and oxymoronic terms such as "dark comedy" to describe those plays of which it truly can be said — far more truly than of the tragedies, certainly — that they do hold the mirror up to Nature.

It is worth pausing here for a moment to note, as well, that whenever we shy away from rather than exult in those many moments in Shakespeare that lead us to feel, with Blake, that "joy and woe are woven fine, a clothing for the soul divine," we not only deprive ourselves of much emotional and intellectual joy but prove ourselves singularly insensitive to one of Shakespeare's greatest and most distinctive talents. For after all, what is it that makes an Othello, a Timon, a Leontes, or a Richard III so tiresome in comparison to many another vibrant and inwardly variegated Shakespearean creation, but that they are the living embodiment of only one quality — be it jealousy, misanthropy, or vaulting ambition — and that the plays in which they appear seem to us devoid of those epiphanies Shakespeare was such a master at evoking, moments that make us laugh and cry almost simultaneously?

For instance, is there any finer moment in *Much Ado*, or any more genuinely poignant moment in literature, than that in which Benedick presents his challenge to Claudio ("You have killed a sweet lady") and suddenly awakens us, along with Claudio and Don Pedro, to the startling fact that the eternal joker and the confirmed bachelor is at last serious about something, and that that something is love? Is there any more comical moment in Shakespeare, or at least any that so effectively frees us in a trice from the terror and pity that had held us in their grip, than Shylock's sudden change of heart the moment Portia's decision seems to be going against him ("I take this offer, then; pay the bond thrice/And let the Christian go.")?[1] Or does any moment in *Measure for Measure* or *Merchant*, plays that have much to say overtly about the need for forgiveness and pity, tug at our heartstrings so insistently as that sublime moment at the end of that "mere farce," *Merry Wives*, when Falstaff, in despite of all his sins and follies, is readmitted warmly to the human fold ("Yet be cheerful, knight; thou shalt eat a posset tonight at my house; where I will desire thee to laugh at my wife, that now laughs at the . . . . ")?

Having come thus far in our look at how misconceptions about the term "comedy" cause us to be unfair not only to Shakespeare's "comedies" but, far more importantly, to our students and to ourselves, we might wish to assume that so seemingly innocuous a term couldn't possibly have wreaked any more havoc than that which we have already poked about in. Alas it can, and has. For while a play such as *Merchant* almost certainly

---

[1] I had never dreamed there could be any comic potential in this line until I saw the Hoffman performance on Broadway, where it got a big laugh as played. By contrast, there's not a hint of laughter anywhere in the scene as it's played (with far less inspiration and verve) in the BBC video.

has suffered in critical esteem ever since Heminges and Condell put it (for lack of any fourth category) in with the "comedies," *Troilus and Cressida* has had to pay a far higher "critical rent," if you will, ever since it was relocated there by some scholars and editors.

I say "relocated," because the fact is that *T & C*, having originally been slated by the compilers of the First Folio for inclusion with the tragedies (and tragedy it certainly is; not any one person's tragedy, but the tragedy of the human race as a whole), ended up, apparently owing to some delay or snag over copyright etc., between the histories and the tragedies — the perfectly logical spot! Yet in this one case some Shakespeare scholars, they who usually are the most reluctant to depart from the precedents set for us by the First Folio, have seen fit to ignore their sacred oracle and chuck *T & C* into that odds-and-ends bin known as the "comedies."

While one can appreciate the rational motives they had for so doing — *T & C* seeming to be neither a tragedy nor a history when judged by the more routine and superficial criteria — I for one can't help but feel that the banishment of *T & C* from the tragedies was almost an act of psychological repression. For given how deeply this play seems to trouble most readers — the very inanity of most of the critical comments it elicits making it seem almost a kind of Rohrsach test, in which everyone sees his or her own fears and insecurities: "oddly disquieting," "fascinating but not altogether satisfactory," etc. etc. — I suspect that once *Troilus and Cressida* had been buried deep beneath the clutter of its utterly unalike bin-fellows (*Comedy of Errors, Much Ado*, etc.) many a scholar let out a long pent-in sigh and got his first good night's sleep in many a moon.

Appendix II

WHY TEACH SHAKESPEARE?

I n this book's Introduction, I declared that it was my intention only to examine Shakespeare's papers (i.e., the plays) not to subject the Bard himself to a body-search (i.e., analyze precisely what it is that makes him as great as he is assumed to be). Such a declaration seemed a sensible and appropriate one, given both the avowed purpose of this project — to do some creative thinking about the secondary school Shakespeare syllabus, rather than about Shakespeare himself — and the absurdity of thinking that anyone could adequately assess Shakepeare's greatness within the compass of so relatively few pages as these. Yet I find I cannot utterly forbear from making a comment on this issue, and this for two reasons.

First, all of the hard thinking that has gone into this book will have served no useful purpose if, particularly given the rising tide of "multiculturalism"[1] and the ebbing tide of literacy and bookishness among young people, Shakespeare finds himself more and more being crowded out of the modern secondary curriculum. It is at least conceivable that, just as the disappearance of the Greek and Roman classics from the classroom

---

[1]My reader will get a good idea of just how much I detest that term from the fact that I can't even use it in passing, as above, without pausing to throw in my two cents' worth about the debate that swirls around it. Thus I would simply ask my reader to note what savage irony there is in this: At precisely the moment in human evolution (our own) when the barriers of class, nation, and race that have in the past held humans back from the life more abundant are beginning to fall, those who deem

179

marks the watershed between an earlier educational era and our own, so too seventy-five years from now we will look back in wonder at those benighted days when we allowed this one particular "dead white male" to rule the curricular roost. If there is in fact any such tendency at work in schools today I would like to do my small bit not simply to stop it, in a spirit of unthinking conservatism, but to provide a few doubtless inadequate reasons why it *should* be stopped.

Second, I feel that in a sense I am obliged to comment on this issue, if only because one of the most eloquent and candid of my survey respondents had the courage to ask (rhetorically, he assumed!), in the second sentence of the following comment, a question many an English teacher doubtless has often asked himself, probably without daring to share it with a colleague or to hope for a genuine answer:

> Sometimes I wish we could have a moratorium on William Shakespeare in school — he gets used like castor oil — it's "good" for kids to read him. Well, I'd like to know, good for *what?* I know all the standard answers — culture, etc., etc. — but they all ring hollow — I feel like a phony sometimes — I know why *I* like him, or sometimes *dislike* him, but can't quite plug him into my students and don't always know what to make of that. I feel like a heretic!

It is my hope that some of my comments in the "Envoi" section have given my marvelously plain-speaking colleague a new insight into the whole "culture connection" vis-à-vis Shakespeare, and when it comes to "plugging kids into" Shakespeare some of my advice in the appendix that follows this one may be of some

themselves liberal and progressive prove themselves pure reactionaries by talking about *multi*culturalism.

Clearly the challenge and opportunity of the rest of human history will be to build *one* culture, a culture that draws on the best of all past human cultures and that includes people of all races. It says something about just how utterly boring and homogenous these "progressives" must find this wild and wooly world to be (their attitude being all the more startling to a Blakean like me, for whom the world is by definition not merely "diverse" but *infinite*), that to them it would be more exciting to live in a world of a thousand different carefully delimited cultures than in a world of one polyglot culture, where each human being would be free to fashion for himself or herself a character and a spirit that was a "rainbow coalition" in and of itself.

use. But for now I'd like to concentrate on that second sentence, and see if I can give my reader some idea of just what Shakespeare *is* "good for." Let me begin with a few very personal reminiscences and reflections.

When I assumed my first responsibilities as an English teacher, I had the great good fortune to be teaching at a school that gave me a free hand to design the curricula for my own courses. Naturally I was elated by this, and a good part of that elation stemmed from the fact that I was free to teach the poetry I wanted to teach. For me this meant introducing my students to both the purest lyric beauty and the knottiest moral complexity in the *Songs of Innocence and Experience*, and to democratic and amorous passion in the poetry of Burns, while to a great extent avoiding the sublime vapidities (many of them of dubious intellectual value even to adults, and guaranteed to evoke nothing but yawns from students full of rising sexual passion and rock and roll) to be found in too much of the work of the other Romantics. For instance, what a world of difference there is between strong and weak Wordsworth! The great "Ode" and "Resolution and Independence" are chock-full of "matter," whereas "Tintern Abbey" or "I Wandered Lonely as a Cloud" are mere picture-postcards, lovely but intellectually negligible.

Yet perhaps because my very freedom to explore only the most intellectually potent and life-affirming of poetry had spoiled me, I found that far too often, when I had students dip into our anthology to sample this or that poem, I was disappointed. (No, the fault was not that of the anthology in question, *Sound and Sense*; its selections are sensible and standard ones, and they are very well presented.) Far too much lyric poetry, in my own view, tends to teach at least one of the following negative lessons, if not two or three of them:

1. That life, when it is examined closely, is found to be intrinsically "tragic," and that the sensitive soul's reaction to it can only be one of at least a gentle melancholy, more likely of outright horror. In this regard one only needs to think of the intense lugubriousness of most of Emily Dickinson's verse, or of the excessively elegaic quality in A. E. Houseman's, to see what I'm getting at.

2. That it is the mark of an enlightened intellect to expend a great deal of thought on romantic love, in the manner of the Shakespeare sonnets or the poetry of Donne.

3. That when a poet (and by extension, all of us) is not being romantic in the conventional sense, he (and we) should be so in the grandiose sense: exalting both childhood and death and neglecting all the mature years in between (*vide* Dylan Thomas); dismissing the need for sexual morality and for imaginative and emotional restraint (*vide* Byron and too much of Blake); running roughshod over common sense and common syntax (*vide* Cummings and many more of the free-versists); purveying an incomplete and dangerously one-sided view of Nature, as a pretty place for a muse and a stroll where farmers never break their backs nor cheetah those of young impala (*vide* Wordsworth, and a passel of others); and — perhaps most crucially of all — peddling the false and immensely dangerous notion that the rare spirit, whether she or he be unusually fragile (as in the case of a Sylvia Plath or a Hart Crane) or unusually robust (as in the case of a Whitman or a Thomas) has no more pressing business in this great yet screwed-up world than to "celebrate" itself, its fears and its raptures, and to congratulate itself (implicitly at least) on its evident superiority to the dim-souled herd all around it.[2]

Now what makes Shakespeare not merely a great poet but in most respects *the* great poet, not just a representative of a species but almost a species in and of himself, is that he not only doesn't teach any of these negative lessons, he teaches the positive lessons that counteract their malign intellectual influence. Let us briefly take note of each of these, dealing with them in the same order as those we have listed above.

While Shakespeare does now and again slip into that juvenile mood of pessimism and misanthropy (*Timon* being the notable example) that so many poets spend a lifetime glorying in and extending the boundaries of, Emerson is right in asserting that there is a certain sovereign cheerfulness in Shakespeare, a cheerfulness strong enough to sustain him whenever he takes one of his many unblinking looks at evil (as in *T & C*) and sadness (as in *Lear*). Although Shaw would like to convince us that Shakespeare is un-affirmative, largely because there are some strong statements against life and the human race to be found through-

---

[2]Seeing as I have not only mentioned Whitman's name in this context but also have alluded to one of his most famous lines of verse, I am compelled by the spirit of historical honor to remind both my reader and myself of one vital fact: Whitman's heroic conduct as a male nurse during the Civil War shows that he himself knew full well that a great human being must be a doer and a healer, not just a celebrator.

out the canon, the really noteworthy fact is that such curses invariably come from the mouths of Shakespeare's evil, disappointed, or emotionally crippled characters (Macbeth on life as a walking shadow, Lear on "this great stage of fools," Thersites on war and lechery). The worst we hear from the Bard's most obvious surrogates — Prospero, Hamlet, etc. — is that life can be both sad ("We are such stuff... ") and hard ("And in this harsh world draw thy breath in pain... ").

As for the plays' treatment of sex and love, one might simply note that while both are examined from every conceivable angle, we find in the plays relatively few of those supposedly uplifting but in my opinion rather absurd "conceits," of the Donne variety, wherein the most elemental of human drives and emotions are not so much analyzed as they are romanticized and intellectualized. It seems to me highly doubtful whether the kind of "lofty thinking" that abounds in Shakespeare's sonnets or Donne's poetry, of the "you and I are one mind in two bodies" variety, bears even a distant relation to sex and love as the troubling realities most men and women are forced to come to terms with. In notable contrast to this, the relatively straightforward acceptance of sex and love that one finds in the plays seems both more sane and more cheerful.

Whether one chooses to think of Shakespeare (the playwright, not the sonneteer) as romantic or anti-romantic in his view of sexual love, what strikes one most forcibly is how far Shakespeare is from being a Romantic of the capital R variety. Let's enumerate a few of his attitudes as they contrast favorably with those of the Romantics, as listed earlier.

1. There is no glorification of childhood here (not much treatment of it at all, of course), and while there's a certain reveling in the dramatic possibilities inherent in a good death — "Et tu, Brute?"; "The rest is silence"; "Howl, howl, howl!" etc. — his maturest reflection on mortality is probably Prospero's monody on the bittersweet evanescence of life — an indulgence in pathos so short and sweet, so *sensible* almost, that it seems a world away from the chest-beating theatrics of "Do Not Go Gentle... " and all its lesser imitations.

2. Far from suggesting, as Romantic poets of whatever era perpetually are wont to do, that there is something glamorous about excess of all kinds, Shakespeare sees to it that the melancholic, "poetic" Jacques is well mocked by Rosalind for being excessively

"humorous"; that Achilles is baited with his own pride and self-love by Ulysses; that the choleric and splenetic Cassius is rebuked by the phlegmatic Brutus; that the hotly burning Romeo is hosed down (however ineffectively!) by Friar Laurence; and that Duke Vincentio is made to represent a middle road between too much sexual frankness (Lucio) and too little (Angelo).

3. While there is of course much great "nature painting" in Shakespeare, the world's greatest dramatist plainly understands what Wordsworth and many another nature poet does not: that the human drama is about humans, not trees. There is no surer sign of intellectual deficiency than the tendency to think that Nature, merely by dint of being bigger than man in a physical sense, therefore deserves to be thought of as man's senior rather than junior partner in the adventure of living. While clearly Shakespeare does believe in a divine will, he is too sharp a thinker to associate this, as the uncritical invariably do, with mere wind and rain.

Thus how ironic it is that Shakespeare should ever have been thought of as a nature boy, warbling his native wood notes wild, when the one great Ode to Nature in his work issues from the mouth of the villain Edmund, and when his greatest scenes of Nature are far more in keeping with that ancient peasant wisdom that sees Nature as man's bitter antagonist in the struggle for life than with the modern Sierra Club mentality, that which can conceive of Nature only in absurdly sentimental and anthropomorphic terms, as a wise and guileless virgin being raped by man.[3] Among those great scenes: the shipwrecks in *The Tempest* and *Pericles*; the prodigy- and lightning-filled night in Act I, scene iii of *JC*; the witches on the blasted heath in *Macbeth* (what conventional "nature poet" would have risen to that "blasted"!); and — above all — Lear defying the cataracts and hurricanoes and daring the thunder to "crack Nature's moulds."

[3]The reader may falsely conclude from my comments here that I am in the pay of a logging conglomerate, or see recycling as a Communist conspiracy against the American way of life. As with so many of the other hotly debated issues of modern life, it is assumed that whoever does not take the sentimental view of an issue must perforce take the crabbed and reactionary one. To the contrary, one can feel a tremendous respect for Nature without professing any inordinate "love," and one can wish to keep rivers and lakes unpolluted without growing positively rapturous at the prospect of someday being able to visit Teddy Trout and Betsy Badger in their spiffy new homes.

4. Yet where Shakespeare really parts company with the rest of the Romantic herd is here: The average poet, indeed even the un-average poet, is perpetually drawing attention to his or her self, often in the mistaken belief that he or she is vastly different from or superior to the rest of the species. In marked contrast to this, and as noted by many a commentator, the chief characteristic of Shakespeare's genius is not so much that it is self-effacing as that it is self-negating. We scarcely ever feel the presence of Shakespeare himself in a Shakespeare play, but rather reel in astonishment at the manner in which he projects himself into not merely the thoughts but seemingly the very being of characters as infinitely diverse as humanity itself.

It might be objected to this that, after all, the soliloquy is a central feature of a Shakespeare play: What difference could there be between the soul-searching that goes on there and the soul-revealing that is at the heart of so much modern poetry? All the difference in the world. For while at a glance the typical Shakespearean soliloquy might seem to be a character turning in on himself, it would be far truer to say that it is a character getting out of himself. The uncritical think, for instance, of the "To be or not to be" soliloquy as the epitome of solipsistic brooding, when it is of course Hamlet's profound musing not on the most personal of topics but the most general: the nature of life's ills, the best method of dealing with them, the nature of the "other world" and its relation to this one. Even in the "O what a rogue and peasant slave am I" soliloquy, where Hamlet's topic *is* himself, his aim in meditation is not, like the modern poet's, to reveal his own inner beauty, but rather to flail himself for his (supposed) sins and weaknesses as a goad to *action*.

We have seen, then, that the first answer to the question "What is Shakespeare good for?" is that he brings our students the right, not the wrong, answers to many of those questions that most perplex thinking men and women. This is a poet who not only is not intellectually weak in all those myriad of ways that cause so many sensible people to have a low opinion of poets and poetry, but who is in fact strongest precisely where they are weakest. We must now take a moment to see if we can discover why this should be the case, if only because we may thereby discover another reason or two for keeping this dead white male in our curricula a few years longer.

While obviously sheer genius helps us to account for a good bit of Shakespeare's poetic preeminence, one doubts whether the difference in brain power between a Shakespeare and the greatest of modern lyric poets — let us say Yeats — if it somehow could by gauged, would be revealed to be all that appreciable. Nor would it help us to account for our feeling that Yeats, for all his poetic greatness, has about him all the fussy vanity of the modern person of letters, and that this in and of itself consigns him to dwell only on a high plateau of Parnassus, whereas the greatest of poets, all of whom seem almost "faceless" — Homer, the authors of the Bible, Chaucer, Shakespeare, Milton — are perched securely upon its peak.

No, we will never account for what makes Shakespeare a unique phenomenon in literature by putting his brain cells under a microscope, or by pretending that he had simply imbibed more of the heady Elizabethan spirit than such third-raters as Beaumont and Fletcher. What makes Shakespeare the world's greatest poet is that, through whatever happy concatenation of personal and historical factors, he somehow contrived to put the inherently inner-directed mode of knowlege known as poetry — whose sphere is that of human motivations and aspirations — entirely at the service of the outer-directed mode of art known as drama — whose concern is exclusively with deeds and with the irrevocable consequences of those deeds. In so doing, Shakespeare not only lit up drama from within, so to speak, and redeemed it from that obsessive fascination with brute cause and effect that makes Greek Tragedy, even at its finest, seem somehow inhuman, but also did something of which far too little notice has been taken: He redeemed poetry from that petty selfishness, that tendency to conceive of the soul as a private garden rather than as a plot temporarily leased from Oversoul, Inc., which nine times out of ten has the effect of making it far less stirring than a trumpet blowing reveille (not to mention one blowing the Haydn concerto) and not even as intellectually rewarding as several pages of the most awkwardly worded and thoroughly abstruse philosophical discourse.

As might have been expected, William Hazlitt, in observing the birth of "modern" poetry two hundred years ago with the arrival of the Romantics on the scene, was the first (and the last?) to remark upon the fact that what distinguishes the modern poet from the great poets of the past is his wholly different attitude toward the ego and its claims. The passage that follows is a longish one, but seeing as it is one, in my view, that every English teacher would do well to muse upon, and one that I myself wish I could chisel in marble above the lintel of every "creative writing" classroom in the land, I cannot forbear from including it here:

> The great fault of a modern school of poetry is, that it is an experiment to reduce poetry to a mere effusion of natural sensibility; or what is worse, to divest it both of imaginary splendour and human passion, to surround the meanest objects with the morbid feelings and devouring egotism of the writers' own minds.
>
> Milton and Shakespeare did not so understand poetry. They gave a more liberal interpretation both to nature and art. They did not do all they could to get rid of the one and the other, to fill up the dreary void with the Moods of their own Minds. They owe their power over the human mind to their having had a deeper sense than others of what was grand in the objects of nature, or affecting in the events of human life.
>
> But to the men I speak of there is nothing interesting, nothing heroical, but themselves. To them the fall of gods or of great men is the same. They do not enter into the feeling. They cannot understand the terms. They are even debarred from the last poor, paltry consolation of an unmanly triumph over fallen greatness; for their minds reject, with a convulsive effort and intolerable loathing, the very idea that there ever was, or was thought to be, any thing superior to themselves. All that has ever excited the attention or admiration of the world, they look upon with the most perfect indifference; and they are surprised to find that the world repays their indifference with scorn. "With what measure they mete, it has been meted to them again."[4]

It would seem, then, that we must add to the first of those factors that make Shakespeare pedagogically indispensable — his virtually unrivaled intellectual strength — a second one: that Shakespeare's verse is deeply moral, in the sense that it never loses sight of the individual's attachment to and responsibilities toward the "outer" world and the larger human community (all blatant selfishness being not merely immoral, but the source and

[4]William Hazlitt, *Lectures on the English Poets* and *The Spirit of the Age* [this is from the former] (London: J.M. Dent & Sons Ltd., 1955), p. 53.

spring of all immorality). Given the fact that one of our chief
pedagogic objectives, as enunciated early in this book, is to
release secondary students from the prison house of solipsism into
which they were thrown with the onset of adolescence, we would
be foolish not to take and use the key to its doors that Shakespeare has crafted for us.

Now one might think that, if there were any logic in the
world, a poet who is not only intellectually but also morally rigorous would be aesthetically unsatisfying, and that our fastidious
modern poets, while they might not surpass Shakespeare in intellectual rigor or moral sensibility, would at least outdo him in
sheer mellifluousness.

Yet here of course we strike the root of a divine, an utterly
delicious paradox. For the man who has given the world the
most intoxicatingly lovely poetry it has ever known seems to
have churned it out almost as a by-product, his two main lines
of goods being dramatic excitement and power and moral utterance. Even the very critic one would least expect to acknowledge
this, Mark Van Doren (a poet himself), does so: "[Shakespeare
is] not only the finest of poets, but the one who makes the
fewest claims for poetry."[5] Yet it is this very paradox — that
Shakespeare's verse, even at its most precious and overwrought,
still somehow seems to point to something beyond itself rather
than point *at* itself and at the rare spirit who produced it —
that explains to us both why Shakespeare's verse is of such surpassing loveliness and power, and how he has managed to out-
lyricize virtually every lyric poet who has ever come up against
him in competition.

Therefore the third of our reasons for teaching Shakespeare
is simply that in his works poetry, having humbled itself to serve
drama and thereby finding itself exalted as only the humble can
be, attains to a power and significance it rarely does elsewhere. If
we wish to awaken in our students a love for the particular form
of intellectual discourse known as poetry — one that slows the
mind down to a genuinely *ponder*-ous pace, so that it may brood
lovingly over the moral, intellectual, emotional, and aesthetic
aspects of existence as they have been brought together by the
poet into one uniquely satisfying harmony — we will do so far
less successfully by trying to assemble a sort of composite Shakespeare out of scores of lesser lyric poets — his madcap spirit
from Cummings, his tenderness from Auden, his intellectual scope

[5] Van Doren, op. cit., p. 83.

from Yeats, the simple beauty of his songs from Houseman, etc.
— than by turning to the man himself. It is precisely because
Shakespeare is indeed "the indispensable man" that we should
make every effort to "sell" him to students in some of the ways
detailed in Appendix III (and in countless other ways known to
my colleagues but not to me).

Having thus, it is hoped, reconciled the teacher whose faith
in Shakespeare in the classroom was waning to the Bard's virtual
pedagogic *inevitability*, bringing us as he does moral, intellectual,
and aesthetic gifts we would be hard pressed to find elsewhere
separately, much less laid out in one dazzling array, I would like
to address one final word to my colleagues as to what Shakespeare's vast poetic preeminence, and the probable reasons for it
that we have glanced at here, bode for the future of the study of
poetry in the secondary school.

The Greek ideal, whereby everything that is useful is also
beautiful, and vice versa (the amphora that is also a work of art,
the religious ceremony that is also great theater, the athlete who
is also the artist's model of godlike perfection of form), is one
that will always be worth striving after. Yet the historical evidence, as I read it, suggests that those moments when the aesthetic and the utilitarian have come together are relatively rare.
The poetic dramas of William Shakespeare surely represent one
such moment, in that they do have a function — to uplift and
to instruct us — but that function is so admirably interwoven
into their poetic and dramatic form that we scarcely take note of
it at all.

Now I would suggest that, even as we do honor to the
Shakespeare canon as one of the few places where poetry, by dint
of being drama as well, becomes something much more than
mere "ditties of no tone," but where to the contrary the tune
swells symphonically and the tone becomes one of genuine philosophical dignity, we will prove ourselves wise (rather than merely
quixotic) if we do not look to most other poetry to do likewise.
In my view the canon represents a glorious anomaly in the history of literature — a place where beauty and social usefulness,
form and function, have joined forces — and Shakespeare himself
is another of literature's rarest phenomena, the author in whom
the lyric and the philosophic impulses are of more or less equal
strength. For as far as I can make out, both from my reading
and from my observations of my fellow humans, their tastes and
aptitudes, these two impulses — the desire to break into song as
an expression of the joy of life, and the compulsion to examine

experience as a means of understanding, appreciating, and better-
ing life — have virtually nothing to do with one another. It is
precisely because the most common human types are the more or
less pure lyricist — the person who can sing far more ably than
he or she can (even granting his or her general intellectual distinction) think: Byron, Chopin, Dylan Thomas, Joni Mitchell,
Neil Young, etc. — and the pure thinker — Herbert Spenser,
John Dewey, etc., who can philosophize but who, if they tried to
sing, would croak like ravens — that we pay such homage to
those rare figures who can sing philosophically (Shakespeare) or
philosophize musically (Beethoven).

Now if it should indeed be the case that over the years the
average singer in words (or, to use the term Shaw loved to apply
to Shakespeare, "word-musician") has been neither so ravishing a
lyricist as Beethoven nor so profound a thinker as Shakespeare,
but has in fact, in attempting to bring together with his lesser
talent two very different expressions of the human spirit, failed to
do either anywhere near as well as he might have done if he had
concentrated more fully on one or the other, it is the duty of
every pragmatic educator to take note of that fact.

If the true and the beautiful, while perhaps in some ultimate
Keatsian sense one and the same, are in most respects attracting
opposites rather than identities, and should it perhaps be true
that the treasure-seeker in search of the beautiful will be far
more certain to find it in those lustrous pearls that are musical
notes than in those immensely fascinating but rather grubby and
well-worn coins of the realm known as words, then perhaps the
time has come for English teachers to leave off their essentially
quixotic efforts to make of the average teenager a sensitive rhap-
sodist and concentrate on the far more doable tasks of making
him a cogent thinker and an honorable actor.

Yet if my colleagues are ever to come to the conclusion
that English teachers really should teach only the most intellectually sturdy of poets — the Bible authors, Homer, Shakespeare,
etc. — and use lyric poetry only as a caulking of sorts to fill
seams in the curriculum between the major works, they will
need to be far more convinced than they probably are at present that their attempts to cajole into song the latent lyric
impulse within their students are far less likely to succeed than
those to instill good sense and moral sensibility. Therefore I
now offer them a few final words on the lyric impulse, its history and its present prospects.

In my view (and if my theorizing here, like much else about

me, reveals me as being very much a child of the sixties, so be it), the lyric impulse, which began, as its name tells us, with the plucking of a lyre, has come back to roost at the very spot from which it flew away so long ago, although the name of the modern lyre is of course the guitar. For two thousand years it wandered far away from the sunny and vine-covered land where it was born (Music by name) into the gray northern landscape of Literature, a land sicklied o'er with pale clouds of thought.

This rather errant pilgrimage was by no means in vain, in that over the years this little bird — let's call her Ariel, in that the two spirits seem to have much in common — whispered sweet somethings into the ear of Chaucer, gladly did the bidding of her master Prospero/Shakespeare, and with her call guided the blind Milton toward Paradise. Yet like her namesake she longed throughout those long years for the freedom that had been promised her, and in our own day it has at last been granted her. We hear her singing sweetly and freely in the genuine poets of our day — the James Taylors, the Bob Dylans, the Joan Armatradings, the Stings, the Jimi Hendrixes — but when we return to that "cloven pine" where she was for so long imprisoned — the too-too-solid structure, compared to music's infinite plasticity, of formal written verse — we find her forever fled.[6]

I'm well aware that many of my colleagues, confronted with this assessment of poetry as being only a provisionally satisfactory form of music, will dismiss it out of hand as being the trendiest of rubbish. I can only point out to them a few of the ill effects of their doing so.

First, it will mean, in all likelihood, that an entire side of their students' affective/aesthetic lives will be completely hidden from their view. One only needs to look at the senior pictures in any yearbook, inevitably embroidered with quotations from the students' favorite rock lyrics, to realize that the poetry that really lives for young people, the poetry that actually sustains and inspires them from day to day, is rock music. Whether rock lyrics are good or bad "poetry," or were ever meant to stand alone without the accompanying music, are of course separate questions. Here it is enough to note that, while of course many of them are sentimental and many more rather ridiculous,

---

[6]Of course I don't mean to imply by this that much good verse isn't being written in our own day; I merely suggest that by far the most powerful current of lyricism is now flowing through musical lines rather than printed ones.

many have the sort of gnomic or aphoristic quality we associate with Blake, and most of them are far more life-affirming than the average piece of modern verse (despite the attention given in the media to many of the frightening and nihilistic "heavy metal" lyrics).

Second and last, and bringing these reflections to a close, the teacher who conceives of the lyric impulse not so much as a visiting nightingale in the lovely grove of literature but as the very voice of the grove itself, will also be she who conceives of Shakespeare not so much as a great thinker gifted with song but as simply one word-musician among many, a man different in degree but not in kind from a Robert Herrick or a Richard Lovelace. The whole purpose of the sketchy natural history of the lyric impulse that has been presented here has been to suggest that Shakespeare is indeed something of a miracle and a prodigy in literature (from which fact flow the thousand and one errors of "bardolatry") and that the wise pedagogue would do well both to revel in that miracle and to abstain from attempts at miracle-working himself: For try as he may, he will never turn the refreshing and healthy water of his students' expository prose into the wine of poetry, nor the small beer that is most lyric poetry into the divine Shakespearean ale, fit for a Falstaff.

Appendix III

ON INTRODUCING SHAKESPEARE

I suppose I should dedicate this section of the book to a certain female 10th-grader, for it was her oh-so-innocent response to my innocent question "Do you like Shakespeare?" that first set me musing as to the best methods of overcoming students' distaste for the Bard. That response consisted of a shake of the head to indicate "no," and the appended comment "People don't really talk that way." It has been by mulling over the significance of student comments such as that one — comments which, I would guess, many teachers dismiss as being too absurdly unsophisticated to merit thoughtful response — that I have arrived at the thesis that I hope will hold this section of the book together.

My thesis is this: English teachers would have far more success teaching Shakespeare than they do (and I'm sure they already have a great deal) if they began with the assumption that Shakespeare is all but unteachable, rather than with the reverse assumption. That assumption, deeply imbued with the bardolatrous spirit, is that God and the Board of Education sat down together one day and, at the Board's fervent request for an absolutely perfect pedagogic food, as delicious as it is nutritious, God showered manna on them in the form of the complete works of William Shakespeare.

For while I have no real way of verifying my intuition, my guess is that nothing makes it so unlikely that our students will conceive of Shakespeare's plays as representing a genuine cultural and spiritual value, rather than as just some more books that have to be read in school, than the bardolatrous teacher's belief that Shakespeare is so manifestly wonderful "he sells himself." It seems far more likely that he does *not* sell himself (after all, sweet Will didn't even try to sell himself to posterity by seeing to it that his plays be published in a uniform format within his own lifetime), and that every effort should and must be made by teachers — perhaps even before the student has read a word or seen a scene of Shakespeare's — to sell him.

Of course we take the first and most important step in the selling of Shakespeare when we give students a glimpse, by means of lecturing, visual aids, and assigned independent study, of the Elizabethan Age, the Globe Theatre, and the life of Shakespeare. This certainly can be accomplished in one or two class sessions, and I presume that most teachers are in the habit of making such a presentation. Thus it only remains to be noted that those teachers who either consciously or unconsciously reject the notion that they are duty-bound to give such a lecture — they might say, "It seems stilted," or "I'm an English teacher, not a history teacher," or "The plays speak for themselves" — do a deep disservice to their students. If only because certain points about Shakespeare and the English language (more on this anon) cannot be made effectively unless the student can place Shakespeare historically, these types of introductory lectures must come to be regarded by all teachers as definitely non-optional.

While I'm addressing this topic of introducing students to the Globe, its denizens, and the world surrounding it, I would like to pause here for a moment to share with my colleagues what I consider to be one excellent prospective method of doing so (I've not yet had the opportunity to try it myself).

In watching the Olivier *Henry V* for the first time in many years recently (on video), I was struck dumb with delight not just by how much of the play's opening (all of Act I, and the first scene of II) is played right in the Globe (I had remembered it as being not much more than the Prologue), but by how patently perfect a pedagogic tool this opening is. While it might be objected that teachers already have better tools in hand, i.e. various filmstrips or videos that introduce students to Shakespeare and his age, I doubt greatly whether any of these makes it possible for students to *feel* the Elizabethan stage in all of its vitality and glory in the way the first thirty minutes of this movie do.

Ironically, the one such video I myself have viewed does make use of a few minutes from Act I, scene ii of the Olivier *Henry V*. However, the moment its producers have chosen to feature (that of the gift of the tennis balls from the Dauphin) is one that features *none* of the pedagogically perfect moments I'm about to describe below. To watch scholarly people putting together a video such as this one and choosing, with uncanny accuracy, virtually the *only* moment in the whole first act that has nothing to teach young people, is enough to make one conclude they are acting out some sort of professional death wish. Also utterly self-defeating is the habit such videos have (this one certainly did) of intersplicing gloriously alive moments from productions of the Bard with the pedantic and largely irrelevant glosses of some droning and dry-as-dust don. Surely any competent teacher can provide her students with whatever pertinent information about Shakespeare and his times she feels they should have, and then sit back and let video do what it does best, inspire and excite.

Among the many remarkable and noteworthy features of the first thirty minutes of *Henry V* are these: the long but lovely panning of the camera over Renaissance London, finally descending into the Globe; glimpses both of the musicians in the third-"floor" music gallery (reminding students as it does that even Shakespeare's plays had "soundtracks" of sorts) and of backstage life in all its chaotic energy (particularly the sight of boys in women's costumes, preparing to don their wigs); the rain that at one point comes showering down on the pit, dampening clothing but not spirits; and, most notably, the complete view afforded us of the interior of the Globe, both of the stage and of the different "classes" as they file in and either take a seat or stroll about in the pit. Yet there are three moments here that stand out above the rest, as being ones certain to fascinate and delight the student receiving her first introduction to the life and times of Shakespeare.

First, the fact that the Archbishop of Canterbury's learned disquisition on "the Salique law" is played here as slapstick (the tipsy Bishop of Ely — we saw him raising a tankard with a fellow player backstage — has thrown the genealogical documents into the air in a fit of exasperation, leaving the actor who plays the Archbishop at a loss for his lines) is of course a pure pedagogic boon. It convinces young people that Shakespeare's fellow actors (the point having been made in the teacher's first lecture that Shakespeare made his living as an actor in the most noted company of his day) were not only human, but oh-so-human — funny, in fact!

Second, the moment when Olivier walks onstage to a great ovation and, with that thousand-volt voice, takes charge of it, reminds young people that even before the world was blessed with the likes of Madonna and Jon Bon Jovi there were such things as stars, and that the average Elizabethan took as much delight in a great entertainer as the average American does.

Third, the general vociferousness of the denizens of the pit — and particularly the great shout that goes up when the name "Sir John Falstaff" is mentioned by the Archbishop (the single most marvelous moment in this opening, and one we have Olivier to thank for, as this bit of text seems to be of his invention) — makes students aware as nothing else could that in those poor, benighted, entertainment-starved days before TV and movies, Shakespeare was not a subject for term papers but a source of infinite joy and delight. Perhaps even more importantly, the fact that the show goes on even after an audience member has mocked (in true adolescent fashion) the effeminate Bishop of Ely by parroting the line he has just spoken, reminds the sarcastic male student that Shakespeare's greatness was drowning out the catcalls of callow youths four hundred years before he had contemplated adding one of his own to that fading chorus.

If we do indeed have here a pedagogically providential thirty minutes of videotape, why is the Olivier *Henry V* not being widely used (as I can only *assume* it is not) to introduce students to the world of the Globe? Almost certainly because teachers are instinctively chary of lopping off one section of an organically whole work of art, or perhaps because they're afraid students will clamor to see the rest of the film.

Yet when one considers that what we're talking about here is a vital moment in the education of young people, and when one notes as well that all of the material covered in this opening segment is in effect only an extended prologue to the action in France that constitutes the play proper (hence Olivier's own decision to demarcate it from the rest of the film), such scruples seem entirely misplaced. If the teacher simply introduces the film with a few words as to what is transpiring in this opening section, and outlines its general relation to what will follow, it seems certain that when she hits the "stop" button and tells the students they are free to watch the rest of the video at home, neither she nor they will have any reason to feel discontented.

Two last points, by way of stressing yet again just how ideal the opening of this film would be for classroom use. First, teachers who wished to (and I would surely be one of them) could take this opportunity to have students memorize some or all of the Prologue. Can one conceive of any other words in all of Shakespeare better suited to enter and remain in the first-time reader's brain than "O for a muse of fire" and those that follow them?

Even more strikingly, the subject matter of the Prologue — the need for a viewer (and even more for a reader!) to put his "imaginary forces" to work if what is about to be seen or read is to attain to its full splendor — is one the student about to spend four-six years reading Shakespeare plays would do well to keep in mind. So too, by seeing the Chorus speaking the speech to a real Globe audience, the student will be made vividly and lastingly aware that a) Shakespeare's plays *are* plays, first and foremost, and that b) if even the Globe audience members are being asked to use their imaginations to bring what they see before them to life, he, being at an even further remove from the "real thing" by dint of usually being a reader rather than a viewer of Shakespeare, must make an even greater imaginative effort.

At any rate, whether one chooses to use the beginning of Olivier's *Henry V* to do so or no, clearly the first step in introducing students to Shakespeare is to provide them with some sort of historical overview. It seems likely that some teachers opt not to take even this first step, and that even those who do so consider it not only the first but the last in this pedagogic pilgrimage. As I see it it must be the first of a minimum of three. The second step entails speaking directly to students about the difficulties of language inherent in the plays of Shakespeare for every reader, be they academic or lay, old or young. Before I speak a bit more fully about how and why this should be done, let me offer an opinion as to why most teachers (I assume) decline to do so.

Knowing as all academics do that the study and appreciation of the plays of Shakespeare is perhaps the most central of all cultural pursuits in the West, doubtless many assume that it is wisest not to confess to their colleagues (and even to themselves?) any difficulties they themselves have had with many a passage in the plays, and to repress any doubts they may have as to the pedagogic suitability of Shakespeare to adolescents. Then too, those of them who are performance- and theater-oriented are likely to point with pride to such facts as that Shakespeare was standard theatrical fare in this country in the nineteenth century (even being performed in mining boomtowns, etc.), to proclaim with pride that "you don't have to study Shakespeare to enjoy him," and to assume that all the difficulties modern young people have with Shakespeare are solely the result of their addiction to

MTV etc. If we could just wean kids from television for a year or two, this line of reasoning goes, and feed them a relatively steady diet of Shakespeare on the stage, all of the problems they have with the Bard would disappear.

Now while the educated person probably doesn't go too far wrong when she guesses that the pre-electronics generations brought to Shakespeare's works, whether seen on the stage or closely read on the printed page, a greater imaginative capacity, a better power of concentration, and far superior language skills than the same qualities as found in modern men and women, it is my personal guess (and we are in a strictly intuitive area here) that all of this can be, and too often is, overstated. Yes, a receptive listener can comprehend an extraordinarily high percentage of Shakespeare's lines on first hearing, yes, this does redound thoroughly to Shakespeare's credit and makes us marvel at the unique power he has over the English language, and yes, if the modern listener is less capable than his nineteenth-century counterpart of comprehending these lines (or even if they simply mean less to him), the blame almost certainly is to be laid at the doorstep of the nearest TV or video store.

Yet it seems almost as sure as any of the points just enumerated that the silver miner who saw *All's Well* in Virginia City (should there have been such a fellow!) missed virtually as many of the more abstruse lines as today's zonked-out teenager, and that even those he did "get" would have made a far deeper and more lasting impression on him if he had had the chance to study the text, or had been able to get out of his head that rich new vein he'd be working tomorrow.

Then too, if we were to leave Virginia City by time machine and travel three hundred years into the past and several thousand miles to the east, we would probably find that the average habitué of the Globe, while he thought this Shakespeare bloke put on a jolly good show and wrote an immense number of marvelous lines, was also prone to miss the sense of a huge number of those lines, and to mistake a man whose life marked a spiritual watershed of sorts in the history of humankind for a mere "master of the revels." Were this conjecture somehow to be proved true, it would certainly go a long way toward explaining what Emerson, with typical acumen, has dubbed "the most extraordinary fact in literary history,"[7] the fact that only Ben Jonson (and more often than not, not even he) thought of Shake-

[7] Emerson, op. cit., p. 307.

speare as being much more than an extraordinarily adept show-man, a man strictly for the age and certainly not for all time.

Now if it is in fact the case that the average person through-out history, and even the un-average academic, has always had trouble with certain passages in Shakespeare, surely nothing would be more certain to put the first-time reader at ease than to *tell* him so, and to give him a few likely reasons to account for this. First and foremost among these is the simple fact that Shakespeare is a poet, but as my suggested Step Three, to be discussed more fully in a moment, addresses that issue directly I will not do so here.

The second factor that helps us to explain why some passages in Shakespeare give us trouble is of course that many of them are "corrupt"; therefore the student should be given (as part of the teacher's opening lecture) at least a rough sketch of the rocky road so many of the plays had to travel down (through bad quar-tos, etc.) before they at last found a haven in the First Folio, itself by no means entirely reliable.

Yet while students may have trouble with a corrupt passage here and there, and while poetic diction is sure to throw them even more often than that, their biggest single difficulty is sure to be with words that the passage of time has either rendered meaningless to the modern mind or whose meanings have thereby been subtly yet profoundly altered. Therefore while an essential part of our Step Two should be a description of the process whereby the plays found their way into print (including, always, the staggering fact that Shakespeare, while seemingly never too busy to press litigation over this or that property matter in Strat-ford, seems not to have lifted a single finger to ensure his own immortality), most of it should be devoted to giving the student an overview of Shakespeare's important place in the history of the English language.

The kind of extremely modest and not very scholarly presen-tation I've successfully given on two occasions is a relatively brief lecture/discussion that begins by unearthing the language's twin roots in the classical world and in Germany, moves on to give students a taste of Middle English by having the teacher recite some of the *Canterbury Tales* prologue, and next makes the point that Shakespeare was the right man at the right place at the right time, a poet who took an incredibly vibrant and malleable new language and left it even stronger and richer than he had found it.

Yet the real point of the whole presentation is its conclusion, which goes something like this: "We have seen that language is a technology of sorts, and that like any other technology it has grown and altered immeasurably over the centuries, as have the countless trades, customs, etc. that Shakespeare used this wonderful technology to describe. Therefore, whenever you students are tempted to throw down your texts in disgust and shout, 'Why does this guy have to write this way?!', remember what a miracle it is, and what a tribute it is both to Shakespeare and the English language, that we can understand even as much of Shakespeare as we can without resorting to footnotes. Sure, we do need those notes — only the most pretentious of types pretend they don't, and insist that the miracle has been one-hundred-percent successful rather than about seventy-five — but how many other technologies from circa 1600 A.D. are still in such good working order as that of Shakespeare's English?"

The teacher who has taken both Step One — the historical overview — and Step Two — the linguistic overview — might readily assume that by then the rather slow and unimaginative student who had objected "People don't really talk that way" had been given enough food for thought to put her objections on hold. This is doubtful, because the main thing that makes Shakespeare's characters "talk that way" is that they are the fancies of a poet's brain who themselves speak poetry. Therefore the third important step in our journey toward a less dissatisfied and querulous group of English students must be that which addresses directly the whole question of what poetry is and who a poet is.

Now I have no intention whatever of telling my colleagues what should go into Lecture/Discussion Number Three — I am entirely confident that their own will be all that anyone could hope for, and more. I would like to make two points about it, however.

First, such discussions as to the nature of poetry are generally held, I would guess, in connection with the reading of lyric poetry, perhaps when the students are working from an anthology such as *Sound and Sense*. It seems likely that whatever points are made in those discussions are reinforced too rarely during the study of Shakespeare's plays, given the fact that all of us tend to become so smitten with Shakespeare the dramatist that we have nary a lingering look to spare for Shakespeare the poet. Believing as I do, and as I've explained in Appendix II, that virtually no other poetry can hold a candle to Shakespeare's, I would strongly urge teachers to make their best possible case for poetry in conjunction with the reading of the Shakespeare plays, regardless of whether they also plan to make that case as part of a unit on lyric poetry.

Then too, while I do have great faith that in most of its aspects the presentation on poetry my colleagues already are offering their students is of very high quality, there is one point I'm not sure they've been making as a part of it that I would now politely ask them to include in the future. To wit, that a poet is a person who is concerned with saying things not merely in the most euphonious way, and the most profound way, but also the most *interesting* way. In other words, he or she is not only an "artist" and a "philosopher" but also a kind of crossword-puzzle maker, a person who knows that if the reader's brain is to be set on fire with delight a kindling of sorts must first be laid, a kindling consisting of ellipses, inverted constructions, occasionally farfetched figures of speech, etc.

In this respect Shakespeare is the supremely poetical figure. Far from being a "natural" warbling his native wood notes wild, he is as mannered as they come, writing verse that continuously fascinates and inspires but that more than occasionally causes us to shriek and tear our hair, or to write in our margins (as I often do), "*Only* Shakespeare would have dared that!" It is my belief that if we teachers could bring our students to have not only great respect for Shakespeare and the guild of poets he represents but also a bit of *dis*respect — a recognition that a poet, like every other type of "artist," is more than a bit of a mountebank — we would also increase the odds that someday they too will become margin-scribblers — which is to say, genuinely critical thinkers.

It is to be hoped that those who have followed these thoughts thus far will indeed decide to give their students not only the historical but also the linguistic and the poetic overviews, if only so that they will have to overhear less often such questions as "Why does this guy have to write this way?" It seems likely, however, that many will balk at the idea of telling their students directly that Shakespeare, as a poet concerned at all times with saying things in a refreshingly new and different manner, of necessity oversteps himself on occasion and in doing so loses not only us but probably himself as well.

Let it be noted in closing, then, that these fears almost certainly are groundless. The above-average student is generally a bardolator-in-the-making anyway, convinced that Shakespeare's works were brought down from Mt. Sinai by Moses, and the below-average student may be academically rejuvenated by his new knowledge that no, people (even Elizabethans) *don't* talk that way, that that's a thing called poetry, a thing his teacher says he hopes he will learn to like but that he understands he may have lots of trouble with.

As I've stated earlier, but as cannot be stated too often, cultures stand or fall not so much on the strength of their intellectual elites as on the willingness of the average Joe or Jill to go through life evincing at least a modest respect and liking for the things of the mind. We are far more likely to arouse that respect and liking in Joe and Jill by beginning our presentations, "You may not like this, and if you don't I bet I know why," than "You'd better like this — or else!"

Appendix IV

SHAKESPEARE ON VIDEO

A s I've noted or implied in a few previous contexts, the dawn of the Video Age is also quite clearly the dawn of a new age in the teaching of Shakespeare. Teachers, who in ages past have grown exceedingly weary of hearing themselves tell students, "Always keep in mind that these are *plays*, meant to be performed, not read," can now simply push a button and *prove* to those students that "these are plays." Perhaps even more importantly for the purposes of this book, the fact that all thirty-seven plays are now available to the teacher on the BBC video-tapes means that all of the "borderline" plays — those that teachers generally have steered clear of as perhaps being too much of a hassle to teach — now seem infinitely more likely to succeed in the classroom: *Richard II*, *Henry IV*, *Measure for Measure*, etc.

For the record, and for my reader's convenience, let it be noted that the BBC videos may be purchased from Ambrose Video Publishing, Inc., Suite 2245, 1290 Avenue of the Americas, NYC, 10104. The price is $249.95 for each, $5,000.00 for the set of thirty-seven. While I'm sure every teacher's initial reaction will be the same as mine was — "$250.00 for *one* video?!" — I would ask my colleagues to consider well whether an investment at that price in a genuinely great production of *Richard II*, *T & C*, etc. is really money misspent. Surely we are making not merely a good deal but a great deal when we bid a tearful farewell to $250.00 but thereby allow generations of students to say hello to Derek Jacobi as Richard, Helen Mirren as Imogen, or Anthony Quayle as Falstaff. Of course many a school doubtless already has the whole series on tape from its initial PBS airing, and then too I believe many public libraries across the country have purchased at least a few of the thirty-seven. Let teachers be warned, however, that the policy at their local library may be the same as the utterly inane and pointless one at the New York City public library branch where I checked out all thirty-seven: that they are *not* to be shown in schools!

Before moving on, I'd like to make one other point about the Video Revolution. For me at least, there could be no clearer indication of just how hugely these BBC videos are transforming the study and teaching of the canon than the fact that this book itself probably couldn't have been written without them. Like most of the members of my generation and unlike most of our parents and grandparents, I am not much of a playgoer, and thus the opportunity these videos provided me with to take a crash course in the plays in performance was entirely invaluable.

Now for a few thoughts as to what prompted me to put together this section on Shakespeare on Video. The idea of doing so first came to me as I was working my way through all thirty-seven of the BBC videos in a shockingly (and rather exhaustingly) short period of time: somewhere around seven months. Needless to say I never would have speed-viewed my way through the canon at that rate if it could have been avoided, but the one unexpected benefit of seeing the videos virtually back-to-back was that I could compare and contrast the quality of the video I had seen on, say, a Tuesday, the memory of it still being fresh in my mind, with the one I was watching on a Saturday.

Although I ended up doing more comparing than contrasting (the overall quality of this series being astonishingly and quite consistently high), after quite a few weeks of the kind described above — weeks that might begin with a sublime video such as the *Richard II* and end with a somniferous one such as the *R & J* — I at last decided that I would be performing a valuable service for my colleagues if I were to steer them toward the *Richard II*'s and away from the *R & J*'s. It also occurred to me that, like me, my colleagues might be avid PBS watchers, and therefore enjoy hearing which of their favorite British "stars" appear in the series, invariably proving themselves marvelous Shakespearean actors in the process.

Two last points about the series, and its pedagogic usefulness. First, it is worth noting that someone goofed in a big way when they assured the actors that for once (and how they must have reveled in this opportunity, freeing them as it did from the need to "project" in a theater!) they could speak as softly as they wished, even in the most hushed of whispers at times, because the sound stage had been miked to pick up even the faintest of mutterings.

Sorry, guys, you blew it. In play after play, priceless dialogue is all but lost as it is mumbled into the actor's own beard, or someone else's ear. Of course this will be even more annoying for the teacher than the general viewer, in that it will give the inattentive student just one more reason to put his head down on his desk and tune out.

Second, while one can only commend all of those many teachers who, it is clear from their survey responses, make every effort to take students to see live Shakespeare whenever possible (some even choosing the text to be read by what productions are in the area, a dubious course of action in my view), it is perhaps worth pointing out one distinct advantage of (in the great American fashion of the 1980s and 1990s) staying "home" (in school) and watching the video. To wit, the performances in this BBC series are, almost without exception, absolutely top-of-the-line, a pure joy to behold.

All those who hold that Shakespeare's greatness will somehow manage to shine through even the most wretched of performances (or even the kind of mediocre-to-good live performance it is likely most kids will end up seeing) should do as I did recently, and see *Twelfth Night* performed by some college players only a month or so after viewing the utterly sublime BBC version. Were they to do so, they might well come to the same three conclusions I did:

1. Despite all the talk-show hype on the subject, there *is* such a thing as great acting, and — heaven knows! — there is *certainly* such a thing as bad acting.

2. However much one resists the assumption that good looks (or at least striking or distinguished looks) are necessary to an actor, one only needs to see a performance in which *none* of the players is conspicuously attractive to feel less cynical about the part sheer physical beauty plays in the making of a great actor (Laurence Olivier being a prime example).

3. No, Shakespeare *cannot* survive a bad performance! And wouldn't he, consummate man of the theater that he was, be the first to shout that into every modern player's ear, if he had the opportunity?

Finally, let me make it clear that in titling this appendix "Shakespeare on Video" I have by no means sought to imply that it is a comprehensive listing. Obviously there are scores of taped productions of Shakespeare out there, many of which my colleagues have been making good use of for years, that I have no knowledge of. Reviewed below are all thirty-seven of the BBC videos, plus some of the other well-known films such as the Olivier *Hamlet* and the Zeffirelli *R & J*, *Shrew*, and *Hamlet*. They have been arranged in alphabetical order.

All's Well — Superb. Perfectly cast, with a marvelous (and lovely) Helena (Angela Down), a great King of France (the veteran British actor Donald Sinden), and an extraordinary Parolles (Peter Jeffrey). The great Michael Hordern is Lafew, and Ian Charleson (of *Chariots of Fire* fame) is Bertram. Charleson, as far as I can tell, can play only one role, that of the cold fish, and therefore he's just right for Bertram.

Antony and Cleopatra (BBC versus Heston) — The BBC production is a real turkey, owing to three pieces of miscasting. Colin Blakely, the perfect physical type for Kent in *Lear* (which he plays in the Olivier version) — short, stocky, a man you can lean on — makes an utterly ridiculous-looking Antony. If this guy is a romantic lead . . . ! Jane Lapotaire, angular, thin, and not at all sensual, just *isn't* Cleopatra for me, however capable her performance. Last and definitely least, Ian Charleson turns in his usual lifeless and wooden performance (even "British reserve" can't begin to account for it) as Octavius.

Given the fact that the BBC *A & C* definitely is not worthy of being put to use in our classrooms, teachers might be forgiven if they made at least some use of the Heston film. It's by no means a great one, and well below the level of the Heston *Julius Caesar*, but at least it has the sensuality and the epic, outdoorsy feel a filming of this play should have. It also has Eric Porter as Enobarbus, who (like Gielgud in the Brando *Julius Caesar*) acts everybody else off the set.

As You Like It (BBC versus Olivier/Berger) — In my opinion the BBC production is a disappointment, primarily because of its two poorly cast leads. One need not demand absolute physical perfection in one's leading ladies and gentlemen, yet for me both Helen Mirren as Rosalind and Brian Stirner as Orlando are simply not attractive enough for this most attractive of plays. One might note as well that in this series the British have fallen into what is, for me, a typical Britishism — the overuse of an admittedly good actor, in this case Helen Mirren. In this series she is Imogen, Titania, *and* Rosalind, and clearly the last role is the one role too many.

No two productions could possibly be more dissimilar than these two, the BBC having been filmed outdoors, the Olivier on the stagiest of sets. While students may find the latter set a bit fantastic, and cause for a giggle or two, if they are like me they will have an even greater problem with the BBC "staging," for the outdoor settings make the suspension of disbelief all but impossible. Of course the very difference between these two productions might be made good use of in the classroom if bits of each were shown. (If one were indeed to show portions of each, I would suggest that the BBC's Touchstone, more human and less frenetic than the film's, is the one more likely to engage the student viewer.)

On balance, I think I would choose to show students the creaky but very charming old antique, in that somehow the magic and above all the *energy* of this work come through here far more successfully than in the BBC version. For this we should thank Elisabeth Berger, who is an infinitely more joyful and dynamic Rosalind than is the rather mopey Mirren, and of course Lord Larry, who is the absolute beau ideal of Orlando. Shaw tells us, in typically Shavian tongue-in-cheek fashion, that the role calls for an "athletic stockbroker," and those of us who love our Larry but don't consider him God's gift to the acting trade would say that that's him to a T!

By the way: Even the wrestling match is more fun in the Olivier version!

Comedy of Errors — Lots of fun. Those of us who have always thought that Roger Daltrey of The Who has more than a bit of the rude mechanical to him can't quite suppress a smile at what an effective Dromio he makes!

Coriolanus — Marvelous. It is, of course, all Alan Howard's show — a true tour de force. Mike Gwilym, who also plays Pericles in this series, is a solid Aufidius, and Irene Worth is outstanding as Volumnia.

Cymbeline — Excellent, and certainly a very good adjunct to the text should teachers decide to nibble at my bait and begin to teach *Cymbeline.* Helen Mirren and Michael Pennington are equally good as the lovers, Claire Bloom is well cast as the Queen, and — last but definitely not least — Michael Hordern declaims magnificently from on high, as Jupiter.

Hamlet (Olivier, BBC/Derek Jacobi, Richardson/Williamson, Zeffirelli/Mel Gibson, PBS/Kevin Kline, Richard Burton) — First I will offer some remarks about each of these productions, then I will attempt to render a verdict as to which would be best for classroom use.

Olivier — To anyone who has spent a good bit of time with the Olivier *Hamlet,* it can only be a source of wonderment that his performance therein should have played so large a part in convincing people that he is an actor of utterly unique gifts. For while Oliver the director certainly is to be commended, and while the film itself is a solid enough achievement, the astonishing fact is that Olivier does about as little with the title role as any person of great intelligence, charm, and physical beauty could have contrived to do. His is not so much the melancholy Dane as the phlegmatic Dane, an absurdly *English* Hamlet who speaks at all times in a hushed, uninflected singsong (except for those moments when Olivier is indulging in that utterly absurd vocal swoop from pianissimo to fortissimo that is his trademark as an actor — or rather as a ham).

Even more remarkable, perhaps, is the fact that, when Olivier does add a bit of inflection to his lines, more often than not he shows grotesquely bad judgment in where he places his accent marks. For instance, after sending the players off with Polonius, Olivier does a little pirouette and, just before blackout, cries out in that phony stentorian voice of his, "The play's the *thing,* wherein I'll catch the conscience of the *king.*" That he should have chosen to accent the last word in each clause, turning Shakespeare's verse into little better than a nursery rhyme, is all the more mystifying when one considers that even the rankest amateur could probably intuit that the accent here simply *has* to fall on "play's."

BBC/Derek Jacobi — It is only when one turns from Olivier's Hamlet — a man who has only two moods, completely tranquil and quiet or wildly roused and passionate — to another one, in this case Derek Jacobi's in the BBC production, that one realizes just how laughable it is to consider Olivier's a great or even an interesting performance. Olivier strolls placidly through the role, seemingly unmindful of the the thousand and one bits of theatrical "business" crying out to be made much of in this play, but Jacobi is not so great a fool as to pass up this, the single greatest opportunity of any actor's lifetime. He makes hay while the spotlight shines, and gives us a far funnier and more openly disaffected Hamlet than Olivier's.

The debit here is that Jacobi is, to put it mildly, not the macho type, and Hamlet needs to have more than a touch of manliness to him if he is not to dissolve into the weepy nervous Nellie hackneyed productions insist on giving us (see Ian McKellen in *Acting Shakespeare*!).

Richardson/Williamson — I'm not sure how many of my colleagues are even aware that this 1969 film, directed by Tony Richardson and with Nicol Williamson as the Prince, is available to them from RCA/Columbia Home Video. (I myself only stumbled upon it on a visit to a college library.) For me it's not a very appealing production, the two chief debits being Richardson's quintessentially "sixties" style of direction (for my money, this movie already looks even more dated than the 1936 Olivier *As You Like It*) and Williamson himself, an actor I myself have never able to "buy" for some reason. Another rather absurd aspect of this *Hamlet* is that Williamson looks all of forty, and Laertes (Gordon Jackson, the butler Hudson on *Upstairs, Downstairs*!) old enough to have once dandled his friend on his knee!

The only real reason for paying any attention at all to this *Hamlet* may be given in four words: Anthony Hopkins is Claudius. Why is every Claudius I have ever seen closer to Hyperion than to Hopkins' lustful, sleazy satyr? At any rate, whether this fascinating conception of the role is Hopkins' or Richardson's, it is certain that it is Hopkins, one of the greatest actors working today, who brings it to life.

Zeffirelli/Mel Gibson — In making up my mind about this movie, I had to substantially revise my verdict on seeing the film for the second time (on video). My initial judgment, when I saw its final third in a theater (I came in about two-thirds of the way through, and had no desire to remain in the theater to see what I had missed), was that both it, and Gibson's performance in it, were pitiably poor.

After a second look, however, I have come to realize that Gibson's Hamlet — an American/Australian Hamlet, a Hamlet for the masses — is worthy of greater respect than the average academic snob such as myself is at first inclined to give it. For while Olivier's delivery of many of the lines seems so profoundly wrongheaded as to be almost perverse, it simply can't be denied that those same lines do come alive for us as Gibson speaks them. Zeffirelli's *Hamlet*, for all its color and excitement, really is "intellectually vacuous" (I quote Pauline Kael of *The New Yorker*), but Gibson — however unpolished and even slightly oafish he often strikes us as being — has made the title role his own simply by having had the manly courage to *claim it.*

If it is indeed true that this film, despite the real interest of Gibson's performance, is intellectually shallow, it is perhaps worth pausing a moment to consider why this should be the case.

The first problem here, certainly, is that this production is all Hamlet and virtually nothing but Hamlet — the supporting cast has been stripped of most of its lines and all of its importance. The second problem, I think, is that one character who doesn't appear in this play's Dramatis Personae, but who does appear to excellent effect in the Olivier film, has been given its walking papers here: the castle itself.

For while of course there is a castle very much in evidence throughout the Zeffirelli film, both it and the stunning natural vistas we are allowed to view from it are all too spacious and lovely. Even more importantly, the characters come and go from this castle with too great ease.

For surely the appropriate staging of *Hamlet* is that which makes the viewer feel almost claustrophobic, as if she, like Hamlet, really were "bounded in a nutshell," and Denmark was to her every bit the "prison" Hamlet tells Rosencrantz and Guildenstern it is to him. Probably the greatest achievement of the Olivier film is the way in which it makes the viewer feel that she is in "the belly of the beast." As the camera moves along walkways and up and down stairways, we seem almost to "go a progress through the guts of a beggar" (or a king). That said, it must be admitted that Zeffirelli's alfresco *Hamlet* does give us at least one sublime cinematic moment: the sight of the brilliant blue sky that haloes Hamlet's head as he speaks of "this brave o'erhanging firmament, this majestical roof fretted with fire."

Kevin Kline (PBS's "Great Performances") — Having just watched Kevin Kline in the first TV airing of John Cleese's brilliant comedy *A Fish Called Wanda* on one night, and his *Hamlet* on the next (I assume that many teachers, like the one I borrowed this video from, did indeed tape it when it aired on PBS in the winter of 1990), I am still wandering about with my head in my hands, wondering whether reason still "holds a seat in this distracted globe." It seems a thing simply beyond the bounds of possibility that the very man who, in his portrayal of the fanatically anglophobic hit man "Otto," has given us one of the most howlingly funny comic performances of our day, should also be he who has given us this unbearably prissy, anglophilic *Hamlet*. Of course many a critic will insist, with reason, that it's one thing to turn in a great comic performance, quite another to create a great Hamlet, but when one considers that the comic performance in question was virtually a thing of genius, and remembers as well what a rich vein of comedy there is to be mined in the tragedy that is *Hamlet*, one feels one's disappointment all the more keenly.

At any rate, let it be entered into the record, without delay or equivocation, that of all the *Hamlet*'s on video I have thus far reviewed, Kline's is the only one that is truly embarrassing — and truly wretched. One is reminded as one watches him in the title role that there is really only one test of a performance, believability, and Kline fails that test miserably. Clearly he has not managed to think his way into this part, and thus we are presented with that most painful of spectacles, that of an actor plainly puzzling over his lines as he speaks them but still pretending, by means of a studiously wrinkled brow, to be the character he is portraying, lost in deepest thought.

Richard Burton — When a number of survey respondents mentioned the fact that they make use of the Richard Burton *Hamlet*, my curiosity was whetted. Having at last tracked it down in the Lincoln Center branch of the New York Public Library (it is a taped performance of the 1964 Broadway show, directed by Gielgud), I offer these comments on it not because it is widely available, for I don't believe it is, but for those who, like me, have at some point wondered whether it might be that elusive great *Hamlet* all of us are always in search of.

What more can I say, but that it sure isn't?! For if Olivier often strikes us being much more a ham than an actual actor, that impression strikes us about a hundred times more forcibly when we find ourselves in the presence of an essentially vulgar showman such as Burton. How to describe his purely stagy voice here (hugely different from the one he treats us to in *Shrew*), one that gives us only cheap *effects*, not lovely or intellectually interesting inflections? The rest of this modern-dress production is as completely one-dimensional as Burton's performance, which means that the whole thing is virtually a carbon copy of the wretched Kevin Kline production (or the other way around?).

Summary — If teachers are at first disheartened by the fact that all of the Hamlet's reviewed above (I refer more to the title role than to the play) seem defective in one way or another, two considerations should serve to cheer them. First, given just what a splendid human being Hamlet is, it should hardly surprise us that so few actors come even close to compassing his greatness. Second, if small portions of different *Hamlet*'s were to be shown to a class, students could hone their critical faculties by assessing the weaknesses — and strengths — of each.

While I myself almost certainly *would* choose to show excerpts from a minimum of two *Hamlet*'s (more on this in a moment), what advice can I offer the teacher who feels she has the time to show only one? First of all, I would suggest to her that she narrow the field by eliminating the Olivier and the Kline right off the bat. As for the Olivier, feedback from a few teachers has confirmed me in my suspicion that adolescents, with their X-ray vision when it comes to seeing right through phoniness, will always see Olivier's Hamlet just as their main man, Holden Caulfield, sees him, as "a helluva handsome guy, but more like some goddamn general than a screwed-up guy" (I quote from memory). As for the Kline, the aforementioned X-ray vision is likely to travel through his airy-fairy Hamlet more swiftly than through Caspar the Ghost.

The choice between the remaining two videos, the Jacobi and the Gibson (I'm assuming few teachers have, or will go to great lengths to get, the Richardson/Williamson), is one every teacher will have to make for himself. Most likely, the Gibson will prove itself the smart choice for slower groups, the Jacobi for more advanced ones.

What approach would *I* take? I think my course of action here would be charted in relation to the position I took at the beginning of my commentary on *Hamlet*, to the effect that there are two different *Hamlet*'s, the "intellectuals' *Hamlet*" and the popular *Hamlet*. As the reader will recall, it is my contention that relatively little of the "intellectuals' *Hamlet*" will get through to secondary students on first reading, hence I see little harm in exposing them initially to the Zeffirelli/Mel Gibson. However, I would show them most or all of that film only after I had pledged myself to awaken in them some curiosity about the "intellectuals' Hamlet." This would be done primarily, of course, through class discussions, but also by giving students a taste (almost certainly *after* the Gibson had been seen) of Hamlet the black-humorist (Derek Jacobi), and perhaps also of Claudius the black-hearted (Anthony Hopkins).

Henry IV — Marvelous. I found David Gwillim's Hal more than a bit offputting at first (he literally "mugs" for the camera by moving his lower jaw around a great deal) but he brought me around in the end. The real attraction here, however, is Anthony Quayle's Falstaff, which is a true joy. Far better this kind of Falstaff, rotund but not gargantuan and with only an *aura* of being bigger-than-life size, than the kind of Rabelesian man-mountain we catch a glimpse of in the Kenneth Branagh *Henry V*.

Jon Finch is superb as Bolingbroke (and sure to break many a female student's heart with his unrivaled handsomeness), Tim Piggot-Smith (of numerous PBS roles) gives a bravura performance as Hotspur, and Gordon Gostelow, as Bardolph, is a sheer delight (as are Leslie French and Robert Eddison as Justices Silence and Shallow).

The only notable drawback to watching *Henry IV* on video is that one feels Falstaff to be almost hemmed in by the borders of the small screen — he needs a whole stage to stretch his limbs on. Thus the scenes at the Boar's Head Tavern, while expertly played, do seem a bit *cramped*.

Henry V (Branagh, Olivier, BBC) — While I've long been a proponent of the theory that the silver screen emits a deadly ray, capable of turning even the best-toned critical faculty to mush, now that I've revised my original estimate of the Kenneth Branagh *Henry V* by seeing it on video I may have to start referring to my theory as proven fact.

When I saw the Branagh film in a theater I, like most people apparently, enjoyed it immensely. What a surprise then, on re-viewing it, to note, first of all, what an immensely *boring* movie this is in its first ninety minutes. Things pick up only with the Saint Crispian's Day speech, which is more affecting than the Olivier rendition primarily because we feel that plebeian Branagh, more so than patrician Olivier, really *means* it when he tells his men that they will soon be his brothers in battle.

So what are the factors that go to make this film's first ninety minutes so unsuccessful? First and foremost, Branagh's utterly wrongheaded conception of Henry. Branagh has to have known that everyone would be comparing his film with the Olivier, hence his obvious decision to go on the offensive and make his Henry every bit as anti-heroic as Olivier's is heroic. Yet while it would have been permissible for him to give us a Henry darker and more complex than the boyishly charming warrior-king we have come to think of him as being, it simply is *not* permissible to turn him into the brooding, tight-lipped tyrant we meet in the opening scenes. Indeed, when Henry makes his first entrance, framed in the light of a doorway while ominous music plays, one might mistake him for some Wagnerian Wotan rather than good old Hal. Yes, I know, Henry is no longer Hal, but that doesn't make him Richard III.

The second major defect of this film is that the comic roles of Fluellen, Macmorris, and Jamy (that who's who of the Celtic British Isles!), and Pistol, Bardolph, and Nym, not only have been stripped down in terms of number of speeches but *played* down. The latter in particular just cannot be allowed. These characters really *are* characters in the sense of beings created for the stage, and to forbid them to overact is to deny them the breath of life.

Two other somewhat lesser defects. First, for me at least Branagh is too little the natural prince among men to make his eve-of-the-battle eavesdropping very affecting. The true patrician — be he Olivier, Gielgud, Scofield, or any other of their rank — can make us feel in this kind of scene that an uncommon man is keeping in touch with common humanity. Branagh, however, is just too likable and ordinary a Joe to do likewise. (Pauline Kael speaks of him as having an "earthy, doughy presence.") Second, the casting of Branagh's wife as Katherine all but scuttles the scenes in which she appears, for one can't buy her as a Frenchwoman for a minute. No one could look more quintessentially English than she.

My advice, then, to those of my colleagues who choose to teach *Henry V*, is to avoid the Branagh and choose either the Olivier or the BBC. My own choice would be the BBC, for this is a solid production which, even confined to a sound stage and without benefit of a stirring outdoor battle scene, holds its end up very well. As for the Olivier, my colleagues may come to find, as I have, that post-Branagh Olivier seems more than a bit stuffy and starchy. David Gwillim's Henry in the BBC, more fittingly heroic than Branagh's yet more warm and human than Olivier's, seems on balance the best of these, and truest to the play Shakespeare wrote. Finally, let it be noted that the comic performances in the BBC production and the Olivier film are equally first-rate, so the teacher trying to choose between these two videos will have to let other factors guide his decision.

Henry VI — Beggars description. Peter Benson *is* the King (hard to imagine him playing any other role!), Trevor Peacock (an actor previously unknown to me who appears to sensational effect in numerous roles throughout the series, including Titus and Feste) is marvelous as both Talbot *and* Jack Cade (there's a lot of doubling of roles throughout the three parts of the play), and Brenda Blethyn (Cordelia in the Olivier *Lear*) burns up the stage as Joan "la Pucelle."

To both counteract and comment on the unabashed jingoism of Part One, the whole production has been camped up, with the French broadly caricatured as "pansies" (the troops who first march in look like something from *Privates on Parade*).

Henry VIII — Excellent. Claire Bloom is perfect as the queen, as is Timothy West as Wolsey. John Stride (Banquo in the Polanski *Macbeth*) is a very good, if not quite corpulent enough, Henry.

Julius Caesar (Brando, Heston, BBC) — While the Brando/ Gielgud movie seems to get "four stars" from just about everybody, a recent viewing convinced me that it is in fact the worst kind of bland, homogenized, Hollywood Shakespeare. Louis Calhern as Caesar is a complete stiff, James Mason is a boring and featureless Brutus, and — heresy though it be to assert as much, condemning one to wander forever in the realm of the Untrendy — Brando's hokey, method-actor's Antony is simply a lousy performance. I'm convinced that throughout academic history there must have been several thousand junior high students who have done a better job of declaiming "O pardon me, thou bleeding piece of earth" than Brando does. His oration in the next scene is thoroughly lackluster, but this one is simply bad beyond belief.

The Heston performance, by comparison, is entirely superior, and that film, while flawed in many ways, has an energy and a human interest the Brando/Gielgud utterly lacks. The big drawback here of course is Jason Robards as Brutus, without doubt one of the worst performances by a great actor anywhere on film.

The BBC production is entirely solid, with a good Brutus in Richard Pasco (wasn't he the marvelously poncey mastermind in PBS's *Brat Farrar*?), a lean Cassius in David Collings, and a Mark Antony (Keith Michell) who, unless I'm crazy, looks like a *perfect* cross between Heston and Brando! A teacher would certainly do better to show his class this than the Brando/Gielgud, although there's far more verve and moxie in the funeral oration scene as played by Heston.

King Lear (BBC versus Olivier) — As these two productions originally were aired on public television, the BBC predated the Olivier. My first impression, after viewing both, was that the Olivier had made mincemeat of the earlier production. In taking both out of the public library in recent months, it so happened that I saw the Olivier first and then the BBC, and my mind was changed completely.

While both are of course first-class productions, and while a teacher could make effective use of both in comparing speeches and scenes, it's hard not to feel that, here as elsewhere, what is called "great acting" in Olivier is at least one third sheer charisma and another third his extraordinary physical beauty. In my judgment Michael Hordern, Lear in the BBC production, is an actor with a far better claim to greatness than Olivier, but of course his lack of movie star good looks ensures that that claim never will be validated. Plainly Hordern's interpretation of the role has been far better thought out (or better directed by Jonathan Miller?) and engages the *mind* in a way Olivier's more strictly emotional performance does not.

Hordern's Lear is, in my opinion, the "real" Lear, a man cursed, even in old age, with too much energy and will power in proportion to brain power. By contrast, Olivier plays Lear as a somewhat irascible but generally lovable old dotard, more weak than foolish. Interestingly enough, at least one aspect of the comparison made a moment ago of the Jacobi and the Olivier Hamlets holds here as well, in that Hordern gets many more intensely interesing moments of "business" from this role than Olivier does. Yet in this case that doesn't seem to detract from his larger conception of the role, but in fact subserves it.

As for the other performances, in my opinion Brenda Blethyn's Cordelia (in the BBC) — sensible and pragmatic, with only a few evidences of emotion in the last scenes — is infinitely preferable to Anna Calder-Marshall's consistently sentimental and weepy performance in the Olivier. Blethyn give us a new perspective (probably simply the *right* perspective) on Cordelia's words in the first scene, by portraying her not as a goody-goody making a show of her honesty but as a genuinely tough-minded individual, not afraid to speak truth to power.

Frank Middlemass's Fool, while perhaps on balance no match for the perfectly cast John Hurt in the Olivier, also clearly has been well thought out. This is a *loud* Fool and a physically large Fool, one who seems determined to *shout* some sense into Lear's foolish head rather than cajole it in. By contrast, Hurt's performance — in line with Olivier's and Calder-Marshall's — is based on sentiment: He seems more concerned to weep at (and along with) Lear than to attempt to "wise him up."

Love's Labor's Lost — Along with *Two Gentlemen* and *Much Ado*, one of the loveliest plays in the series to look at. There are good performances all around, and the eighteenth-century settings and costumes are just right for a work that strikes us as being a before-the-fact satire on that rationalistic age.

Macbeth (BBC versus Polanski) — *Macbeth*, perhaps more than any other Shakespeare play, tends to polarize reader (or viewer) opinion — you either love it or you hate it. Perhaps the simplest thing that can be said by way of lauding the Polanski and denigrating the BBC versions of it is that the latter is as certain to confirm the haters in their hatred as the former is likely to reveal to them a vibrant and unhackneyed work utterly unlike the *Macbeth* they felt they had come to know all too well.

While there is no space here to analyze exactly how Polanski achieves his cinematic miracle, or why the BBC production strikes one as being precisely the kind of quintessentially "traditional" staging of *Macbeth* (complete with the requisite gaunt, dark-haired Lady Macbeth — Jane Lapotaire — rather than Polanski's surprisingly effective lissome blond beauty) that even we who are partial to this play are apt to find a dreadful bore, the essential point certainly is that *Macbeth* makes for a rather hokey stage show but a *bloody* good movie. We all have good reason to cheer when film, which degrades us intellectually far more often than it exalts us, proves itself capable of all but reinventing a classic work of art, scouring it clean of the cobwebs and mildew that have for centuries tended to obscure its greatness.

One final thought: Nothing could reveal more clearly something essentially weak-minded in our culture than the fuss that is made over the violence in the Polanski *Macbeth*. We blithely send our children out to see a "comedy" such as *Beverly Hills Cop* that is filled to overflowing with mindless, gratuitous violence (much of it *literally* gratuitous, in that it was part of the screenplay of a previous drama that *Cop* was turned into!), but we cry out in disgust when a genuine artist such as Polanski uses violence to achieve two perfectly valid ends: the creation of a drama that is true-to-life and historically accurate, and the arousing in the viewer of that terror without which there can be no subsequent catharsis.

Measure for Measure — Excellent. The great Frank Middlemass — known to PBS viewers as Algy Herries on *To Serve Them All My Days* — is a wonderfully effective Pompey, and John McEnery proves just how extraordinary an actor he is by being every bit as perfect a Lucio here as he was a Mercutio in the Zeffirelli film. Kate Nelligan, in whom I've always thought I detected a trace of priggish superiority (perhaps not to be wondered at, given her great beauty and, I would guess, intelligence), is ideally suited to the role of Isabella.

Merchant of Venice — Nothing could be more interesting than the psychology that clearly was at work when many of the reviewers of the Dustin Hoffman performance as Shylock on Broadway gave him a critical drubbing. Clearly their thinking went something like this: "I want to convince my reader that I find anti-Semitism loathsome and intolerable. *The Merchant of Venice* is an anti-Semitic play, one designed to make us hate Shylock. The Shylock I saw last night wasn't hateful. Therefore this wasn't a good production, and I prove myself a good person by saying so."

Could anything be more pathetic — both in the true and the colloquial senses of that term — than such nervous self-righteousness and such blinkered critical vision? "Thinkers" of this type are so intent on remaining in the well-worn rut of conventional thought that, rather than let a genuinely new and valid interpretation of a play nudge them out of it, they sit there bawling loudly, like a child who refuses to leave the sandbox.

Clearly, the performance Hoffman would have had to have given to satisfy such critics would have been one essentially the same as Warren Mitchell's in the BBC production. Shylock must be old and gray, small of stature, and speak with a thick, Yiddish-like accent. What irony there is in this! The very critics who wish to show themselves utterly right-thinking on the issue of racism positively swoon with delight at the sight of a pure racial caricature!

Let it be noted here, as well, how genuinely racist it is to have Shylock be the only person in such a production (with the minor exception of the various suitors for Portia's hand) to speak with an accent. The hidden message of such an approach, in which Jews sound "foreign" but Italians speak perfect English, is clearly this: Jews really are outsiders, are aliens. While of course a director could argue that a heavily accented Shylock only serves to point up the fact that the Venetians do *see* him as an alien, another director such as Peter Hall is entirely within his rights (*pace* the critics) if he decides to emphasize the larger, more important truth — a truth *implicit in the play Shakespeare wrote* — that, however the Venetians looked upon Jews, from a higher vantage point all humans look — and sound — the same.

Now this review is meant to be strictly of the BBC video, for I'm quite certain that the video of the Hoffman performance I have viewed at the Lincoln Center branch of the New York Public Library is not available through any distributor. Nonetheless I have dwelt this long on the difference between Hoffman's and Warren Mitchell's portrayal of Shylock to make it clear that the latter, while every bit as able as all the others in this superb production, is for me old-hat and simply not acceptable for use in the classroom.

This is a great pity, in that the casting in this production is otherwise simply flawless, as good as any in the series, and the production as a whole a delight. Nonetheless, unless I could also show my students a Shylock over 5' 5" in height, distinguished of mien and noble of voice, I would have grave reservations about "exposing" (just the right word) them to the old anti-Semitic Shylock, the one the non-anti-Semites so love to hate.

Merry Wives of Windsor — Joy itself. A whole village seems to have been constructed for the set, which in itself is worth the price of admission. Ben Kingsley as Master Ford is far more winning here, in my opinion, than in many of his serious dramatic roles — it's a great performance. And what fun to see Prunella Scales — Basil Fawlty's missus — as Kingsley's missus here! The only debit here is the *extremely* lackluster Falstaff; one can agree with the scholars that this Falstaff isn't the real one anyway, and still wish this actor had put at least a *little* oomph into the part. No such luck — he's absurdly phlegmatic and reasonable.

Midsummer Night's Dream (BBC versus Reinhardt) — The BBC production is a mixed bag, but on balance not all it should be from a teacher's point of view. The debits here are the extremely static quality of such scenes as those in Theseus's palace and in Peter Quince's house (in both, everyone seems just to *sit there*), and a cockney Puck, whose speech is thereby rendered even harder for the student to follow than it otherwise would have been. Also perhaps worthy of noting, or at least humorous to note, is the fact that the group of 7th-graders with whom I watched the video all were unanimous in their opinion that the actors playing the lovers were physically unattractive. "Why are they all so ugly?" someone asked, to an assenting chorus, and clearly they were genuinely perplexed by this. Perhaps we have here confirmation of my hunch that the British have a certain genius for the dowdy that *will* "out," so to speak.

While it might be fun to show a class parts of the classic film directed by Max Reinhardt, to give them a taste of the special effects, the Mendelssohn score, and Cagney as Bottom, in most respects this is relentlessly cutesy Hollywood Shakespeare, with Rooney's half-demented laugh (as Puck) enough to drive anyone around the bend. Then too, the text has been cut up and rearranged with gay abandon.

Much Ado About Nothing — A marvelous production, and *very* lovely to look at. Robert Lindsay is a wonderful Benedick, and Cherie Lunghi is more than his match as Beatrice. And what fun to see Jon Finch smiling and laughing for a change, as Don Pedro!

Othello — While I have never seen a film starring Anthony Hopkins in which I was able to give any other actor my attention for more than a few seconds, the real attraction of the BBC *Othello* is Bob Hoskins, that East End Cockney par excellence, acting up a storm as Iago. It's a mesmerizing performance. Hopkins is of course excellent, but for me at least his (or the director's?) strategy — that of making Othello *incredibly* reasonable, soft-spoken, and "laid-back" in the early scenes, in order to heighten the contrast with his later jealousy-maddened self — is too transparent to be believable. Also, while Hopkins in his makeup obviously is meant to be a brown-skinned "Moor" rather than a black-skinned "Negro," it's hard to buy him as being either.

Pericles — Marvelous. A play perfectly suited to video, in that its improbable happenings and abrupt changes of scene bother us far less on the small screen than they would on stage. If one needed any proof that Edward Petherbridge (Lord Peter Wimsey on public television) is an accomplished Shakespearean actor, one would only have to point to his death-defying feat here: He grapples with Gower's unspeakable verse, and somehow emerges victorious!

Richard II — Simply flawless. Derek Jacobi was never really meant to *be* Hamlet, but he *is* Richard in this, one of the true bravura performances in the series. As Bolingbroke, Jon Finch is a treat for the eye — he's as handsome as every king should be — but above all for the ear — what a magnificent baritone! As for Gielgud as John of Gaunt — should anyone but he ever be allowed to intone the great "this sceptred isle" speech?

Richard III (BBC versus Olivier) — The BBC is a great production, staged on the same nearly bare set as that used for *Henry VI*. Ron Cook is excellent in a relatively understated portrayal of Richard — far superior, to my taste at least, to Olivier as the Big Bad Wolf. My verdict on the two productions as a whole is the same as that on the two stars.

Romeo and Juliet (BBC versus Zeffirelli) — All those who have grown bored (if such a thing is possible!) or disenchanted with the Zeffirelli *R & J* are advised to do as I have done, and sit through the first twenty minutes of the BBC video (I could stand no more). The first thing that strikes one here (as it does also in the Falstaff scenes in *Henry IV*) is the sense of being boxed in; clearly *R & J* can be blown *up* from its usual stage proportions with great success, but it just can't be sized *down*.

Equally fatal to the BBC production are some of the performances. This nurse, in marked contradistinction to the movie's, actually *doesn't* get on the nerves of Lady Capulet, who chides her gently ("Enough of this . . . ") rather than in utter exasperation. This Act I Romeo seems absurdly cheery and well-balanced, and as for this Mercutio . . . let's just say that his Queen Mab speech, in comparison to John McEnery's, is a complete bore (*oh* so fey), confirming me in my belief that the latter's is a piece of genius. And as if to make the festivities complete, we have here John Gielgud — the very incarnation of the spirit of romantic love! — as the Chorus . . . .

Let it also be noted here, for the benefit of those whose curiosity perhaps has been whetted by seeing late-night TV listings for two filmed versions of this work (the 1936 Leslie Howard/Norma Shearer, and the 1954 Laurence Harvey/Susan Shentall), that teachers and students aren't missing much. To see productions such as these, both of which (but the Howard more than the Harvey) are relentlessly prissy and fey as only things upper-class-English can be, is to make one realize that it took an Italian (Zeffirelli) to restore to us Shakespeare the universal genius, and deliver us from the stiff-upper-lip Englishman some have tried to turn him into.

Taming of the Shrew (BBC versus Zeffirelli) — While both productions have much to recommend them (and much for a critic to carp at, if she were to feel so inclined), if I had time to show only one of them to a class I certainly would choose the Zeffirelli. It is every bit as gorgeous to behold as his *R & J*, and the physical comedy is played to the max — and beyond. By contrast, and rather oddly perhaps, given John Cleese's extraordinary prowess as a physical comedian, the BBC production is understated to a fault (presumably the static having been judged, here as with *Midsummer*, as being better suited to the small screen than the kinetic). In marked contradistinction to Liz Taylor's hissing, pouncing wildcat, the BBC Kate (Sarah Badel) is a tame little kitten, rubbing herself against John Cleese's leg and staring up at him in his immense height.

The understatement that characterizes Cleese's performance extends even to the delivery of the lines, which is vintage BBC-parodying Cleese but more than a bit hard on the Bard, as even the non-purist might admit. Compounding the difficulty presented by Cleese's offhand delivery is the rapid clip at which dialogue is rattled off in this production. This means, for instance, that the lovely cadences of the speeches by Tranio and Lucentio that open Act I are entirely lost to the listener.

Needless to say, by his sheer presence Cleese makes *Shrew* fun and watchable, and he has contrived a number of very funny, if relatively understated, bits of "business." Yet on balance he is no match for Richard Burton, who brings to the role not merely a great comic touch but also his sexual presence and, above all, that magnificent speaking voice, better suited to "I come to wive it wealthily in Padua..." than to "And now, for something completely different...." For whatever else one might have to say about Richard Burton, one thing seems certain: He was sent to this earth for the sole purpose of playing Petruchio!

Note that the wedding of Kate and Petruchio, the events of which are of course only related, not seen, in the play, is shown in full in the Zeffirelli film, and to riotous comic effect. Like Polanski's decision to actually show the murder of Duncan, this clearly was a filmmaker's decision to make the most of his medium. Can anyone doubt that Shakespeare heartily would have approved of it?

The Tempest — Sublime, with Michael Hordern perhaps even a better Prospero than he is a Lear. A fascinating directorial touch: Prospero's last words in Act V, "Please you draw near," which were intended to be addressed to his assembled guests as he invites them into his "poor cell," are here turned into the first lines of the Epilogue, with Prospero beckoning the camera closer and speaking directly to the viewer. This is not only a brilliant gambit but an immensely effective one, in that those last words, spoken to us "up close and personal," bring a tear to the eye and a lump to the throat.

Also note two fun PBS connections here, which caused me to just about jump out of my skin for joy when they finally "clicked" in my mind. Stephano is played — brilliantly — by Nigel Hawthorne (Sir Humphrey in *Yes, Minister*), and Gonzalo is played by John Nettleton, who plays Hawthorne's older civil servant crony in the same PBS series!

Needless to say, the chief selling point of *The Tempest* on video is an Ariel who really can appear and disappear at will, and all of this works wonderfully well here.

Timon of Athens — A solid production. Jonathan Pryce, star of the movie *Brazil* and the musical *Miss Saigon*, is Timon.

Titus Andronicus — A real crowd-pleaser — or rather, stomach-turner, with the great Trevor Peacock as Titus. This production also boasts a perfectly cast Saturnius in Brian Protheroe (he also plays Edward in *Henry VI, Part Three* and *Richard III* — he's perfect as a craven, immoral monarch) and an even more perfectly cast Tamora in Eileen Atkins (*every* Tamora should be required to have her leonine mass of red, frizzy hair!).

Troilus and Cressida — Extraordinary. Suzanne Burden brings to Cressida *exactly* the right blend of innocence and sex appeal, and Anton Lesser (something of a Robin Williams look-alike) is an even better Troilus than he is Edgar in the BBC *King Lear*. The finest acting here, however, comes from the great Charles Gray as Pandarus — one of the series' standout performances. And who will ever forget "The Incredible Orlando" (who *is* this guy anyway, perhaps a London street performer thought to be just right for the role?) as a drag-queen Thersites?!

Twelfth Night — Utterly sublime, and perfectly cast. While I have no other Malvolio to compare him with, if any other actor can top Alec McCowen's performance here I'd love to see it — this one is a joy to behold. Also great are Robert Hardy (known to PBS viewers as Churchill in *Churchill: The Wilderness Years*, among many other roles) as Sir Toby, Felicity Kendall (of PBS's *The Good Neighbors*, and the film classic *Shakespeare Wallah*) as Viola, and Trevor Peacock as Feste. Ronnie Stevens is the absolute spitting image of Sir Andrew Aguecheek, but Clive Arrindell is unimpressive as Orsino — he has no feeling for the blank verse.

A personal note: For me, the pathos and beauty of Peacock's rendition of the final song ("For the rain it raineth every day") was utterly overwhelming.

Two Gentlemen of Verona — *Gorgeous* to look at — without a doubt the production most ravishing to the eye — and a complete success. Nicholas Kaby is extraordinarily winning as Speed, and in themselves the close-up shots of Crab the dog are worth the price of admission.

Winter's Tale — A good production, if you like this kind of thing....

Appendix V

SURVEY RESULTS

In October of 1989 I sent out a two-page survey on the teaching of Shakespeare to 384 English department chairpersons nationwide, and 212 of them were so good as to respond. When one considers just how busy these men and women are, the fact that over half of them took the time to respond, often in detailed and anecdotal fashion, is a real testimony to just how seriously they take their work and how eager they are to share their experiences — both of success and of failure — with a colleague.

Then too, the fact that so many of them went out of their way to express an interest in seeing my findings suggests that they have an understandable desire to know exactly how their colleagues are approaching a central aspect of the teaching of English. Indeed, if I'm proud of any one aspect of this book it is that its publication allows me to perform a vital service for my colleagues, a service for which, unless I am mistaken, there has been a crying need up until now. For surely every English teacher has a right to know (among other things) just how often each of the Shakespeare plays presently is being taught, even if the conclusions he or she goes on to draw from the data are entirely at variance with mine, or with those of some other colleague.

I'd now like to say a word or two about my motivation in sending out the survey, about how I've compiled the data, and about the conclusions I have (or sometimes, haven't) drawn from it. First, let it be noted that what really prompted me to send out the survey was my desire to know exactly which plays are being taught and at which grade levels. (Because this was primary for me I've placed those results first, even though the question happened to fall at the end of the survey form itself.) In most respects all of the other questions were included either as adjuncts to that central one (for instance, those that seek to ascertain which plays are popular with students or teachers) or simply because I was curious to know whether teachers like video, have kids act out scenes, etc.

Second, I'd like to make it clear that I am no statistician, but have simply done my best to present the data as clearly as possible. Indeed, because teachers' responses were sometimes incomplete, illegible, or self-contradictory, the data presented here could *not* have been made completely "scientific," even by IBM. Thus I suggest that my reader take it in the spirit and the manner in which it is offered, i.e., as being suggestive rather than definitive.

Third, I must point out that the "Comments" which follow most but not all sections are just that, my comments, not probing statistical analyses. Doubting as I do my ability to carry off the latter, even if I had more of a penchant for it than I do, I've simply spoken out about whatever seems to stick out, so to speak. That much having been said, let's look at the data.

1.   "Whichever of the Shakespeare plays you have taught in the last 5-6 years, please indicate grade level."   Data below has been arranged so as to show in which grades, from 7-12, each play is being taught, with the total showing how many of the 212 schools say they have taught that play in the last 5-6 years. Plays have been ranked from most to least taught. The reader will note that totals are greater than the sum of the figures given for each grade level. The reason for this is that sometimes a teacher checked a play, to indicate that he or she does teach it, but failed to provide a grade level. Note too that if a respondent indicated "11-12 elective" as his or her answer, as I toted up the responses I simply put the first such response in the 11th-grade column, the next in the 12th-, and so on. Thus the totals for grades 11 and 12 are slightly less "definitive" than the other grade totals, but they should be quite accurate nonetheless.

	7	8	9	10	11	12	TOTAL
Hamlet	0	1	1	9	60	109	195
Macbeth	1	4	19	86	36	28	189
R & J	9	46	92	17	4	2	181
Othello	0	1	2	22	38	74	151
J. Caesar	7	23	74	28	6	4	151

	7	8	9	10	11	12	TOTAL
Midsummer	28	27	24	10	16	18	134
Tempest	1	3	4	16	31	53	121
King Lear	0	0	0	3	28	61	109
12th Night	1	7	10	20	20	27	97
Merchant	1	6	28	18	18	13	92
Shrew	1	9	10	16	20	23	90
H. IV, One	0	1	6	23	27	25	90
As You L. I.	3	3	6	14	20	18	69
Rich. III	0	2	4	8	10	26	55
A. & Cleo.	0	0	2	2	14	29	50
Rich. II	0	0	0	2	11	24	40
Much Ado	1	1	0	8	13	12	37
H. IV, Two	0	0	0	7	4	11	25
Henry V	0	0	1	3	4	11	21
W.'s Tale	0	0	0	2	3	12	21
C. of Err.	1	1	1	4	4	6	20
M. for M.	0	0	0	0	4	9	17
Merry Wives	0	0	1	0	1	6	10
All's Well	0	0	1	0	2	5	10
Troilus & C.	0	0	0	0	2	4	6
Love's L. L.	0	0	1	0	2	1	5
Titus And.	0	0	0	0	0	5	5
Coriolanus	0	0	0	0	0	5	5
Henry VIII	0	0	0	1	0	3	4
Henry VI	0	0	0	0	1	3	4
Two Gentle.	0	1	0	1	0	1	3
King John	0	0	0	0	1	2	3
Cymbeline	0	0	0	0	1	2	3
Pericles	0	0	0	0	0	2	2
Timon of A.	0	0	0	0	1	0	1

COMMENTS: If one looks at the "total" column, one notes that the plays break down roughly into three groups: a Top Twelve (down through *Henry IV, Part One*), a middle ten (through *Measure for Measure*), and a bottom thirteen. Clearly there are "play lists" of Shakespeare plays in the independent school, and if I could be disc jockey for a term or two I would give far more air time to *T & C* (above all), to all (or at least most) of the full *Henry IV*, to *Richard II*, *Measure for Measure*, and *Cymbeline*.

2. **"In what grade do students read their first Shakespeare play?"** Virtually all of the 9-12 schools teach their first Shakespeare play in the 9th grade. In the 154 7-12 schools who responded to this question,

    43 start Shakespeare in the 7th grade
    70   "   "   "   8th grade
    39   "   "   "   9th grade
     1   "   "   "   10th grade
     1   "   "   "   11th grade

COMMENTS: My more experienced colleagues may well have learned, after years of experimentation, that it is wiser to wait until the 8th grade to introduce students to Shakespeare than to try but fail to do so in the 7th grade. Granting that very real possibility, I do wonder whether that decision has been arrived at by teachers who have seen only three plays as being "possibles" for the 7th grade — *Midsummer*, *JC*, and *R & J* — and who have learned from experience that none of them actually works at that grade level. Should that be the case, I would urge them to give it the old college try yet again, but this time with *As You Like It*.

I also wonder whether those who have tried but failed to begin Shakespeare studies in the 7th grade have made "introducing Shakespeare" an important week or two of study before a word of the first play is read. For while some of the hints I have shared with my colleagues in Appendix III perhaps would be put to better use in 9th or 10th grade (for instance, the frank discussion of Shakespeare's preciousness as one of the factors that make him a genuinely difficult "read"), there is no reason why most of them (such as the recommended use of the first half hour of the Olivier *Henry V*) shouldn't work with 7th-graders. Indeed, the younger and more impressionable the student who receives this "freshman orientation" to Shakespeare is, the more likely it is that he or she will be genuinely impressed by it — and by him.

How many Shakespeare plays do your students read between grades 7-12, and how does that break down on a yearly basis?" (Obviously, 9-12 schools had to read that as "9-12.") Note that, because the breakdown on a yearly basis varied very widely from school to school, I have made no attempt to reproduce that data here. Note also that these totals do not include plays taught in Shakespeare electives, which most (or at least many) schools do seem to offer. Here is the data indicating how many plays, total, are taught by the 152 7-12 schools who responded to this question:

2 plays —	9	7 plays —	13
3 plays —	25	8 plays —	6
4 plays —	35	9 plays —	4
5 plays —	30	10 plays —	1
6 plays —	27	11 plays —	1
		12 plays —	1

34 9-12 schools responded to this question:

2 plays —	4	5 plays —	3
3 plays —	11	12 plays —	1
4 plays —	15	(three per year)	

COMMENTS: As someone who is not a department chair, and who therefore has never had to put together curricula for all grade levels, or squeeze a Shakespeare syllabus into an already crowded curriculum, I am not about to pontificate in my comments here. Thus I will simply offer my personal opinion that, given Shakespeare's central importance in Western culture, students should not have graduated from high school without having read a minimum of five of his plays. As the above data seems to show, at the moment that goal is not being reached by many schools.

Doubtless one factor skewing the data is that it makes no mention of Shakespeare electives, but I'm not sure we should take too much comfort from the fact that our brighter students are leaving high school having read many *more* than six plays while the slower students have read far fewer. As I have stated at least twice previously in this book, it is the "cultural status" — in every sense — of the less fortunate members of a society that in the long run makes or breaks that society, and if vast numbers of high school graduates have vivid memories of Holden in the prostitute's room but none whatever of Hamlet in his mother's bedchamber, or Troilus in Cressida's, we all have cause to be concerned.

4. **"In order of preference [1 to 3], please list those plays you feel work best with students encountering Shakespeare for the first time."**   Let it be noted that, in framing this question, I decided to go with the more general wording ("encountering Shakespeare for the first time") rather than say "with 7-9 students," although I assume that's what most respondents were thinking of anyway. The totals given below were arrived at in the same fashion as all of those that will follow: Every respondent's first choice was weighted as a 2, second choice as a 1.5, third as a 1, and then the totals were added. This means, of course, that all such totals have only a relative rather than an intrinsic significance.

Romeo and Juliet	283
Midsummer Night's Dream	155
Julius Caesar	142
Macbeth	113
The Merchant of Venice	36
The Taming of the Shrew	21
As You Like It	20
Twelfth Night	20
Henry IV, Part One	15
The Tempest	13
Hamlet	11
The Comedy of Errors	7
Othello	3
The Two G. of Verona	3
Henry V	2
Much Ado About Nothing	2
Richard III	1

COMMENTS: If respondents were thinking of *R & J* as best for the first-time *freshman or sophomore* reader their position seems at least a tenable one, but (as my reader knows by now) I don't agree with the proposition that *R & J* is junior high Shakespeare. As I have also made clear, I don't think *Midsummer* is good beginner's Shakespeare, even if that beginner *is* a freshman or sophomore.

What I find rather interesting here is that my "baby," *As You Like It*, taught less than *Twelfth Night* in the grades (7-9) I presume most respondents were thinking of here (it received 12 votes to the latter's 18 in the "most taught" category), managed to tie its rival here. Perhaps mildly supportive of my thesis that it's by far the stronger work at those grade levels? Also intriguing is the fact that *Two Gentlemen* — a work that I do indeed feel has many qualities suiting it to young readers, although I have been unable to recommend it — "made the cut" here at all.

5. **"Across all grade levels, what three plays would you say students *enjoy* most?"**

Romeo and Juliet	215
Macbeth	212
Hamlet	125
Midsummer Night's Dream	82
Othello	33
Julius Caesar	32
The Taming of the Shrew	29
King Lear	26
The Merchant of Venice	24
Twelfth Night	22
The Tempest	16
Henry IV, Part One	12
As You Like It	5
Much Ado About Nothing	4
Richard II	3
The Winter's Tale	2

COMMENTS: Needless to say, responses in this category have to be taken with a very large grain of salt, in that teachers are giving *their* opinions about *student* opinions.

Comparing the figures in this category with those in the most taught category is doubtless the statistical equivalent of comparing apples and oranges, these figures being the tabulation of a teacher "vote," the others representing the actual number of schools presently teaching each play. Nonetheless, it does look as if the popularity of *R & J* and *Macbeth* is about what one would have hoped given how often those plays are taught, whereas *Hamlet* and *Midsummer*'s showing here is less strong than one might have expected. Given the apples-and-oranges factor I may well be guilty of special pleading when I make the following two observations, but I suppose I don't sin too greatly if I offer them merely as hypotheses.

As for *Hamlet*, while one isn't surprised that this problematic work has been outscored here by the sexy *R & J* and the gory *Macbeth*, perhaps teachers should entertain anew my theory that this work is a puzzlement to the student of average or below-average intelligence, and that the seemingly highfalutin *T & C* might actually be a more rewarding read for that student. As for *Midsummer*, doesn't it appear at a glance that this play isn't as solidly popular with students as some have supposed it to be? If so, that fact is of considerably more importance in this case than in that of *Hamlet*. For while one could plausibly argue that, given all that *Hamlet* has to teach students, it is a relatively minor matter whether it thrills them to the marrow, doubtless *Midsummer* is taught so widely not on the supposition that it has a lot to teach students, but in the hope that they will fall in love with it, and thereby with the Bard.

Another noteworthy aspect of this data is the way in which *Twelfth Night*, the ninth most commonly taught play nationwide, has here been outscored by both the tenth and eleventh most commonly taught, *Merchant* and *Shrew*. While the believer in the pedagogic *Twelfth Night* presumably could face with equanimity the fact that so robust a farce as *Shrew* has beaten it out here, I would think he or she would be a bit surprised or disconcerted to see that *Merchant* has done so as well. For one would think that if students were delighting in the comic moments featuring Malvolio as much as their elders do, they would prefer this work to a darker one such as *Merchant*. Particularly when one takes note of the fact that *Twelfth Night* is a far more popular work with teachers than the other two (see question seven), the fact that teachers have here "admitted" it is not so popular as those is perhaps somewhat significant.

Finally, note that two plays that are taught more often than the last four plays on the above list — *Richard III* and *Antony and Cleopatra* — are, if we may judge by the fact that they received no "votes" at all in this category, not popular with students.

6. "Regardless of student enjoyment, what three plays do you as a teacher feel are most educationally enriching?" I took a bit of flak from some respondents about that piece of jargon I was forced to employ here: "educationally enriching." Yes, the phrase is a bit pretentious, but the point seems clear enough. The results:

Hamlet	253
Macbeth	173
King Lear	118
Romeo and Juliet	77
Othello	46
Julius Caesar	43
The Merchant of Venice	30
Henry IV, Part One	28
Midsummer Night's Dream	28
The Tempest	24
The Winter's Tale	5
As You Like It	4
Twelfth Night	4
Antony and Cleopatra	2
The Taming of the Shrew	2
Measure for Measure	2
Troilus and Cressida	1
Richard II	1
Henry V	1

COMMENTS: No surprise, certainly, to see *Hamlet* topping this list. As for *Macbeth*, if teachers took "most educationally enriching" in its widest conceivable sense of "best classroom experience," which they certainly had a right to do, I have no quibble with them. I would suggest, however, that if one were to take my bit of jargon to mean "arousing the most vivid interest in moral issues," there are grounds for doubting whether *Macbeth* does this as well as many another play. Granted, the very simplicity of *Macbeth*'s moral as to the dangers of ambition makes it in most respects well suited to the secondary classroom, but one can still wonder how effectively the student who has learned that "it's bad to kill people" (which is how a friend of mine humorously recollects what *he* got from the study of *Macbeth* in high school) has been "educationally enriched."

As for *King Lear*, I can't help but wonder if it really does enrich the lives of adolescents as much as these teachers say it does, or if they ranked it so high simply because it's a great work and they enjoy the challenge of teaching it (or trying to). In support of that suspicion I might cite a comment that was made by one of those respondents who was exclaiming over what he perceived to be the stupidity of the phrase "educationally enriching." In the margin he wrote, "For *whom*, students? teachers?" Surely it is rather distressing to find a teacher who wonders whom education is *for*, teachers or students, and I myself wonder whether those who teach *King Lear* are more intent on enriching their students' lives or their own.

What really delights me here, however, is the fact that *Merchant* and *Henry IV, Part One* — three and five rungs, respectively, beneath *The Tempest* in the most-taught category — outrank it here. Particularly given what a favorite *The Tempest* is with teachers (see next question), I take this result to mean that even they have to admit that this work brings less to students than they imagine it does.

Note also that, once again, *Richard III* (that rightly unpopular fellow!) is the only one of the fifteen most commonly taught plays to have failed to receive a single vote here.

7. "Your duties as a teacher to one side, please list in order of preference your own three favorite plays."

Hamlet	213
King Lear	165

The Tempest	74
Macbeth	73
Othello	65
Twelfth Night	37
Midsummer Night's Dream	33
Romeo and Juliet	28
Henry IV, Part One	18
Richard II	17
Measure for Measure	17
As You Like It	17
Richard III	16
Antony and Cleopatra	14
Much Ado About Nothing	12
The Winter's Tale	12
The Taming of the Shrew	11
The Merchant of Venice	11
Julius Caesar	7
Henry IV, Part Two	4
Troilus and Cressida	3
Henry VIII	3
Coriolanus	2
Love's Labor's Lost	2
The Comedy of Errors	2
Cymbeline	1
Merry Wives of Windsor	1
All's Well That Ends Well	1

(No votes for *Pericles*, *Timon*, *Titus*, or *Two Gentlemen*.)

COMMENTS: A few interesting things here. First, it seems to be true that teachers like the plays they teach — or teach the plays they like? The only exception to that rule is *Measure for Measure*, which seems to have a few fans out there but still is very rarely taught. As I've argued earlier, teachers who refrain from teaching *Measure* out of fear that students will have trouble with its difficult verse have relatively good grounds for their anxiety, but in the final analysis I don't think that fear is justified. If instead it is either *Measure*'s sexiness or its moral complexity that is keeping teachers from teaching it, I would refer them again to my discussion of those factors in the play commentary.

While of course many teachers exclaimed in their comments — and for good reason — of the absurdity of trying to reduce their love of the whole canon to any "Top Three," and while it was inevitable that *Hamlet* and *Lear* would crowd most other plays out of the number one and two spots on the survey form, I am somewhat disappointed that my colleagues don't seem to cherish a number of very great plays more than they do: *Henry IV*[1], *Richard II, Measure for Measure, Merry Wives, Coriolanus,* and — especially — *T & C* and *Cymbeline.*

I would also be remiss in my duty to students — always a teacher's first and in most respects *only* duty — if I didn't ask publicly whether *T & C, Henry IV, Richard II, Cymbeline,* etc. aren't being taught much simply because teachers don't like them. There were a good many marginal comments written in on survey responses about the *Richard II*'s and the *T & C*'s, to the effect of "I think this one is hard for kids," but even as one grants that possibility one wonders whether that's really the factor keeping these works out of our syllabuses.

8. "Imagine for a moment that you are participating in an experimental program that encourages teachers to throw caution to the winds and teach some Shakespeare play that until then they had always thought of as pedagogically unsuitable. What play(s) would you choose? Please list in order of preference [1 to 3]."   This question elicited many marginal exclamations of disbelief, horror, and anger, from those I would characterize as bardolators, as to how *any* Shakespeare play could *possibly* be thought of as being "pedagogically unsuitable"! It was also left blank by a very large number of respondents, who presumably were equally nonplussed by it.

While I admit that I myself might not have known what to make of the *motivation* prompting the surveyer to pose such a

[1] While one needn't endorse Van Doren's assessment of this play — "No play of Shakespeare's is better than *Henry IV*" — no sensitive critic could fail to see his point. Op. cit., p. 116.

question, I don't think I would have had trouble understanding what I was being asked to do. As for the motivation, it was this: to see which plays, if any, teachers are very enamored of, or at least intrigued by, but feel aren't right for the classroom. With this data in hand, I hoped I might be able to comment on the issue of whether teachers' fears as to lack of pedagogic suitability are or are not justified. The reader will note that the totals given below are somewhat lower than some that have appeared in earlier questions, this being because so many respondents left this question unanswered. Of course, totals in almost all categories have only a relative rather than an intrinsic significance anyway.

Measure for Measure	48
The Winter's Tale	38
King Lear	38
Troilus and Cressida	36
Antony and Cleopatra	35
The Tempest	32
Coriolanus	28
The Merchant of Venice	27
Richard III	26
Titus Andronicus	25
Richard II	24
The Taming of the Shrew	20
Othello	17
Henry IV, Part One	17
Midsummer Night's Dream	13
Timon of Athens	12
Much Ado About Nothing	12
Pericles	12
Henry V	8
As You Like It	7
Cymbeline	7
Henry IV, Part Two	5
Twelfth Night	4

All's Well That Ends Well	4
Love's Labor's Lost	3
Henry VIII	3
The Comedy of Errors	2
Henry VI	1

COMMENTS: I'm immensely gratified to see that two of the plays I had been "angling for" when I designed this question have taken the bait in splendid fashion. Clearly, many teachers would love to teach *Measure for Measure* and *T & C*, but feel they shouldn't for one reason or another. Again, I can only urge them to make their own classrooms the "experimental program" described above, and to indeed "throw caution to the winds."

Also noteworthy to me here are a number of plays, now widely taught but deemed by me to be pedagogically unsuitable, that some teachers clearly feel *are* better suited to an experimental program than to the secondary classroom: *King Lear* (by far the most significant of these), *The Tempest*, *Richard III*, and *Othello*. I'm also glad to see that even *Midsummer* and *Antony and Cleopatra*, plays I do feel are teachable but only under the right circumstances, are thought by a few teachers to be best approached with circumspection.

Some disappointments, or at least surprises. The fact that *Merchant* ranks so relatively high here makes me all the more certain that teachers are being scared away from this pedagogically ideal work by its perceived anti-Semitism. *Cymbeline*'s very low ranking confirms my hunch that this is a play most teachers don't even *consider* teaching, much less teach. Also, I would have expected that more teachers, particularly those who already teach *Henry IV, Part One*, would have been eager to drive Part Two around the block, if only to see how it handles compared with the earlier model.

As for the high score *Winter's Tale* has logged, I can only assume it tells us that this is a work quite a few teachers either like or are intrigued by. Having nothing nice to say on that subject, I shall remain mute. . . .

9. "Which edition (publisher) of the plays do you use?"
Some departments use more than one edition (different at different grade levels, etc.), so I simply logged one vote for every edition a chairperson said they presently are using. Note as well that

some of the less common editions at the bottom of this list have
perhaps been mentioned twice inadvertently, in that I have no
way of knowing whether the titles I have jotted down directly
from teachers' survey responses are in fact the same book being
referred to in different ways.

Folger	90
Signet Classic	45
Penguin (Pelican)	20
Harcourt	6
Arden	5
Kittredge	4
Boynton	4
Bantam	3
G. B. Harrison	2
Amsco	2

Maynard Mack; Oxford School Edition; Hayden; Little, Brown's
Introduction to Literature; Harcourt's *Theory of Tragedy*; the Norton
annotated; Yale University Press; the Norton Anthology; Viking;
and Scott, Foresman.

COMMENTS: I have no experience whatever with the choosing or ordering of texts, so I will limit my comments to the
competition between the Folger and the Signet editions for the
title of most commonly used secondary school Shakespeare text.

A very large number of respondents, in explaining why they
like and use the Signet Classic editions, made reference to the
"truly splendid" critical essays included there, and to the fact that
they like to expose their students to these. Thus a number of
respondents said that with younger students they tended to choose
the Folger, with their juniors and seniors the Signet Classic.

Now while all of this seems eminently sensible, I would like
to argue strongly for the Folger edition, not because I am in that
publisher's pay (in fact, I once worked for New American
Library, publishers of Signet Classics!) but because I feel the
uncluttered Folger format (notes on the left side, text on the

right) is the only one *certain* not to put off students more than they're already put off by Shakespeare himself.

If it has been the major thrust of this book to say that students should always come first whenever pedagogic decisions are being made, and a minor thrust to suggest (in Appendix III) that we will have our best luck in teaching Shakespeare if we think of his works as being genuinely knotty and complex, and by no means "self-teaching," then surely we should see to it that the actual physical format in which the plays are presented to our students is the optimal one. While quite a few respondents who use the Signet Classic editions noted parenthetically "readable format" or some such, as I see it these editions are in fact *less* readable than the Folger, and that by a fairly significant measure. Also very far from ideal, of course, is the fact that in the Signets footnotes are at the bottom of the page, where it is harder for students to find them. It seems certain that, in a huge number of cases, this discourages students from consulting them at all.

While I had thought from the very start of this project that the Folger has *the* format for secondary school Shakespeare studies, as I worked on it over the months my conviction on this score was deepened, and in a rather amusing fashion. As I prepared to study a particular play in preparation for writing about it, I found myself so loath to pick up my Signet (or sometimes Pelican or other) edition that I would trek off to the bookstore and plunk down a few of my very few dollars for the Folger. My rationale for this was, "I want to read the play in the format most kids are reading it in," but after I'd purchased Folger after Folger I realized my *real* rationale was, "I want to read the plays in the format *I* like the best and find least daunting"! I would suggest that if even an educated adult likes a clear, uncluttered page, our students are almost certain to *need* a clear, uncluttered page if they are to get a handle on Shakespeare's works and develop a fondness for the man himself.

A couple of thoughts for those who use the Signet with older students. While I very much understand the desire teachers have to expose their students to the kind of superb critical essays one finds in the Signet, what I'm not sure I do understand is why teachers can't simply xerox an essay or two and hand those out to the students, rather than let that factor alone guide their choice of one edition over another. I also wonder whether it isn't fallacious to assume that the average junior or senior has become so acclimated to Shakespeare that no edition, however un-ideal, could make his studies less palatable. I would suggest that it is far wiser to assume that the road to a full comprehension and appreciation of Shakespeare is *always* a rocky one for *all* students, be they brilliant or dim-witted, eighteen or thirteen, and that we teachers have an obligation to clear from their path as many of the stones, regardless of their size, as we can.

10. "When a class is studying a Shakespeare play, do they also see it on videotape?"

Usually/Always   85

Often/Sometimes   108

Very Rarely/Never   7

"If they do see it, do you show it before reading, after, or during (after each act or scene)?"   Note that because some teachers said they use, or have tried, different techniques in this area, some hybrid categories had to be invented here ("During and After," "During or After").

Before reading   5

During reading   37

During and After   13

During or After   16

After reading   86

COMMENTS: The pedagogic rationale for not showing the entire video *first* — because to do so would be to rob students of interest in the actual text of the play, and cause them to slack off in the days of study ahead — is perhaps a compelling one, but I'd be failing in my duty as gadfly if I didn't take a minute to challenge it.

I can conceive of speaking very frankly to students in this manner: "I'm a real believer in letting you students enjoy the *play* Shakespeare wrote — and let's always remember he did write *plays*, not 'books' — and letting you enjoy *all* of it from the first scene to the last. Thus we're now going to watch the Polanksi *Macbeth* [or whichever], and I hope you like it. However, let me say this. As the price of your enjoyment in the next couple of hours, I'm going to be *demanding* in the next couple of weeks that you become experts on the *text* of the play Shakespeare wrote. And anyone in here who thinks she's going to do that just by recollecting her viewing of the film, or even by watching it again on her own VCR the night before the test, is sadly mistaken."

A possible approach? I by no means wish to suggest that it is necessarily a winning approach, but I do think students generally respond in a mature fashion to a bargain struck in this fashion, along the lines of "I'll scratch your back if you'll scratch mine." For some thoughts as to what the possible pedagogic pluses are of showing the video before reading the text, I would refer my reader back to my commentaries on *Richard II* and *Henry IV*.

"Do you feel positive or negative about using video as an aid to teaching Shakespeare?"   The response here was virtually unanimous, as one would have hoped and expected it to be: Teachers clearly feel that being able to use video in the classroom gives them a tremendous advantage when it comes to teaching Shakespeare. The "tremendous" may be a bit of an overstatement, in that not all waxed ecstatic on this subject, but enough did to convince me that the adjective pretty faithfully reflects the general feeling out there.

In responding to this question, only seven teachers expressed ambivalence about video (presumably most teachers *feel* some ambivalence — primarily because showing the video takes up lots of class time — but their delight in this pedagogic resource seems to far outweigh their reservations), and only six said outright that they have no use for video in the classroom.

COMMENTS: In my view the "video revolution," now so clearly upon us, has two definite classroom implications. First, there simply is no longer any excuse for failing to reward the student who has made the long, hard slog through Elizabethan

English by showing him the video. While one can sympathize with all of those survey respondents who complained that showing the video takes up an inordinate amount of valuable class time, surely teachers should force themselves to admit that this is not wasted but highly valuable time, for student even more than teacher.

Second, I would suggest that every school now has an obligation of sorts to have as many VCRs and TV screens as are needed to allow teachers to show videos virtually whenever and for as long as they wish. A quixotic vision, doubtless, but a dream that *shouldn't* be such an impossible one.

11. "How often do you have students listen to recorded performances?"

Often	56
Occasionally	53
Seldom/Never	89

COMMENTS: Although clearly recorded performances loom less large for most teachers than they did in the pre-video era, many of those respondents who said they do often make use of recorded performances were quite enthusiastic in their comments. My own guess is that that enthusiasm is of deep pedagogic significance, and that all of us English teachers should pay it very close heed.

First of all, there can be no doubt that we English teachers have an obligation to do anything and everything we can do to make our students less video-conscious and more word-conscious. Immersing them in the *spoken* word is surely one excellent way of achieving that goal. Second, demanding that students *listen* to a play rather than watch it should serve to restore to them at least a bit of that imaginative capacity that our TV-and-video culture has so wantonly stripped them of. Third, when we recall that Elizabethans routinely would make statements such as, "Tomorrow we're off to *hear* the new Shakespeare play," we teachers can console ourselves, as we endure student jeers because we have chosen to have them listen to a recorded performance rather than watch a video, that we are helping to turn these bratty little moderns into model Elizabethans!

12. "How often do you have students on their feet, acting out scenes?"

Often	93
Occasionally	41
Seldom/Never	58

"Have they memorized their parts, or do they have book in hand?"

Book in hand	76
Memorized	22
Sometimes one, sometimes the other	37

COMMENTS: I myself have done so very little in terms of teaching Shakespeare through performance that I'm in no position to render an intelligent judgment in this area, but perhaps what I can do is ask (in the manner familiar by now to my readers!) an innocent question: Does book-in-hand acting by students (even if they've studied their parts the night before, as a number of teachers said they assign them to do) ever really amount to much? It may, but in my only attempt at it it struck me as being simply too awkward and stilted.

Note that one respondent made mention of a technique that struck me as intriguing: Some students read the lines, while others act them!

Thank you, friend reader! If you'd
like to share with me thoughts and
comments about this book and/or
your own experiences teaching
Shakespeare, feel free to write me c/o
Pripet Press, P.O. Box 8, Cathedral
Station, N.Y., N.Y. 10025-0008.

ORDER FORM

To order additional copies of *Shakespeare and the Moral Curriculum*, provide the information requested below and mail this form along with check or money order to:

> Pripet Press
> P.O. Box 8
> Cathedral Station
> New York, N.Y. 10025-0008

Name: _____

School (if part of address): _____

Address: _____

City, State, Zip Code: _____

Book price is $17.95 per copy. Please add $2.00 for shipping and handling for first book, $.75 for each additional copy.

New York State residents must add 7¼% sales tax ($1.48 per copy).

Number of copies @ $17.95: _____

Shipping: _____

Sales tax if applicable: _____

Total amount enclosed: _____